Monks Hall

For Philip Hudson and Stephan Deare-Bilham

This book is dedicated to the memory of Andrew Francis Gray, 1935–2015, who modestly called himself the Syleham 'Village Recorder'. A teacher, skilled artist and local historian, his painstaking transcription work of medieval documents and early wills and his vernacular study of Monks Hall have been an invaluable help to the author. Without his unpublished work this volume could not have been written. I hope he would have approved of this history to which he contributed so much.

Elaine Murphy 2018

Monks Hall

The History of a Waveney Valley Manor

Elaine Murphy

Poppyland Publishing

Copyright © Elaine Murphy
First published 2018 by Poppyland Publishing, Lowestoft, NR32 3BB
www.poppyland.co.uk

ISBN 978 1 909796 54 6

All rights reserved. No part of this publication may be reproduced, stored in a retrieval system or transmitted by any means, mechanical, photocopying, recording or otherwise, without the written permission of the publishers.

Designed and typeset in 12 on 14 pt Caslon Pro

Picture credits:

Alamy Ltd. (Everitt Collection) 111
Author cover, 3, 6, 14, 30, 56, 66, 74, 91, 95, 96, 97, 99, 100, 101, 106, 107, 109, 166, 222
Author's collection 98
British Library 8
Chapman, J. and M. 217 bottom
Colchester and Ipswich Museum Service 135
Deare-Bilham, S. 125
Evans, T. 188, 189
Gainsborough House Society 154
Grosvenor Prints 137
Haddesley, R. 55
Leader, G. 218
Lyndon-Stanford, I. 232
Monks Hall Archive 164, 207, 210, 212, 214, 216, 217 top, 219, 224, 225, 226, 227, 229
New Walk Museum & Art Gallery 132
Norwich Cathedral Library 18
Page, M. 35
Poppyland collection 10, 29, 144, 156
Salisbury and South Wiltshire Museum 67
Suffolk Record Office 1, 118, 223

Acknowledgements

The author owes huge thanks to all the people who helped with the research for this study, especially the patient staff at the Suffolk Record Offices at Ipswich and Lowestoft, at the Norfolk Record Office and also at The National Archives, Kew. I am especially grateful to Mary Lewis, Churchwarden of the Parish Church of St Margaret, Syleham for the loan of many volumes of work given to the parish by Andrew Gray, to Diana Spelman once more for her palaeographic transcription skills and to Elizabeth Walne Budd, for providing sufficient clues to allow me to hunt down one of her 18th century relatives, James Walne. Thanks also to Simon Lake, Curator of Fine Art, Leicester Arts & Museums Service; to Ruth Stokes, local historian of Bardwell, Suffolk; and to Jim Corbett for information about R. H. Winn. Sue Dixon, George Bullingham's great-granddaughter, was able to tell me about her family connections with Monks Hall. Margaret and John Chapman kindly supplied the photo of Minnie Roberts and clarified who came from Devon with the Leaders to Monks Hall. Many friends of the Leader family were willing to talk about them and I am especially grateful to Charles Michell, Stuart Greenwood, Inga Lyndon-Stanford, Prue Day and Geoffrey, Anne and Alan Leader for their personal insights and factual information. Sarah Patey, my copy editor, gave me much needed advice to improve the first manuscript, Peter Stibbons for redrawing the maps and Gareth Davies, at Poppyland, has been an enthusiastic and interested support. Finally, Mike Robb as ever was on hand as computer expert and constant moral support.

Contents

Acknowledgements	v
Contents	vi
Foreword	vii
Introduction	1
The Saxon Manor and Landscape 1000–1066	5
The Normans, Roger Bigod and Thetford Priory, 1066–1380	13
Syleham's Day of Fame, 1174	26
The Manor and the Monks 1300–1400	33
Monks Hall in the Fifteenth Century	53
The Dissolution of the Priory and a new era for Monks Hall	62
Emery Tilney, Protestant and Poet, 1545–1606	73
Tilney's Hall	90
The Fuller Family 1605–1722	102
The Brainy Wollaston Family 1723–1867	131
Monks Hall Tenants in the 18th Century	143
The Read Family – Victorian farmers	163
Bullingham the Bigamist and Other Tenant Farmers, 1895–1935	180
Richard Horry Winn, 1900–1942, owner of Monks Hall 1935–1936	200
The Leader Family at Monks Hall 1937–2016	209
A Manor through Time	237
Bibliography	242
Index	250

Foreword

I first met Elaine Murphy by sheer chance, several years ago, when she and I turned up in Ashwellthorpe in Norfolk at the same time, on the same day, to visit the church, which was, unfortunately, locked, with the keyholder nowhere to be found. She had gone there to look at the splendid Thorpe tomb, in connexion with research which she was then undertaking on the history of her house, The Grange at Brockdish. My own visit to Ashwellthorpe was to further my investigations into a Yorkist soldier from the village, who had fought at Bosworth and who may have been a retainer of Thomas Howard, Earl of Surrey (and, later, Duke of Norfolk). Howard, at the time of the battle, was residing there with his first wife, Elizabeth Tilney, in the manor which her family had held for several generations. Thwarted in our attempts to get into the church, we got into conversation instead and, discovering mutual historical interests (some of which, coincidentally, have surfaced in this book), have remained in contact with one another ever since.

Baroness Murphy's research into the history of her own home saw its embodiment in *The Moated Grange. A History of South Norfolk through the Story of one Home, 1300-2000* (Book Guild, 2015), a book which has since received wide acclaim. On the back of that success, she has now embarked on a second in-depth study of another fine, historic East Anglian house, the subject of this present volume, with the encouragement of its current residents. The Grange in Brockdish lies on the northern side of the Norfolk/Suffolk border, but for this, her latest research undertaking, she has gone just south of the River Waveney, into the adjoining Suffolk parish of Syleham.

It is easy to see why such a very attractive house as Monks Hall would generate widespread interest and appeal. Indeed, it is not only the author herself who has been struck by its charm, but also many others, including the Suffolk writer, environmentalist, film-maker and broadcaster, Roger Deakin, whose extensive archive, now held at the University of East Anglia, contains references to the house.

As well as being a house which has a striking visual impact, Monks Hall's appearance and name instantly suggest that it is a building with a long history. But how does one go about unravelling that history? Often, researching the story of a house over a long period – especially one which spans many centuries – can be fraught with pitfalls and disappointments, particularly when solid documentary evidence may not always be forthcoming. Indeed, there are many examples even of famous historic buildings where a dearth of archival data has resulted in gaps in the historical narrative, thereby necessitating intelligent guesswork on the author's part. Moreover, an imbalance of source material often forces house historians to concentrate on more recent periods, where the fullest survival of records usually occurs.

Fortunately, in the case of Monks Hall, there is a quite exceptional *corpus* of primary source material, with an excellent sequence of archival records from at least the thirteenth century, through to the present day. Furthermore, the virtually undisturbed terrain around the building enables meaningful interpretation of a landscape which appears to have been largely unchanged since pre-Conquest times. In addition, the study of the house and its fabric has also been facilitated by the existence of valuable secondary sources, not least, unpublished studies by the local historian, Andrew Francis Gray, to whom the author has dedicated this book.

This is good news for an historian and Elaine Murphy has put all those sources to excellent use, telling a compelling story, not just about the building and its residents, but also placing it within its wider local, regional and even national settings. In so doing, she has woven a fascinating tale. Beginning with a consideration of the Anglo-Saxon estate and landscape, she then moves on chronologically to take full advantage of the extensive records relating to Thetford Priory's manor at Syleham, which survive in an almost unbroken run from the early fourteenth century onwards. These have permitted her – and the reader – a remarkable insight into the operations and development of the medieval manor, its officials and inhabitants, as well as providing a detailed description of Monks Hall itself, as it stood in the 1430s. Moreover, the long connection of the site with the monks of Thetford Priory during the middle ages seems almost certainly to be reflected in the house's name.

The excellent survival of documentary evidence continues into the modern era, taking the story beyond the dissolution of Thetford Priory in the mid-sixteenth century, when Monks Hall was acquired by the Tilney family and the house substantially rebuilt by them, in a form which is recognisable today.

The records allow the timeline of ownership to be further pursued in very close detail right up to the present day, chronicling owners such as the families of Fuller, Wollaston, Read, Winn and Leader, together with tenants, who included George Bullingham, James Backhouse and the Redgrave family. Each brought their own identity to the house and, as the author shows, each contributed to its story. Few house historians have the good fortune to find a survival of sources such as exist for Monks Hall and which have allowed such a detailed and even insight into its history at almost every period of its existence.

In her 2015 volume on *The Moated Grange*, Elaine Murphy described herself as 'A novice explorer in local history'. From the evidence of this, her second study on the history of a house, she is a novice no longer. Her diligent research, skilful analysis of the sources and, most particularly, her ability to bring the story forward in a most comprehensive way have combined to make this book an absorbing historical account of what may well be the oldest continually occupied house in Suffolk.

Dr John Alban

Former County Archivist, Norfolk

Introduction

    Monks Hall is a house that knocks you sideways, it's so lovely. I was driving along the lane from Hoxne to Syleham along the River Waveney, a world away from the busy Scole to Yarmouth road on the northern bank of the river, and suddenly there ahead, part hidden by a chestnut tree on the bend, was this arrestingly beautiful ancient house. Though painted now in an 21st century interpretation of Suffolk pink, a bold rose madder, its colourwash cannot detract from the quality of the timber framing and mellow brickwork, time having bent its timbers into curvaceous maturity. It is simply one of those houses that you have to slow down to get a better look at as you drive by. I have

Sketch of Monks Hall, by Wilson Smith, 1981

Sketch of Monks Hall by Wilson Smith for cover of Syleham Festival Programme 1981. North East Suffolk Photographs and Illustrations. SRO Ipswich, 932/4/56/4/1.

been driving by enviously now for over forty years.

Of course when you live in the locality you quickly realise many others feel the same pleasurable longing for this house. Roger Deakin, the Suffolk writer and 'wild swimmer', who lived in his own Elizabethan timber-framed house in Mellis, hinted that even the birds recognise the quality of the place:

> Yesterday the ash arch began to come into leaf, just sprouting at the tips of the laid horizontal branches at first, and then a few flowers. Wild hops suddenly leaping and grappling up the grey, smooth ladies' stockings ash bark. The quince and cow parsley and ash blossom/leaf all began on the same day, when the wind went round and four swallows appeared. They flew over the house and then turned left and disappeared somewhere else. How I longed for them to stop here instead. They took a turn or two overhead, then just went. To Monks Hall in Syleham, perhaps.[1]

A house like this is always steeped in local legend and I must have been told a dozen times that the house is called Monks Hall because it was the hunting lodge for monks living at Thetford Priory, a notion that conjures up some wonderful Chaucerian images but sadly probably isn't true, although the connection with Thetford Priory is solid enough. And then a dozen architectural historians, Nikolaus Pevsner being the most famous and oft cited, decided after a cursory glance that the west crosswing is the oldest part of the house and the central main building is 17th century with later additions.[2] In fact the documentary evidence gives an earlier date for both parts of the house. I dare say that in the following chapters I too shall make mistakes that some future historian will delight in exposing but I will try my best to back up the story with documentary references that can be rechecked by the enthusiast.

First, a word must be said about my personal approach to house history. The story of a dwelling must include something about the building and its development, that's the nuts and bolts. Mostly though it is the story of the people who lived and worked here, owned or rented the house, farmed the land, were shaped by the terrain and the economic, political and religious context of their times. Above all, what we learn should inform local history and add to an understanding of the region we live in.

When the current residents, old friends who know my enthusiasms well, suggested I might like to "do something on the history of Monks Hall", I jumped at the opportunity but I envisaged a long and often fruitless search for evidence. It had taken me five years and a lot of professional help to unearth the history of my own home in neighbouring Brockdish and I thought it was likely to be just as painful a process for this Syleham house.[3] I had not expected to find the fabulous array of documents preserved in public and private archives, from medieval manorial extents and accounts going back to the 13th century, through to deeds from the Victorian era and household accounts through the 20th century. What emerges is an extraordinarily colourful pageant of characters who shaped the manor and the history of farming in this quintessentially agricultural corner of the Waveney Valley on the northern border of Suffolk.

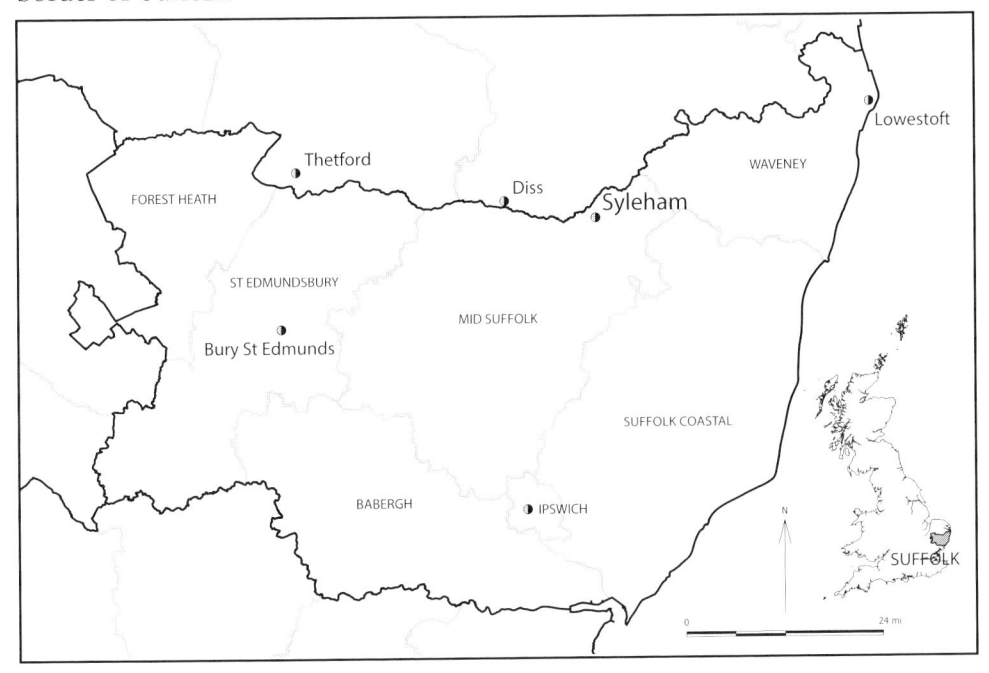

Map of Suffolk, showing Syleham

The following chapters tell the story of the manor, the estate and the people who lived at the hall, and has to start when the manor was created in Saxon times. There must be very few estates where the contours of the Saxon manor are broadly the same today. The acreage has varied in size from 250 acres to more than 500 acres as the owners added or sold land in the vicinity, but the continuity is remarkable. The changes in agriculture reflect the development of the Waveney Valley from subsistence farming in the valley bottom and slopes, through sheep and dairy farming with hempen fields, to the well-drained arable land of a modern farm in the 21st century. The contours of the land in

Syleham parish have been mercifully untroubled so far by urban development.

The manor was owned by Thetford Priory religious settlement throughout the medieval period and, miraculously, surviving records tell us quite a lot about that time in Syleham. After the Dissolution of Thetford Priory in 1540, the manor estate was sold to ambitious Thomas Tilney who bought it for his fervently Protestant son, Emery, who matched his father in ambition and deviousness. Emery sold the estate to the Fuller family of Puritan yeomen farmers, who weathered the trials of the 17th century at the hall. Then followed a long period of absentee ownership by the wealthy but scientifically gifted Wollaston family. Their remote ownership of Monks Hall explains why the hall was preserved largely intact from the 17th century without major alterations. The 18th century tenants made a good life at Monks Hall, part of a local social circle. The Read family farmers who followed were keen Victorian improvers and James Read was able finally to buy the estate in the 1870s. The last Read did not live at Monks Hall but rented the estate out to a motley crew of tenants during a period of agricultural recession at the end of the 19th and beginning of the 20th centuries. An eccentric property developer owned the estate briefly until the attractive Leader family arrived in 1936. Their ownership ended only in 2016.

The characters in this pageant who called Monks Hall 'home' have a surprising amount in common. The house is not a grand house compared with many today, although its 16th century occupants were grand in aspiration. The residents generally belonged to a social stratum of educated articulate people, mostly prosperous farmers who made a comfortable living from the land, mixing with the local gentry but not always a part of them. This may be the oldest continuously occupied house in Suffolk.

Notes
1. Roger Deakin (posthumously) and Robert Macfarlane. 2015. 'Spring, in Fragments'. *Granta Magazine* 133 Autumn. Granta Publications online at https://granta.com/fragments/.
2. Pevsner, N. and Bettley, J. 2015. *Suffolk: East: The Buildings of England*. Pevsner Architectural Guides (revised edn, London: Penguin; originally published Penguin 1961).
3. Murphy E. 2015. *The Moated Grange: A history of south Norfolk through the story of one home 1300–2000* (Hove: Book Guild).

1

The Saxon Manor and Landscape 1000–1066

Monks Hall manor has changed surprisingly little since late Saxon times. Of course the crops have changed over the years, the productivity of the land now unimaginably greater than before the Norman Conquest, and the lives of the residents are certainly very different. Nevertheless it is possible to trace a direct connection between the manor of Anglo-Saxon days and the estate as it is now. So the Saxon period is a good time to start.

The Waveney Valley landscape has always set it apart from the countryside around. There were very good reasons for settling on this land. Before the slow revolution in agricultural science in the 17th and 18th centuries, farming on the light gravelly valley soils was far more productive than on the heavy boulder clay soils found on the plain at the top of the valley. For thousands of years this better drained sloping farmland supported crops and grazing and the river provided the added bonus of fishing and otter hunting. The heavy clay soil at the top of the valley even today remains seasonally waterlogged if not artificially drained. Monks Hall is where it is for very good economic reasons.

The surrounding farmland south and east to 'Upper Syleham' and west towards Hoxne is part of a gently undulating plateau that dominates most of north Suffolk, a huge area, about 165 square miles, bounded by the Waveney in the north and stretching from Great Ashfield and Walsham-le-Willows in the west to the South Elmhams and the north side of Halesworth in the east to the edges of the Gipping and Deben valleys in the south.[1] This plateau landscape has an ancient field pattern with sinuous and substantial hedges and ditches, often in 'co-axial' patterns, where the boundaries aggregate into long parallel lines which run at right angles to the principal water-courses.[2] These field systems probably originated in the late Saxon or early medieval periods and a high percentage of the fields were originally used as pastures for dairy cows.

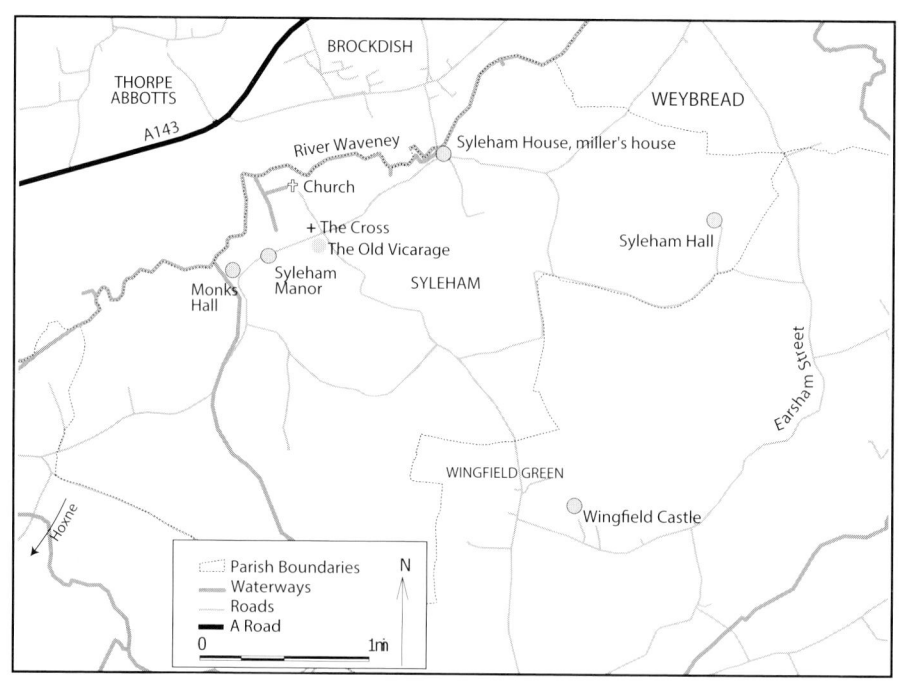

Map showing Syleham's locality

The great agricultural writer Arthur Young described this area in 1804 as being the 'dairying region' of the county.[3] In the late 18th century the introduction of clay drains for under-field drainage enabled the conversion of many dairy pastures into more lucrative arable units. However, a certain amount of arable farming has always been practised in this area, especially on the valley slopes, as is clear from the Domesday survey of 1086.

The poorly drained areas of the clay plateau are covered with numerous greens and commons. The greens, used for common grazing by the surrounding inhabitants until the advent of enclosures, seem to be the result of expansion into former marginal or 'waste' areas in the 12th or 13th centuries, and this is sometimes reflected by the green being shared by several adjacent communities, the Great Green at Syleham for example being contiguous with Wingfield Green. The evidence suggests that these greens evolved through prolonged grazing from areas of woodland or wood pasture documented in Domesday Book. Upper Syleham was probably a secondary settlement that developed on the edge of the green, whereas the area around Syleham Cross, down in the valley, was the primary village settlement around the church and river.

According to Andrew Gray, a local historian who did so much to explore the history of the village in old documents, phonetic spelling of the village name was variously recorded down the ages as Seilham, Seilanda, Sillham, Sulham, Silham, Sulhamstead, Sylam, Seelham, Scilham, Sealam, Sileham, Sylehame, Sylham and Syleham, but this diversity is not unusual, indeed it is normal for a village name to be differently spelt in every document.[4] Nineteenth century scholars concentrated their attention on the later and somewhat more common twelfth century spelling of the name 'Sulham', interpreted as a corruption of the Saxon word 'Sulh' or 'Sylu', meaning muddy or boggy place.[5] That makes sense to those who have tried to reach the church after several wet days! Others choose Seilanda as the correct name, interpreting it as meaning 'Sea Isle', perhaps less convincing, although the church may have originally been on an island. The earliest surviving will of a Monks Hall manor resident, admittedly four centuries after Saxon times, a man named John Saghar (Sawyer), who died in 1439, calls himself a 'Skepmaker' or basket maker. He lived at Syleham Cross and would probably be using osiers from willow that grew abundantly by the river.[6] Gray suggests that Syleham could refer to the 'Settlement where the willows grow'. This fits well with the known Saxon method of describing landscape features as a guide to travellers in an age when maps were unknown.[7] In this book the author will call it Syleham but refer to variants where relevant.

Osgood, the Saxon overlord

The earliest document relating to Syleham village is the will of Bishop Theodred of London.[8]

> In the name of the Lord Jesus Christ Amen. I Theodred Bishop of Londoners …. return to my lord the King his heriot ….' [heriot was a type of tax or death duty. The King was either Edmund the Elder 939–946 AD or Edred 946–955 AD.] Theodred leaves the son of Queen Eadgiva by Edmund the Elder, 50 marks in 'red gold', …. And

I give the land at Mendham to Osgood, my sister's son and the land at Seilam and at Isestead (Instead) and at Chickering and at Ashford and at Whittingham …

The will goes on to hand out many other tracts of land in Norfolk and Suffolk to various named individuals. Osgood was probably a 'tenant in chief' or thane, who was bound to supply a number of armed men to serve for three months every year in the Fyrd, the Saxon army. We really do not know which part of Syleham Osgood acquired or whether he kept it, but a century later there was still an Osgood or Osgod with enormous power in the area, who may have been a descendant.[9]

Farming in Saxon times would have been predominantly cattle grazing and dairying, the nature of the heavy clay above the river terraces still preventing any large-scale exploitation for arable purposes. While the late Saxons had an efficient iron plough they could not easily drain heavy clay soil. Where patches of lighter soils existed on the slopes down to the valley, barley, oats, rye and perhaps some wheat were cultivated. The number of people living in Syleham in Saxon times was perhaps no more than ten families, forty to fifty persons,

Anglo Saxon ploughing

British Library, Cotton MS Tiberius B.V/1, f.3

although that is quite a well-populated area for the period. But Hoxne was then one of the seats of the Bishops of Elmham, a larger community that supported a market, and as it is within easy walking distance, it is possible that some of those working the land in Syleham lived there.

If there was anyone living on the site of Monks Hall, we are unlikely to find any trace of the settlement since the timber, wattle and daub thatched dwellings of this period needed replacement every twenty or thirty years and therefore leave little trace of their existence other than post holes or shallow round or rectangular pits when they decay. The reconstruction of the Anglo-Saxon village at West Stow gives us some notion of how a settlement might have looked. It is likely that a small cluster of dwellings was located not far from the church, probably close to where the Cross now stands. This seems to have been the standard village form during the Saxon period.

Early Saxon villages were typically located at such sites, marginally above the flood plain. There would also be small, scattered, single-family farmsteads, situated in a pattern probably not dissimilar to those we see today. Almost all the roads and footpaths around the village clearly reflect traditional routes used by the people at this time. The roads up the valley slopes to the present upper village almost certainly owe their origin to the movement of livestock. These tracks were called 'cattle drifts' where animals were driven to graze on the clayland pastures or 'greens'. Cattle drifts were generally ditched, banked and hedged on each side to prevent cattle straying onto cultivated land.

The late Saxon church at Syleham

The most important building in Syleham during Saxon times would have been the church, of course, sited where it is today but then conveniently on the main road through Syleham from Wingfield that crossed the river by a bridge east of the church and continued up to Brockdish north of the Waveney. This bridge remained in place for many centuries, it is thought up to the 17th century at least, long after Thetford Priory built a new bridge for the mill. The continuation of the old track north of the river can still be seen on ordnance survey maps.

The earliest church would have been built of timber with wattle and daub walls and a thatched roof. In the early 11th century, before the Norman Conquest, the ownership of Syleham village reverted to the church, becoming the property of the Bishops of East Anglia (also called the Bishops of Elmham). An entirely new church building was erected, probably similar in size to the chancel of the present building and including a tower, constructed of flint rubble, but with expensive limestone cornices. The lower flintwork courses of the tower up to the height of some three feet or so above ground level are judged to be from around 1000 AD. The flint is entirely local, probably originating from deposits found on the southern valley slopes between Syleham Mill and Monks Hall. The new church was almost certainly funded by the Bishop.

The establishment of manors

By late Saxon times, Syleham parish had already been divided up into two main estate holdings or manors. One part, which would become Monks Hall manor, belonged to the Bishops of Elmham, called Sielham Episcopi (Bishop's Syleham) in some early documents. The remaining land formed part of the estates of Edric, an immensely powerful Saxon nobleman whose estates stretched from the Roman Pye Road (roughly the modern A140) eastward encompassing almost all the land and villages along the River Waveney up to, but not including, the Elmhams. There is an interesting survival of this estate in Syleham in the medieval document called the ' extent', the manorial land holding survey of 1379. There is a piece of land, the sharply rising ridge to the west of Monks Hall, called 'Edrycheshegg' which means Edric's Hedge.[10] One is tempted to think this formed part of the boundary between Edric's land and the Bishop's land.

During the last years of Edward the Confessor's reign (1042–1066), the final period of Saxon domination, Sielham Episcopi became part of the estates of the phenomenally successful Stigand, formerly Bishop of Elmham, who became Archbishop of Canterbury. Stigand had control over huge swathes of the Waveney Valley. After the Conquest, Saxon Stigand did not last long as Archbishop. He lost his usefulness to William and was quickly deposed, dying in 1072.

Archbishop Stigand as depicted in the Bayeux Tapestry at the coronation of Harold.

Following Stigand's downfall, Seilham Episcopi became the property of the new Norman Bishop of East Anglia, then based at Thetford, while the land in Syleham formerly owned by Edric passed into the hands of the Norman

Robert of Tosny or Count Robert. This larger manor became known as Syleham Comitis (Syleham of the Count or Earl).

And this is as much as we know about the Saxon origins of the Manor that became Monks Hall. Did Osgood's ancient feet walk upon Syleham's meadows green? Probably not, but lots of other feet did, of freemen, unfree serfs and villeins and cottagers and slaves. The late Saxon period witnessed very significant advances and changes in agriculture that were to have far-reaching consequences. The factors driving and influencing these changes include a slight warming of the climate, an increase in population, the development of a more sophisticated plough and the recurrent Viking raids. The creation of common fields or greens may have arisen out the social upheaval caused by the Viking invasions or in the reorganisation following. But in Syleham there was clearly a well developed manorial system of blocks of land that may have had its origins long before, in Roman times.[11]

Almost all Anglo-Saxons lived as farmers and spent most of their time growing food and looking after animals. They mostly grew a type of wheat called einkorn, rye, barley, oats, peas and beans, using wooden tools, such as hoes, rakes, spades, billhooks and forks. It was hard and difficult work and so was ploughing. An iron plough was an expensive piece of equipment. They farmed cows, sheep and pigs, but they also kept goats, geese and chickens and used animals for meat, milk, cheese, butter, eggs, wool, leather, tallow for candles, bone and horn, cooking fat and feathers. Cattle and horses were used for transport. Oxen were most important for pulling the plough although in East Anglia the horse was also used, which was lighter and quicker but more expensive to maintain.[12] It was a hard life but it produced sufficient food, just about, for most in a prosperous area such as Syleham.

Notes
1. Suffolk County Council on Plateau Claylands. http://www.suffolklandscape.org.uk/landscapes/Plateau-claylands.aspx
2. Dymond, D. and Martin, E. (eds.) 1999. *An Historical Atlas of Suffolk, 3rd edn.* (Ipswich: Suffolk County Council & Suffolk Institute of Archaeology and History).
3. Young, Arthur 1804. *General View of the Agriculture of the County of Suffolk* (London: Board of Agriculture), p. 46.
4. Gray, Andrew F. 2004. *Syleham: A village history, Part 1: Glaciation to AD 1605*. Unpublished paper courtesy of Mary Lewis, Churchwarden St Margaret's Parish Church Syleham.
5. Skeat, Walter W. 1843 (later edn online 1913). *The place-names of Suffolk*

(Cambridge: Cambridge Antiquarian Society). Available at https://archive.org/details/placenamesofsuff00skearich (accessed 9.4.2018).
6. Will of John Saghar 1439. NRO Norwich Consistory Court will register Doke 106.
7. Smith, A. H. 1956. *English Place Name Elements, Vol. 2* (Cambridge University Press, Cambridge).
8. Will of Theodred, Bishop of London, A.D. 942–951. Translated by Whitelock, E. H. D. 1930. *Anglo-Saxon Wills* (Cambridge: Cambridge University Press). No 106, pp. 552–4.
9. Henson, Donald 1998. *A Guide to Late Anglo-Saxon England: From Ælfred to Eadgar II* (Ely: Anglo-Saxon Books), p. 47.
10. Monks Hall Manor Extent 1379–80. British Library Manuscript Collections. Ref Add.Ch.16561. Transcription by Andrew F. Gray c.1995. Held at Monks Hall Archive, unpublished, p. 1.
11. Martin, E. and Satchell, M. 2008. "'Wheare most Inclosures be" East Anglian Fields: History, Morphology and Management', *East Anglian Archaeology 124*.
12. A good overview of Anglo-Saxon farming can be found in Banham, D. and Faith, R. 2014. *Anglo-Saxon Farms and Farming* (Oxford: Oxford University Press).

2

The Normans, Roger Bigod and Thetford Priory, 1066–1380

Syleham in the Domesday Survey 1086

Following the Norman Conquest the Saxon overlords in Suffolk were ousted from their lands, and these were allocated by grateful William to his closest and most valuable henchmen. Stigand maintained his ownership of his estates longer than most because William thought he would be a useful mediator between the new regime and the resentful conquered Saxons. But by 1072 Stigand was gone and his East Anglian lands were handed over to a Norman called Herfast, the new Bishop of East Anglia, who based himself at Thetford.

William the Conqueror wanted to know what his new kingdom was worth and how much tax he could expect to get from it, every inch of it. He also wanted to establish exactly which of his rebellious Norman lords owned what and settle ongoing disputes. The Domesday survey of 1086, which locally was conducted by Norman inspectors based at Hoxne, provides a clear picture of the village agriculture but only what was relevant to wealth production. Women, children and other unproductive dependents were not counted, though many would have been working on the land.

Little Domesday, the more detailed survey carried out in East Anglia, describes three manors in Syleham although one of them, Esham, is now classified with Wingfield in the National Archive.[1] The rough illustration shown below is just that, a 'best guess' at the broad position of the manors from the various early descriptions. Esham or Essham may well have been even smaller than shown.

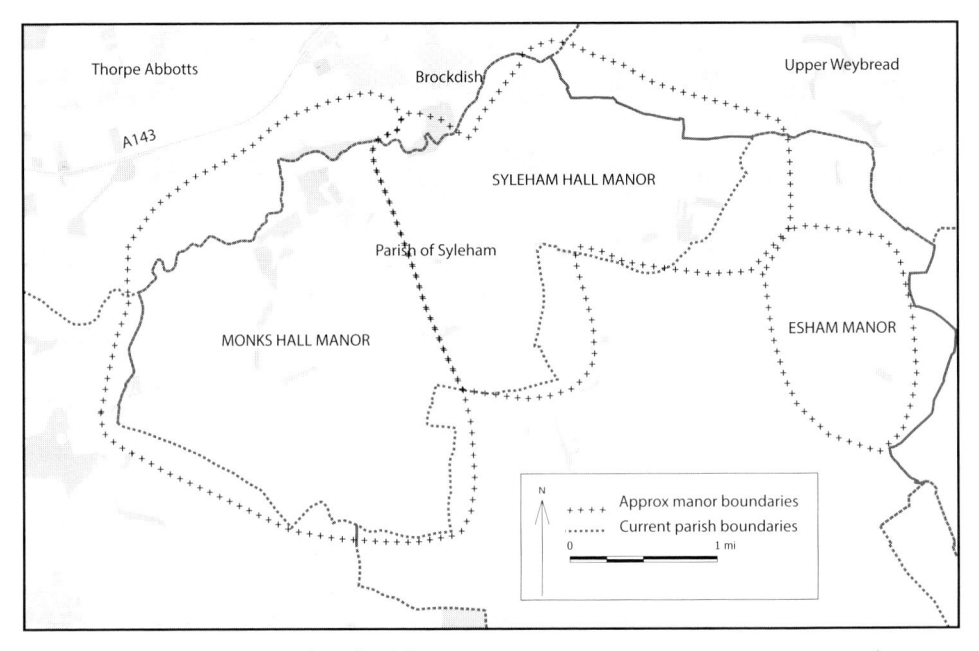

Approximate geography of Syleham manors in Norman times, superimposed on modern parish outline

A manor was an area of land held by a landlord who was not necessarily titled or a knight, but capable of producing sufficient income to maintain the owner, who in Norman times was usually a military man or an individual with military obligations to his lord. The landowner was either a tenant of the King or one of the great lords who had received their land from the King. Each manor consisted of a 'demesne', an area of land for the lord's own use, often around the hall, while the remaining acreage was cultivated by peasants and usually included some land regarded either as common or as 'waste' or uncultivated land. A manor's owner often held multiple manors across a wide area as a result of patronage, heredity and local dispute resolution conducted by powerful men.

People living on a manor, that is, those who actually did the work, could be roughly divided into two classes, the free and unfree. The subtleties of belonging to these two groups all depended on what services one was obliged to perform for the lord and how much one was free to farm on one's own account. Top of the pecking order were the freemen or freeholders, who farmed land they owned in their own right or rented from the lord of the manor but who did some nominal services for the landlord. Freemen also paid some local taxes to the lord but were able to sell or pass on their land to whoever they wished. Freemen did not necessarily live on manor land but often did and could hold land in more than one manor. The manors of southern England had more freemen than northern and western areas of the country, probably reflecting the greater prosperity of the south-eastern areas.

The second class of inhabitants, known as 'villeins' or sometimes 'serfs', were skilled craftsmen who were 'tied' to the manorial lands. They paid all local taxes and rent to the lord while also cultivating their own land and the demesne for the lord. Closely allied to villeins were the slightly superior cottagers or cottars, who worked the land, living in primitive cottages on the manor. Villeins and cottars had few rights, could not move away from the manor and were subject to the authority of the manorial court. These courts were held regularly, usually at two or three weekly intervals. Every freeman and villein who worked the manor land had to attend this court, where fines were imposed on all those who broke the 'Custom of the Manor'. This usually consisted of a set of local rules that regulated almost every aspect of agricultural and communal life. In return for their work and services, villeins were allocated a certain amount of land within the manor that they cultivated to support themselves and their families.

At the bottom of the social ladder were slaves, totally unfree, who worked at menial jobs and whose lives were entirely in the hands of the manorial lord. They could end up in chains if they tried to escape. Slavery diminished over the medieval period.

At a time when there was no police force, law and order was generally maintained by a system known as 'Frankpledge'. Under this system the community as a whole was responsible for the behaviour of all persons over fourteen years of age. Thus villagers living in Syleham would have been divided into groups of households, responsible for reporting and investigating offences against the custom of the manor as well as arresting and bringing criminals to trial, a sort of early Neighbourhood Watch. Each group of households was responsible to a senior man known as the 'Chief Pledge' who represented the group at the manorial court and was responsible for bringing offenders before it.

The three manors of Syleham

The manors, which seem to have encompassed a rather larger area east and south than the 21st century parish, were Syleham Comitis, Syleham Bishops Manor and Esham Manor.

Syleham Comitis, the larger **Earl's manor**, had a taxable value of 2.9 geld units and 7.5 'villtax'; these were the units liable for taxation. The value to the lord in 1066 was £5; the value to the lord in 1086 was £5.4s. Households included three villeins, thirteen cottagers, one slave and five freemen. There were three lord's plough teams, for the demesne land, and 4.5 men's plough teams for the rest of the manor. That is enough to cover about 330 acres.[2]

In addition to the ploughland, which implies good arable land, there were 9 acres of meadow, woodland with 150 pigs and one mill, probably a horse mill. The livestock in 1066 was 2 cobs (sturdy working ponies), 8 cattle and 80 pigs. Twenty years later in 1086 the livestock had dwindled to 1 cob, 2 cattle, 44 pigs, 7 sheep, 3 goats and 1 beehive. The lord and overlord in 1066 was Ulf, the son of Manni Swart; the lord in 1086 was the Norman Robert of Tosny, who was also tenant in chief. The decline in stock suggests that either Robert was a bad overlord or he employed a poor local bailiff or reeve to supervise the work on the land. The manor paid tax, called a 'Scot', to the King of 7½d. a year.

Syleham Bishop's Manor, which later became **Monks Hall Manor** was somewhat smaller and had a taxable value of 2 geld units. The value to the lord in 1066 was £3, in 1086 also £3. There were twelve cottagers and one freeman. There were 2 lord's plough teams and 2 men's plough teams. It has been estimated that this would have been sufficient to plough 240 acres. In addition to the ploughland there were 5 acres of meadow, woodland with 60 pigs, 1 mill and a church with 0.13 acres of land. The lord in 1066 was 'one freeman', the overlord was Stigand. We have no idea of the name of the freeman who actually ran the manor but he would have been in effect the bailiff supervising everyone else.

By 1086 the lord of the Bishop's Manor was Bishop William of Thetford. Probably the most valuable possession in the manor was the water-driven mill, almost certainly located where the converted mill cottages are today. In the later medieval period the mill was a dual-purpose mill used for milling grain and fulling wool but in the 11th century it would be used solely for grinding grain. The value of the entire manor was substantial but as church land owned by a bishop it paid no tax or 'Scot' to the King.

Esham Manor (also Essham or Essam). This was a small manor that seems to have been managed in conjunction with the Bishop's Manor. Its taxable value was 0.1 geld units and the value to the lord in 1086 was one shilling. One freeman was the lord of the manor, again in effect the manor bailiff, the overlord being Bishop William of Thetford. Little is known about the location, extent or size of this manor save that it was small. It probably included the land presently occupied by the group of houses and farms lining the incorrectly named 'Earsham Street' abutting Wingfield, Weybread and Syleham Comitis. The evidence for its location is derived from two 15th century documents in the National Archive at Kew and one in the Suffolk Record Office at Ipswich.[3] In two 13th century legal documents it is called 'Charles Manor' after a local family who owned it briefly.[4]

During the reign of King Edward I, around 1290 AD, a violent dispute broke out over the ownership of land[5] situated to the east of Syleham Hall and the hamlet of Esham. While the manor was small it was important, for it contained a Chapel of Ease dedicated to St Faith that saved local people having to undertake the journey to Syleham church to hear mass. Many people living outside Esham had an interest in the land there either as freeholders or tenants and in the late 13th century there were violent disputes about the ownership of the land. Eventually the manor ended up in the hands of the Seymour (St Maur) family and in 1375 the manor was passed to the De la Poles at Wingfield, along with the Manor of Chickering, eventually disappearing altogether as a separate manor.

The Bishops Manor at Syleham becomes Monks Hall Manor

How did the manor become the property of the Priors of Thetford Priory? On to the Syleham stage enter two of the great characters of early Norman East Anglia, **Roger Bigod** and **Herbert de Losinga**. The Conqueror, Duke William of Normandy, was followed by his second son, William II, called 'Rufus'. His job was to sustain the empire he had inherited and continue the 'Normanisation' of all institutions of the church and state. Introducing Norman prelates to the existing bishoprics and upper echelons of parochial church management was one step; persuading French monastic foundations to cross the channel to establish new monasteries in England was another.

It is hard for 21st century folk to grasp the phenomenal power, authority and wealth of the religious foundations of the church of Rome and the impact they had on the landscape and farming practice. Monasteries owned a quarter of all land in England by the time of Henry VIII and were the wealthiest institutions in the country. Mutual backscratching between the monastic foundations and secular seigniorial lords was a necessary feature of the age.[6]

Looking at the austere, pious figure of Bishop Herbert de Losinga depicted in Norwich Cathedral, one would never guess the machinations he was capable of to get what he wanted.[7] Educated in Normandy, Herbert became prior of Fécamp Abbey and was in that post when William Rufus invited him to become Abbot of Ramsey Abbey in Huntingdonshire. Quite soon after, Herbert seized the opportunity presented by the death of Herfast, Bishop of East Anglia, to buy the Bishopric from the King sometime in late 1090 or early 1091, for the princely sum of £1900, a vast amount of money that he had acquired in the King's service. At the same time, for £1000 he also bought the Abbacy at Winchester for his father Robert de Losinga.

Herbert was therefore guilty of simony, the crime of buying or selling church offices and roles. Repenting, he travelled to Rome to seek absolution. Although he did not give up his prizes he made great show of offering to do so. With the Pope's and the King's consent he was returned

Bishop Herbert de Losinga, c1054-1119, carving in Norwich Cathedral, by C H Simpson 1895.[8]

to his See and was told to build churches and monasteries as penance, which he did with startling enthusiasm and grand style.

Accounts of Herbert's character from contemporaries are divergent but all agree that he was clever, learned, and physically very attractive, wrote a lot and was very popular with his own monks and acolytes. Devious and ambitious too, no doubt, but he was one of the most impressive figures of the Norman period.

Herbert de Losinga's acquisition of the Thetford see gave rise to one of those disputes among powerful churchmen that were a feature of the early Middle Ages. Herbert's new See had three, perhaps even four, seats located at Thetford, North Elmham, South Elmham and Hoxne. None of these were suitably grand enough so he decided to move the centre of his See to Bury St Edmunds, a pilgrimage site that received a rich flow of revenue from pilgrims in the form of endowments and legacies from the cult of St Edmund. As a result, a furious dispute erupted between the Bishop and Baldwin, Abbot of St Edmunds, who did not want a bishop operating in his area, competing for donations from the same population. William Rufus was drawn into this 'holy row', which continued until 1091 when the king's judgement in favour of Abbot Baldwin finally forced Herbert to give up his plans for Bury St Edmunds and turn his attention to the rapidly developing royal city of Norwich, already one of the largest cities in England, with 25 churches and a population of 5–10,000 people. It was a good decision from our point of view, given the magnificent legacy he left founding Norwich cathedral.

Once settled on Norwich, Bishop Herbert began in 1094 to make plans to build his cathedral. To do this, he needed to gain control of a large area of land on the south east of the city with a river frontage. **Roger Bigod or Bigot**, self-styled 'Earl of Norfolk', at that time Constable of Norwich Castle, readily agreed to exchange the extensive burial land he owned in the area of Norwich we know today as 'Tombland', including St Michael's Church, for the manor the Bishop owned in Syleham. This particular piece of land in Norwich was important to Herbert because St Michael's was Norwich's principal church, founded in Saxon times, and if Norwich Cathedral was to be a success it was better not to have a strong local competitor church. St Michael's was indeed demolished by Herbert de Losinga before 1119 and a stone cross was erected on site, now represented by a granite obelisk.[9]

Roger Bigod thus became the owner of Syleham Bishop's Manor and for a very short time it was therefore Syleham Bigod's Manor. Bigod was an interesting character, the father of one of the greatest East Anglian dynasties. Roger came from a fairly obscure family of poor knights. The family may have come from a small domaine in Douvrend in Normandy, called Clos Bigot, but it is also possible that the family name was originally a nickname reflecting a family personality trait. The name remains common in France and in Italy as Bigotti. Robert le Bigot, certainly related to Roger, possibly his father, acquired an important position in the household of William, Duke of Normandy due, the story goes, to his disclosure to the duke of a plot by the duke's cousin.

Both Roger and Robert may have fought at the Battle of Hastings, although the author has been unable to confirm this from academic research sites listing names. After the battle however they were rewarded with substantial estates in East Anglia, which suggests they played some important role in the Conquest even if they were not actually at the battle. The Domesday Book lists Roger as holding 6 lordships in Essex, 117 in Suffolk and 187 in Norfolk. Bigod's base was originally in Thetford, Norfolk, which was then the see of the bishop.

In 1069 Roger Bigod and two other Norman knights defeated one of the intermittent but regular Danish invasions, this one by Sweyn Estrithson (Sweyn II) near Ipswich. In 1074, Roger was appointed sheriff of Norfolk and Suffolk and acquired many of the estates owned by his predecessor, the dispossessed Earl of Norfolk. For this reason he is sometimes counted as Earl of Norfolk, but probably he was never actually created earl. (His son Hugh formally acquired the title Earl of Norfolk in 1141.) Roger gained further estates through his influence in local law courts as sheriff and great lord of the region.

In the Rebellion of 1088 Roger joined other barons in England against William II, whom they hoped to depose in favour of William I's older son Robert, who had inherited the Dukedom of Normandy from his father but not the Kingdom of England. Roger seems to have lost his lands after the rebellion failed but regained them after reconciling with the king.[10] In 1101 there was another attempt to bring in Robert of Normandy by removing King Henry, but this time Roger Bigod stayed loyal to the king; he had learnt his lesson.

At some point Roger married Adelise (also Adelicia) de Tosny (died c.1136), probably daughter or sister to Robert de Tosny who held Syleham Comitis Manor.[11] Roger Bigod and Adelise had five children. Their older son William, who seems to have been an impressive man, founded the magnificent Norman church at South Lopham but died tragically young, drowned in the White Ship disaster of 1120, a national tragedy.[12] Their second son, unreliable hothead Hugh, we will meet again in this chronicle. They also had three daughters who all married suitably well.

Roger got richer and more powerful over the years. His first castle was built at Thetford, where around 1100 he built the first motte and bailey castle there on an old site. In 1101 he consolidated his power when Henry I granted him licence to build a castle at Framlingham, which eventually became the family seat of power until the Bigod downfall in 1307. Another of his castles was at Bungay and another was Walton Castle, at Felixstowe, an old Roman fort strengthened by Roger but now swallowed by the sea.

Wealthy men wanted certainty in the hereafter for themselves and their family. Building churches and founding monastic and other religious institutions guaranteed certain privileges and rights within those establishments but also someone reliable to sing and recite masses for one's soul. Roger Bigod decided to found a priory at Thetford for a relatively young order based in Cluny in France, and as part of his donation, because a new priory needed land to sustain it, he gave the valuable manor at Syleham as part of his benefaction.[13] The manor included the valuable watermill and 'fishery'.[14]

Roger's benefaction was not perhaps as freely given as first assumed. The chronicles written at the time say that Roger had made a vow to the new King Henry I that he would go on a pilgrimage to the Holy Land. He quickly thought better of this idea, perhaps because pilgrimages were dangerous, took many months or years, and were inclined to lead to insurrection and trouble back home. He was allowed to commute his original commitment by applying the money that the pilgrimage would have cost to establishing a monastery, and Henry I's favourite religious order at the time was the Cluniacs. Contemporary Norman accounts say that the decision was taken by Roger 'on the advice of his wife', according to a translation by Dugdale in 1693.[15] We can imagine Adelise's relief that Roger found a way of staying at home!

Roger communicated his intention to establish a new Cluniac priory to Hugh, abbot of the main Cluny house in France, and although the abbot could not spare monks from his house to form the proposed new foundation, he welcomed the addition to the order and asked for a silver mark yearly in token of its dependence. Bringing in 'alien' foundations like the Cluniacs, with a mother abbey house in France, was part of the great Normanisation project. The French monks were however not all that keen at first on crossing the channel to this inclement land and often required inducements. The first Cluniac house had been established at Lewes by William de Warenne around 1080, initially with just three monks but it had since grown into a successful enterprise.

In 1104, the Prior of Lewes agreed to send twelve monks to serve at Thetford, together with Malgod, a man described as living a 'simple life', to serve as their prior. They chose Herbert de Losinga's abandoned cathedral church of the East Anglian bishops as the church of the new priory, and a cloister or cells of woodwork were erected for the accommodation of the monks. Thetford welcomed the monks, and for three years they were busy in building the new monastery within the borough.

At the end of this time Malgod was recalled to Cluny; he was considered not quite up to the job, quite possibly by Bigod. In his place Stephen, 'a monk of noble parentage and of the highest learning and morals, a great friend of the abbot of Cluny and sub-prior of Lewes', was sent to Thetford to complete the foundation. Stephen at once saw that the monastic site, surrounded by the houses of the Thetford town burghers, was inconveniently sited, incapable of expansion and had no room for a guesthouse. The king, who often held his court at Thetford, certainly gave his sanction and may even have applied pressure to persuade Roger Bigod soon to give them a pleasant and open site on the other side of the river.

Herbert, Bishop of Norwich, turned the first sod of the new foundation in July 1107 and the prior, founder and many noblemen laid the foundation stones. But the eighth day after the stone-laying Roger Bigod suddenly died.[16] We do not know the cause. An unseemly dispute then ensued between the prior and bishop as to the place of Roger's burial, although it is clear that Roger himself wanted to be buried in Thetford. One account records that the monks claimed that Roger's body, along with those of his family and successors, had been left to them by Roger for burial in the priory by the foundation charter, as was common practice at the time.[17] It was indeed usual that in return for the endowment gifts, the benefactor/founder gained 'confraternity' with the order, becoming a sort of honorary monk himself. He was thus able to enjoy all the benefits of religious life without having to accept the monastic rule, meanwhile building up credit in heaven. Traditionally when a benefactor lay dying he would be carried to the monastery and on his death be buried dressed as a monk so becoming part of the order, the soul of the benefactor receiving the benefit of endless prayer.

Bishop Herbert decided to seize the body for his own new foundation. Bigod was a sufficiently important local figure to attract visitors but perhaps also Herbert wanted to demonstrate the importance of his new cathedral in providing the resting place for one of the richest men in East Anglia. It is recorded, admittedly by the possibly partisan Cluniac monks at Bermondsey, that Bigod's body was stolen in the night by Bishop Herbert; although this seems unlikely, Herbert was perfectly capable of organising such an outrage.[18] When Bishop Herbert de Losinga had the body buried in the embryonic cathedral in Norwich he was surely depriving Roger of his rights and clearly he had scant regard for Roger's own wishes. However, the Cluniac monastery at Thetford kept Roger's benefaction of the manor at Syleham. As a result **Syleham Episcopi** became known as **Syleham Monarchorum** or **Monk's Syleham.**

Meanwhile the building of Thetford Priory went on, the revenues increased, and Prior Stephen lived to see its completion and the monks moving into their new premises on St Martin's Day, 1114.

Notes:
1. There are now many versions of translations of Domesday online. This account uses the Open Domesday website and National Archive Document References E31/1/3/1515, E31/1/3/995. Phillimore references 22671, 22098 and 22105.
2. Estimates of acreages were calculated by the inspectors from the number of ploughs needed, which gave a very rough idea and took no account of different farming practices or terrain. Roffe, D. 2000. *Domesday: the Inquest and the Book.* (Oxford: Oxford University Press), p. 148.
3. Laurence de Sancto Mauro, parson of Silham [Syleham] and Esham [in Syleham] churches. John de Wyngefeld quitclaims to (2), all lands, tenements, rents and reversions which (2) formerly purchased from Sir Edmund de Sancto Mauro's brother. 10 Edw.III. (Phillipps MS No. 28839). SRO ref HD 1538/376/1. Thomas Donfe to grant land in Stradbroke, Wingfield, and Earsham Street in Wingfield (Esham), in exchange for other land there, to the master and chaplains of the church of Wingfield, Thomas retaining land in Stradbroke. Suffolk. 1401-2. TNA ref C143/433/11. 2. Eleanor late the wife of John de Wyngefeld to grant a messuage, land, and rent in Wingfield, Earsham [Esham, now in Wingfield], Fressingfield, and Weybread and the advowsons of the churches of Wingfield, Stradbroke, and Syleham, and of the chapel of Earsham, to the warden and chaplains of a chantry to be new founded by her at Wingfield, retaining land in Stradbroke and Wingfield. Suffolk.35 Edward III TNA Ref C143/339/1. Quitclaim 8 Jul 1336 Laurence de Sancto Mauro, parson of Silham and Esham

churches. John de Wyngefeld quitclaims to all lands, tenements, rents and reversions which were formerly purchased from Sir Edmund de Sancto Mauro's brother. 10 Edw. III. (Phillipps MS No 28839) SRO. Ref HD 1538/376/1

4. Gray, A. F. 2004. 'Syleham: A village history. Part 1 Glaciation to AD 1605', unpublished paper.
5. Patent Rolls 1301 'Commission on complaint by Thomas Charles that Ralph de Sancto Mauro and Alice his wife, Roger de Clyfton, Richard de Gosebek, WiUiam Cokerd, of Harleston, and Avice his wife, Hugh le Proster of Thrandeston, Robt. de Raveningham, Richard le Prestre, of Neuton Floteman, and Richard Rannespalefreyur assaulted him at Syleham and carried away his goods.' quoted in Copinger, W. 1905–1911. *The Manors of Suffolk: notes on their history and devolution* (Manchester: Taylor, Garnett, Evans and Co).
6. Shirley, Kevin L. 2004. *The Secular Jurisdiction of Monasteries in Anglo-Norman and Angevin England* (Woodbridge: Boydell and Brewer), Chapter 3: 'The Anglo-Norman Period 1066–1154', pp. 55–70.
7. Account of Herbert de Losinga from White, C. H. E. 1885–1900. Dictionary of National Biography, Volume 34, and Greenway, Diana E. (ed) 1971. 'Norwich: Bishops (originally of Elmham and Thetford)', in *Fasti Ecclesiae Anglicanae 1066–1300*: Vol. 2, *Monastic Cathedrals (Northern and Southern Provinces)* (London: Institute of Historical Research), pp. 55–8. Available at British History Online http://www.british-history.ac.uk/fasti-ecclesiae/1066-1300/vol2/pp55-58 (accessed 3.7.2017).
8. Photograph of carving of Herbert de Losinga courtesy of the Dean, Norwich Cathedral Library. Bishop's Choir Throne, by C.H. Simpson, designed by J. L. Pearson, made in 1895 by Cornish and Gaymer of North Walsham.
9. St Michael's Church, Tombland Norfolk Heritage Explorer NHER No 86. Online at http://www.heritage.norfolk.gov.uk/record-details?MNF586-Site-of-St-Michael's-Church-Tombland-Norwich (accessed 9.4.2018).
10. Yarde, L. 2011. '15 minutes of Fame: The Rebellion of 1088', http://unusualhistoricals.blogspot.it/2011/05/15-minutes-of-fame-rebellion-of-1088.html (accessed 3.7.2017). Also Sharpe, Richard, 2004. 1088 – *William II and the Rebels.* Anglo-Norman Studies XXVI (Woodbridge: Boydell and Brewer), pp. 139–57.
11. Keats-Rohan, K. 1998. 'Belvoir : the heirs of Robert and Beranger de Tosny', *Prosopon Newsletter*, 9.
12. In the White Ship disaster in 1120 an overladen ship, bearing the heir to the throne and 300 noblemen and women from France to England, sank after striking a rock off Barfleur. This catastrophe left Henry I without a male heir and led indirectly to the twenty-year civil war for the throne between his daughter Matilda and Stephen of Blois. Story told in Ordericus Vitalis (1075–c.1143) *The ecclesiastical history of England and Normandy,* translated 1853 by Forester, Thomas (London: HG Bohn). Online at https://archive.org/details/ecclesiasticalhi03orde (accessed 4.7.2017).
13. Houses of Cluniac monks: 'The priory of St Mary, Thetford', in and London, William (ed.) 1906. *A History of the County of Norfolk*, Volume 2 (London:

Victoria County History), pp. 363–9. Online at British History Online http://www.british-history.ac.uk/vch/norf/vol2/pp363-369 (accessed 7.7.2017).

14. Copiger, W. A. 1909. *The Manors of Suffolk,* Vol. 4 The Hundreds of Hoxne, Lackford, and Loes, Manor of Esham, p93. (Manchester: Taylor, Garnett, Evans and Co). Online at https://archive.org/stream/cu31924092579576/cu31924092579576_djvu.txt (accessed 9.4.2018). Online at https://archive.org/stream/cu31924092579576/cu31924092579576_djvu.txt (accessed 9.4.2018). See also Page, Augustine, 1841. *A Supplement to the Suffolk Traveller or Topographical and Genealogical Collections concerning that County. Hundred of Hoxne, Syleham or Seilam* (Ipswich and London, Joshua Page), p 421–2.
15. "Rogerus Bygot" founded Thetford Priory, with the advice of "…uxoris *meæ Adeliciæ*", by undated charter dated to the reign of King Henry I. Dugdale, Sir William 1693. *Monasticon Anglicanum, or, The history of the ancient abbies, and other monasteries, hospitals, cathedral and collegiate churches in England and Wales. With divers French, Irish, and Scotch monasteries formerly relating to England.* (London: Sam Keble, Hen Rhodes), Vol. V: Thetford Priory, Norfolk p 148. Online at https://archive.org/details/monasticonanglic00dugd (accessed 4.7.2017).
16. The Annals of Bermondsey record the death in 1107 of Rogerus Bigod, principalis fundator monasterii Beatæ Mariæ Thetfordiæ. Annales de Bermundeseia, p. 431. The Latin annals of the Cluniac house of Bermondsey were not compiled until the 15th century but contain many older items. British Library BL, Harley ms. 231.
17. Ibid.
18. Ibid.

3

Syleham's Day of Fame, 1174

We cannot leave the 12th century without recording the most important event in the history of the manor of Monks Hall. It has often been said that nothing much happened in Syleham before 1174 and nothing much has happened since, for which we can all be grateful. The events at Syleham were of national significance at a time when the crown was under threat. The account here is largely taken from transcribed accounts of original sources. On 24th and 25th July 1174, King Henry II and Hugh Bigod spent a night encamped near the village, with thousands of Fleming mercenaries on Bigod's side and an army with Henry II. The circumstances surrounding this visit are recorded in two contemporary chronicles and confirmed by entries in the royal accounts for that year.[1]

The politics of the period are complicated and to understand them it is necessary to chronicle the series of events that brought the king to this small village in Suffolk. Henry II was by all accounts an extraordinary human dynamo of a man who not only ruled England and Ireland but was also Duke of Normandy. Something of Henry's complex personality and tortured family relationships were captured by Peter O'Toole in the 1968 film 'The Lion in Winter' in suitably manic and extreme fashion, if not quite showing Henry's short stocky body, red hair and striking good looks.

Henry ruled over a large portion of France gained through marriage with the older Eleanor of Aquitaine. Henry's lands in France made him, in theory at least, a 'tenant in chief' but also a vassal of Philip Augustus, King of France, and as such he was required to be obedient to his overlord. There can be little doubt that Henry did not enjoy being an underling, least of all to Philip, who in turn feared Henry's power and never ceased his attempts to undermine Henry's authority and seize control of his lands.

Henry was a reformer, anxious to ensure that both his kingdom of England and his lands in France were well administered and law-abiding. His efforts brought him into confrontation with his nobles, many of whom had acquired a taste for autonomy during the civil wars that had marked the reign of Henry's predecessor, Stephen. Confrontation with the Church followed as Henry attempted to reduce the power of Church courts by making churchmen subject to the king's justice. Conflict between king and Church escalated, leading firstly to the exile and ultimately the assassination of Thomas Becket, Archbishop of Canterbury.

As if these two factors were not enough, Henry's wife Eleanor and his four sons, Henry the Younger, Richard (later called Lionheart), Geoffrey and John were in open dispute with their father. So dysfunctional were family relationships that Henry kept Queen Eleanor prisoner as a punishment for meddling in politics and encouraging her sons to disobey their father. It should also be said that their early tempestuous love match had turned sour and he now had a younger mistress. Matters came to a head in 1173, when the French king, seizing upon Henry's huge unpopularity with his lords and the Church in the aftermath of the assassination of Thomas Becket, planned the great rebellion that would, he hoped, remove for ever the threat to his kingdom of France posed by the English monarch.

When the French rebellion erupted Henry found himself surrounded by enemies on every side, a situation that did no more than galvanise his determination to triumph. With mercenary troops recruited from the Brabant, an area covering part of Belgium and Holland, he inflicted a small but humiliating defeat on the French king. Henry then swept into Normandy, capturing the fortresses of those rebellious Norman lords who had collaborated with Philip Augustus and forcing sons Richard and Geoffrey back into obedience; he imprisoned them with their mother Eleanor. Henry's eldest son, Henry the Younger, who was supposed to be ruling England on behalf of his father, had also joined the rebellion, crossing to Flanders where he joined Philip of Flanders in recruiting mercenary troops and preparing an invasion fleet. He was counting on the support of many great lords who had seen their Norman lands devastated by King Henry, now insultingly called 'the old King' though not yet fifty years old.

England was in uproar. The Scots, encouraged by the French, sent a large army over the border, and the forces loyal to 'the old King', were forced to march north to deal with the invaders. Meanwhile, rebel lords in England led by the Earl of Leicester sacked and burnt Nottingham, and Hugh Bigod, Earl of Norfolk, attacked Norwich Castle with an army of Flemish mercenary troops, burning and looting the city.

Hugh Bigod (1095–1177)

Also known as 'Bigod the Restless' or 'Bold Bigod', Hugh was Roger Bigod's second son and inherited everything when his older brother William died in 1120. After Henry I died Hugh did not support Matilda, Henry's daughter, but gave his support to Stephen of Blois instead. Indeed it was Hugh Bigod's fault that these wars started in the first place since Stephen's claim to the throne rested on Hugh's testimony that Henry I, on his deathbed, had given his kingdom to Stephen. He almost certainly did not.[2]

Throughout his career, Hugh changed sides when convenient to end up on the winning side, although not always with success. He was vacillating and inconstant in other ways, repudiating his first wife and taking up with a second, thus setting up endless years of interfamilial squabbling between the stepfamilies.

In 1140 Hugh again rebelled against Stephen, this time making Bungay his headquarters. He was not successful. 'At Pentecost, the king with his army came upon Hugo Bigot of Suffolk and took the castle of Bunie'. Two months later, though, Hugh had rearmed and Stephen was forced again to march against him. This time Stephen tried the expedient of giving Hugh the Earldom of Norfolk to keep him quiet! This seems to have been just what Bigod needed, and in 1141 we find the new earl fighting *for* the king at Lincoln. Unfortunately for Stephen, the battle turned against him and he and most of his henchmen left the field prisoners. Hugh Bigod fled when he saw the battle was being lost and for the next twelve years joined Matilda's winning side.

When Matilda's young son Henry II took the throne, he showed his strength immediately by putting down with a firm hand the unruly barons who for twenty years had kept the country plunged in the miseries of anarchy; this included Hugh Bigod, who was deprived of his castles, although he was allowed to retain his harmless title of Earl of Norfolk. By 1163, however,

Remains of Bungay Castle (2004).

Hugh Bigod met Henry II at Syleham where he was declared a traitor. He only escaped with his life by agreeing to the destruction of Bungay Castle and a huge 1000 mark fine.

Henry seems to have considered Bigod sufficiently chastened for it to be safe to give him back his castles, which Bigod then fortified to the hilt. Henry built Orford Castle, possibly in response, to keep an eye on what the unreliable earl and his Flemish mercenaries were up to.

When rebellion broke out all over Normandy and England during the Easter of 1173, Bigod seems to have had no hesitation in joining in with the rebellious barons against the king. When the Earl of Leicester arrived in Suffolk with more Flemish troops to join Hugh Bigod, it seemed that no town or village in East Anglia was safe from an involvement in the insurrection. The two rebel earls joined forces briefly at Framlingham Castle, Hugh's main base, then parted, the Earl of Leicester marching on Bury St Edmunds while Hugh stayed further east to prevent Henry II landing in Norfolk or Suffolk. Henry, having brought his French possessions back under control, quietly returned to England in late June 1174 and landed in Kent. Instead of rushing to raise an army, he went first to Canterbury where he prayed at the tomb of Becket before moving on towards Huntingdon, which was being besieged by a small force. Huntingdon surrendered within days of Henry's arrival, while elsewhere events were rapidly turning against the rebels, who were soon in full retreat. The Earl of Leicester's army was defeated by local forces at Fornham

St Genevieve, near Bury St Edmunds. The earl, his wife and the commander of the Flemish mercenaries were captured. Hugh Bigod was left to face the king alone.

Around 20 July 1174, the royal army, after fighting victoriously in Scotland, arrived at Huntingdon to back up Henry's troops. Henry now turned his attention to Hugh Bigod, who retreated to his new fortress at Bungay, a town then surrounded by marshes, making the castle difficult to approach. Henry arrived in Syleham on 24 July 1174, having earlier sent a note to his Exchequer in London ordering them to pay the sheriff of Norfolk and Suffolk to send five hundred carpenters to 'Sileham'. The carpenters were going to make siege machines to attack Bigod's castles at Bungay, Framlingham and anywhere else he might hide.[3] We do not know whether these five hundred carpenters were actually recruited and possibly they were not.

Hugh Bigod was by now ageing. Extraordinarily when men grew old at fifty, he was now in his late seventies and tired, and he realised the game was up. On the morning of 25 July 1174, Hugh rode to Syleham to make his peace with the king.

There is a local tradition that Hugh was so fearful of Henry's anger that he spoke to the king holding on to Syleham Cross (a stone cross now replaced by a wooden one to mark the spot). The enraged monarch had earlier in the day received a painful kick from a warhorse belonging to a certain 'Tosti of St Omer a knight of the Temple' so Henry may not have been in a very patient frame of mind. There is no record in the chronicles of this cross-hugging episode. In fact the record says that neither man got off his horse!

A wooden cross now marks the spot where Syleham Cross once stood.

The two ageing men were both tired perhaps of these endless rebellions. Peace was made and Hugh negotiated a free passage for his Flemish mercenaries to go home via Dover at the king's expense, perhaps one of Hugh's nobler acts.

Hugh Bigod paid a heavy price for his rebelliousness. He was forced to surrender his castles at Framlingham, Bungay and Thetford and promised to depart from England forever, leaving his eldest son Roger in Henry's care as hostage. Henry had Hugh Bigod's castle at Framlingham destroyed but the earl 'ransomed' Bungay castle, saving it from destruction by the king's engineers who were already undermining the massive tower keep. Hugh Bigod did not survive his exile, dying on his way to the Holy Land in 1175 at the grand old age of eighty.

There is one possible trace of Henry's visit to Syleham. In the early list of tenants and landholding in Syleham, compiled by the monks of Thetford in 1379, the road running along the valley bottom from Hoxne to Syleham Mill is called 'Kingswaye', perhaps commemorating the route used by the king on his way to meet Hugh.[4] There is one other possible legacy of that day. The church was extensively rebuilt in the 13th century, and the church was re-dedicated to St Margaret of Scotland, Henry II's great grandmother, who was canonised in 1250.

If several thousand men turned up in Syleham today, it would certainly cause a stir, and it must have then. If village folk thought there was to be a military confrontation they would either have fled the village or possibly sought refuge in the church. We know so little about Syleham's one day of fame. But surely Monks Hall should have a summer party every 25 July to celebrate the king's final triumph over the disagreeable Hugh Bigod at this historic manorial location?

Notes
1. Jourdain Fantasme. 1174. 'An account of the wars between Henry II, his sons, William of Scotland and Louis VII., in 1173 and 1174' recorded in Stevenson J. and Fr. Michel (eds) 1886. Chronicle of the reigns of Stephen (London: Longman pp. 202–307. See also Mathew Paris Chronica Majora, Vol 2. A composite chronicle, containing the St. Albans compilation to the end of 1188, Roger de Wendover's chronicle, 1189-1235, both revised by Paris, now online at https://archive.org/details/matthiparisiens06luargoog (accessed 8.7.17). See also Latimer, Paul 2016. 'How to suppress a Rebellion'. Chapter 10 in Dalton P. and Luscombe, D. (Eds), 2016. Rulership and Rebellion in the Anglo-Norman World c.1066-1215 (Farnham: Ashgate), pp 163–78, p. 176, fn. 59. Pipe Roll evidence of expenses to carpenters etc. in Pipe Roll 19 Henry II pp. 33, 58, 156, 163, 173, 178

and Pipe Roll 20 Henry II, pp. 38 and 82. TNA. Refs E372.
2. Huscroft R., 2016. *Tales from the Long Twelfth Century: The Fall of the Angevin Empire* (New Haven: Yale), Chapter 2: 'The Earl's Tale, Hugh Bigod, Civil War and Royal Recovery', pp. 22–50.
3. Wooden siege machines came in kit form and had to be assembled on site with pegs. See http://www.timeref.com/castles/trebuchet.htm (accessed 10.7.2017).
4. Ministers Accounts 1312–1313. Monks Hall Manor. Suffolk Record Office Ipswich Ref HA411/2/1/12/3/1 NRA Catalogue Ref 4134.

4

The Manor and the Monks 1300–1400

The Cluniac religious order was an offshoot of the Benedictines that originated in Cluny in Burgundy in the 10th century. Cluny Abbey had the largest church in the western world before the construction of St Peter's in Rome. Cluny today remains an impressive site. During its ascendancy, c.950–c.1130, the Cluniac movement was one of the largest religious forces in Europe.

The order was founded to reinvigorate the devotional life of an increasingly worldly Benedictine order. Cluniac monks devoted their lives to constant prayer; they did not preach, teach or work as other monks did. Their 'work' was constant prayer for the good of all mankind. Cluniac monks thought it inappropriate that monks should dirty their hands with manual labour in any way. The Abbot of Cluny, Peter the Venerable (died 1156), remarked that it was unbecoming for monks, 'the fine linen of the sanctuary', to be begrimed in dirt and bent over labouring. In Cluniac houses other elements of their monastic observance, such as the copying of manuscripts, were considered to fulfil the work requirement of the Benedictine Rule.[1] An increasingly rich liturgy stimulated demand for altar vessels of gold, fine tapestries and fabrics, stained glass and polyphonic choral music.[2] So we must be very clear that although they lapsed intermittently from their own high moral standards, the Thetford monks did not work on the land or run the mill in Syleham, nor indeed did they do any hunting or fishing. They managed their manors and church land to produce revenue for the priory to support themselves, just as seigneurial secular lords had before them. They were landlords.

After Roger Bigod's original benefaction had brought monks from Warenne's initial foundation at Lewes to Thetford, other donations followed.3 In 1240 the Priory acquired the revenues of a church in the diocese of London and by 1291 it had acquired the income of six Norfolk churches and portions of the rectory income of eighteen other churches in the county, as well as four in Suffolk. The total annual value of its property and land was then reckoned at £123 12s. 5d. In 1535, the income valuation prior to the Dissolution of the then wealthy priory was £312 14s. 4½d. The gross value was £418 6s. 3d.

Priories depended on the wealth produced on their agricultural land, so the more manors and land they acquired the better. Syleham Monks Hall manor was only one of the manors owned by Thetford Priory. They also owned North Glemham, Darsham, Lynton Santon, West Tofts, Monks Wyk Newmarket, Lynford, and extensive warrens, foldcourses (common pasture with exclusive grazing rights), tithes from advowsons (church glebe land) and other properties.[4] Their job was to manage these resources as best they could.

Thetford Priory was not always financially successful in the early days, nor were its priors all saints. The second prior Stephen 'turned the priory of Thetford into a house of debauchery', carousing night and day with his brothers Bernard, a knight, and Guiscard, whom Matthew Paris, a Benedictine Chronicler from St Albans, describes as 'clericus monstruosus', which hardly needs translation. Finally in 1248 Stephen engaged in a quarrel with a hot-blooded Welsh monk whom he wished to send back to Cluny, from whence he had only just arrived. Angered by his prior's abusive language the monk drew his knife and stabbed Stephen fatally by the great door of the church.

The fortunes of the priory were rescued by the miraculous 'discovery' of relics from the church of the Holy Sepulchre at Jerusalem, given by Hugh Bigod and a monk named Ralph. Bigod's highly convenient 'discovery' was just what the priory needed to attract pilgrims. The priory duly became the scene of miraculous cures, which helped generate revenues, by 1262, however, the debts of the house amounted to 610 marks. The prior's full statement of accounts to the Abbot of Cluny was clear enough about the debts. Inspectors from Cluny in 1275–6 found twenty-four monks all living with sufficient regularity save Ralph the cellarer, whom they found guilty of 'incontinency', a phrase which covered both fornication and drunkenness. A cellarer's work extended far beyond the wine cellar, in effect he managed all supplies. The liabilities of the house had risen to 804 marks, and there was also a debt of 400 marks to the priory's patron, the Earl Marshal.

Thetford Priory, 2014.
Courtesy of Mike Page.

The continuing wars between England and France meant that 'alien' priories like Thetford, accountable to a French mother-house, were poorly supported. Although the priory of Thetford was made formally autonomous in 1376, which enabled it to elect its own prior and set it free from any pecuniary obligation to Cluny, in fact the house did not want formal independence and continued to yield some allegiance to the great abbey and accepted its visitations up to the close of its existence. In 1390 the Cluniac visitors were again at Thetford, and described it still as a direct affiliation of the mother church of Cluny. There were then twenty-two monks participating in six daily masses, three of which were sung. A tenth part of the bread was reserved for distribution to the poor. The visitors found that all monastic obligations ordained by the Cluny rule were being duly observed.

In 1399 the Pope finally exempted Thetford Priory from the jurisdiction of the Abbot of Cluny altogether and authorised the election of their own prior, subject to confirmation from the prior of Castle Acre, another Cluniac foundation. The yearly tax of 13s. 4d., which the priory of Thetford used to render to the house of Cluny, was granted by Edward III in 1462 to the provost and college of Eton.

Hunting monks laid to rest

Why did the myth arise that Thetford monks used the Hall as a hunting lodge? Cluniac monks did not generally come out of their priory although priors did and other religious foundations, of which there were dozens in Suffolk, were less strict in their observance of the rule. We owe to Chaucer's *The Monk's Tale* the image of the hunting monk with worldly habits and vices. of which Chaucer clearly disapproved.[5] No doubt the image reflects a reality for some orders but it was not a Cluniac reality. We do know that there was a hunting lodge at Ashridge in Hertfordshire used by Benedictine monks, and indeed the bishops of East Anglia kept hunting parks. Bishops were altogether more worldly in their behaviour than monks.

Medieval hunting deer parks were common all over Norfolk and Suffolk but so far no deer park has been identified in the medieval period at Monks Hall.[6] The difficult boggy land of the plateau nearby was however used for deer parks, with examples in existence at Eye and Dennington as early as 1086. Many were 'disparked' and converted to farmland in the 16th century, but often the outline can still be traced in the field boundaries, as at Framlingham, Wetheringsett, Thorndon, Hoxne (owned by the Bishops of Norwich: 191 acres), South Elmham St James (also used by the Bishops of Norwich: 199 acres) and elsewhere.

Names such as Park Farm or Lodge Farm are often indicative of these former parks and we can see those names quite nearby Monks Hall, probably associated with the Hoxne medieval park. Many of the parks were wooded, or partly so, and there is frequently a close association with other areas of woodland or greens; examples include Depperhaugh Wood and Reading Green beside the Hoxne park, Hestley Green and Rishangles Green at Thorndon, and Park Street Green, Broad Green and Blacksmith's Green at Wetheringsett. All these suggest the former existence of larger areas of woodland on the plateau. So there may well have been hunting going on near to Monks Hall, and probably indulged in first by the Bishops of Elmham and later the bishops of East Anglia. It seems likely that it was not the monks who hunted but less cloistered religious and secular lords. And hunting was going on sufficiently nearby for the hall to be identified with hunting. One small caveat: the monks did later support the hunting of foxes as vermin in the late 15th and early 16th century, according to the Thetford Register (see Chapter 7) although they may not have participated themselves.

Monks Hall manor also had a fishery. Fresh water fish and eels were highly prized in the medieval period. It would have been possible to send fish in winter from the Waveney to Thetford. Again, it was not monks but manorial peasants who did the fishing.

Syleham Monks Hall manor in the 14th century

Throughout history, East Anglia has been one of the richest and most fertile agricultural areas in the whole of England. As a result it was far more heavily populated than much of England and the two counties of Norfolk and Suffolk received the closest attention from the king's tax collectors. The administrative structure of manorial holdings was quite rigid in the 14th century, a system designed to ensure that farm production continued in the absence of the owner. It is rather reminiscent of the management of large public and private enterprises today. Thetford Priory would have employed a steward, a kind of managing director, or CEO, over all their manors and then a local bailiff.

We know the name of the bailiff at the end of the 14th century, a man called **John Banerynghale**, who compiled the manorial accounts for the monks for 1396–1397.[7] Regrettably that is all we know about him but finding his name in the manorial records is very satisfying. We will meet **John Bole** and the **Cossey** family soon, who filled the reeve and bailiff roles in the 15th century. Each manor farm had a 'reeve', one of the more important villeins, who would be either elected or appointed each year. Reeves often served for many years and were the lynchpin of manorial farming life, being responsible to the bailiff for all production and use of labour.

As always the tenants of the manor paid rent to the lord but paid tithes, a tenth of their produce either in kind or in cash, to the incumbent rector priest. Part of the tithe record for Syleham for 1341 miraculously survives; 13s. 4d. were paid in respect of hay and 'turbary', or peat cutting.[8]

This neat picture of rural England obscures the profound hardship and misery for the estate bailiffs, reeves and the thousands of peasants who worked the land during the first half of the 14th century. The two most devastating human disasters to strike the Monks Hall manor in the millennium from 1000 to 2000 occurred in the early 14th century.

The Great Famine

Between 1315 and 1322, seven years of some of the worst weather northern Europe has ever seen caused a famine. The rain started in 1315 and continued every summer for seven years. The winters were exceptionally cold. Decrease in the food supply was not limited to a drop in grain production, but extended to epidemics in herds and flocks and an acute fall in the supply of salt needed to cure meats and fish that might have supplemented the reduced supply of grain. Wars diverted resources to military demands that might otherwise have been used to feed the hungry. A century of benign weather had lulled individuals and communities into a state of unreadiness for such an extended drop in production. In the late 13th century, yields in the colder parts of northern Europe and on marginal lands were usually low, even as low as two bushels for each bushel sown and probably nowhere higher than about seven for one sown.

Medieval people were accustomed to the vagaries of weather and resultant poor harvests, so no manor was without some means for storing excess grain from bountiful harvests in anticipation of the occasional bad one. There had been an extended period of balmy weather in the 13th century and relative plenty. Barns and drying ovens were too few and too small to store grain to last through more than one bad harvest. England weathered the crisis of 1315 relatively well. It was the continued bad harvests of 1316 and 1317 that brought widespread starvation and disease. It is thought that 15 per cent of the population perished. There were stories of starving peasants resorting to cannibalism; certainly people ate dogs and their precious livestock. Starving people swelled local cities such as Ipswich and Bury looking for work. The manorial courts reveal the anxiety of the times with frenzied litigation over small strips of land, the demands of creditors and arrears in rent.[9] Where landowners paid labourers in bushels of wheat the inflated price pushed landlords into desperation too.

The priory was not immune from depression and famine and by 1321 the monks were said to be 'spiritually and temporally destitute' and its buildings threatened with ruin.[10] There had been a riot in 1313 when the prior and his servants were attacked by an enraged mob and some were killed.[11] Debt continued to be a major problem for the priory throughout the 14th century. They needed the income from Syleham's relatively good land.

Syleham tax return of 1327

Frequent taxation weighed heavily on the countryside throughout the 14th century. In 1327, the king imposed a tax based on the value of each subject's moveable goods. Poor people were exempt from this tax but all those with moveable assets in excess of two shillings (twenty-four silver pence), were to be taxed at the rate of one penny for every twenty pence value they possessed.[12]

The tax lists still exist in part and include the return for Syleham or Silham. Eight people resident in the village had to pay tax, including three wealthy widows, Johanne de Elmham who paid 57d, Caterina Charnel who paid 48d. and Elianora (elsewhere Alianora) Charles, the widow of Thomas Charles of 'Essham', who paid 42d. The tax paid by these three women represented 21 per cent of the total sum raised of £2 18s. 1d. This sum makes Syleham the sixth wealthiest village in the Hundred of Hoxne. While we can surmise that Elianora lived in Esham, we do not know if either Johanne or Caterina were associated with the manors of Monks Hall or Syleham Comitis.

While these tax lists do not include the poor, they do enable us to form a rough estimate of the village population, which appears to have been about one half the size of the present day population (2011 = 180).

The Black Death

In spite of the hard years, when the weather recovered again in 1323 the countryside was quickly restored and the population started to grow again, too much so in East Anglia, a land already overpopulated, given the poor productivity of arable land everywhere.[13] The overpopulation problem was 'solved' by the horrors of the Black Death, the bubonic plague that swept through Europe between 1348 and 1349. A very great deal has been written about the Black Death, the change in economics, demography and agriculture, but it is still hard to capture the human emotional catastrophe behind the statistics that must have produced years of grieving despair and incomprehension for many families. Between a third and a half of the population died of the plague, usually within two to three days of the appearance of the infected 'buboes' or stinking boils that appeared first in groins and armpits.

Historian Mark Bailey has ingeniously used the appointments of new parish priests, who died at a higher rate than the general population, to plot the track of the epidemic in Suffolk in early 1349.[14] It appears that the Waveney

Valley villages were infected via the ports and traffic up the River Waveney. The pestilential onslaught was over quite quickly. Within three months it had moved on, which could explain why the Bishop of Norwich based himself at Hoxne from July 1349 for three months while the epidemic still raged in Norwich.

No family was untouched. There is a local tale that there was a group of houses in the area of Syleham Cross whose inhabitants were all victims of plague. It is quite possibly true although there is no historical or archaeological evidence to support the story. There is however documentary evidence that Syleham had been subject to a measure of population loss during the century following the initial outbreak of the disease, a situation reflected elsewhere in East Anglia.[15] Over a century after the original outbreak of plague, in 1449, there is a tax return called 'Feudal Aid', in which 'Seilam' had its tax reduced by a third, indicating that Syleham had suffered a loss of population.[16] Whether this loss was due to disease or migration it is impossible to tell.

Before the Black Death, a manorial farm comprised a well-differentiated male and female workforce with interlocking skills and chores in a community of carefully ranked status. After the devastation there were insufficient tenants and workers to till the land, so a re-ordering of rents and income had to be undertaken in order for farmland to remain workable. Men and women's roles became more intertwined after the pandemic and although men retained their privileges, the role of women in the home and in work became vital. In Suffolk, arable land was turned to pasture, which required less manpower, and sheep-rearing took over whole swathes of East Anglia. It has to be admitted that a smaller population was easier to feed and diet improved as meat became more widely available. The greater availability of land did not halt the continued flight from country to town, where work in the clothing industry was an attractive alternative.[17]

The Great Rising

The Peasants Revolt of 1381, known as Wat Tyler's rebellion, or the Great Rising, was a short-lived but vicious insurrection that spread from Kent and London to Essex, to Suffolk and Norfolk and then to the north and west. The rebels captured the Tower of London, murdered the Archbishop of Canterbury, and in many towns behaved like an indiscriminately violent mob to anyone thought to be in authority.[18] As with all riots, the leaders thought they had good cause, and the following mob added local resentments and personal antipathies to the *melee*. The historian Christopher Dyer has studied the revolt in Suffolk and it is clear that local resentments fuelled the rioting and murders.[19]

After the Black Death wages rose, but the Statute of Labourers of 1351 forced wages down again, causing resentment. Furthermore, serfs and villeins wanted to be free labourers without having to do feudal labour services.[20] These were simmering discontents, compounded by anger over the poll taxes imposed to pay for the Hundred Years War. In May 1381 peasant anger erupted at the return of tax collectors in Brentwood, Essex, and in Kent. Archbishop Sudbury's palace in Canterbury was burnt down and he was murdered because he was blamed, correctly, for the poll tax. Manor houses were attacked, records destroyed, law courts attacked. Between 50,000 and 100,000 people marched on London from Kent and Essex to take their complaints to King Richard II, a boy of fourteen, who they believed would agree with their demands. Richard tried to negotiate personally but failed when Wat Tyler was cut down by Richard's henchmen. The historian Charles Oman describes the outcome…

> Only a short month separates the first small riot in Essex, with which the rising started, from the final petty skirmish in East Anglia at which the last surviving band of insurgents was ridden down and scattered to the winds. But within the space that intervened between May 30 and June 28, 1381, half England had been aflame, and for some days it had seemed that the old order of things was about to crash down in red ruin, and that complete anarchy would supervene. To most contemporary writers the whole rising seemed an inexplicable phenomenon — a storm that arose out of a mere nothing, an ignorant riot against a harsh and unpopular tax, such as had often been seen before. But this storm assumed vast dimensions, spread over the whole horizon, swept down on the countryside with the violence of a typhoon, threatened universal destruction, and then suddenly passed away almost as inexplicably as it had arisen.[21]

At Leiston, there was a gathering of people from Hertfordshire, Essex, Suffolk and Norfolk, where John Wrawe, the parson of Ringsfield near Beccles, raised a force from them and marched inland, intent on attacking the Abbey of Bury St Edmunds. John Wrawe acted as leader in that area but, because of his priesthood, delegated his deputy Robert Westbrom of Bury to be the rebels' 'King of Suffolk' in his stead, and Bury was to be their first target.

Knowing that the townsmen and peasants were after his blood, the abbot fled, but was hunted down and killed and his head paraded round the town.

With the Abbot of Bury at the time was the king's Chief Justice, John de Cavendish, who was one of the targets of the Suffolk mob, as he had enforced with all his power the hated Statute of Labourers that was passed to keep wages low. He nearly escaped when he fled to nearby Lakenheath, by reaching for a rowing boat that was tethered nearby, but before he managed to get in it a local woman, called Katherine Gamen pushed it away from the shore with her foot, so he was captured and executed with John de Lakenheath, the Collector of Taxes for the area. It is thought about 4 per cent of the rebels were women and they certainly participated enthusiastically in some of the most violent incidents, including hacking off the head of the Archbishop of Canterbury.[22]

The rebels continued across Suffolk, attacking the property of 'traitors' of the people, who included the de Norwich family who lived in Mettingham Castle, near Bungay. Five hundred rebels attacked the castle. The defences gave way, the house was ransacked, and the attackers made off with goods to the value of £1,000. The rebels were intending to create an alternative county government, and James of Bedingfield, a leading rebel, took a band of 100 men and threatened to behead William Rous, the Constable of Hoxne Hundred if he did not immediately muster ten archers from the area to join the rebels, surprisingly promising to pay them at the usual rate of 6d. a day.[23] Rous complied of course. Court rolls were taken from manor houses and burnt, in order to attempt to establish a free new social order.

We do not know what direct impact the revolt had on Monks Hall manor but it is likely to have been considerable. In Thetford the burgesses were threatened and had to provide money and goods to the rebels, but I can find no direct account of the priory being attacked as the abbey at Bury was. The rebels seemed to have been paid off and Thetford people did not participate in the rebellion. The Earl of Suffolk was also lucky. He fled his estates, travelling in disguise to London. But other leading members of the local gentry were captured and humiliatingly forced to play out the roles of a royal household, working for Litster, the Norfolk leader. Violence spread out across the county, as gaols were opened, Flemish immigrants killed, court records burnt, and property looted and destroyed.

Moving through Norfolk to Norwich, the rebels stormed the gates of the city. Peasants and tradesmen manned the defences of the castle and awaited the next move. They did not have long to wait, for the rebels were counter-attacked by the soldier/priest Henry le Despencer, the Bishop of Norwich, and driven from the city. Geoffrey Litster fled for sanctuary to North Walsham Church, but the bishop had him dragged from the altar and drawn and quartered.[24] Thomas of Walsingham described Despenser as 'a man distinguished neither in learning nor discretion', 'unbridled and insolent, incapable of restraint' but he was decisive, effective and successful.[25]

After calm had been restored, Minor Juries were set up in every locality affected by the insurrection. The jury serving at Hoxne was chiefly concerned with cases of robbery, extortion and collaboration with the rebels. The Hoxne jury was made up of local freemen, some of whom were landholders on the manors of Monks Hall and Syleham Comitis: men such as John le Cotelar, William Hynke, Thomas Wolrych and John Page, whose names appear on the Monks Hall extent (survey) of 1379–80 and their descendants in the 'extent' of 1443 (see below). Not all the charges brought by local juries were accepted and the judges seemed to realise there were many old scores being settled in strictly local disputes. There were very few executions by the savage standards of the time and many pardons a couple of years later in 1383.

Poll taxes were dropped after the insurrection. Wages slowly rose and within ten years the government gave up trying to control wages. The dying old feudal system finally disintegrated. By 1500 all labourers were free.

Syleham mill

Existing documentary evidence suggests that there were two mills in Syleham between the 13th and 15th centuries. The oldest site is located at the converted 19th century mill buildings at the southern end of the county bridge to Brockdish, now dwellings. A water mill existed here for near 1000 years until the last disused mill buildings were converted into a garment factory in the late 19th century. The early 19th century miller's house still stands and the mill-race can be seen north of the cottages.

The second mill was probably further east on the Syleham Comitis manor land and may well have been the so-called 'horse mill' referred to in a later will. These donkey or horse-drawn mills are still used in much of the world. Windmills were much less common until later.

Milling was crucial to the medieval economy, without it grain could not be turned into food. The ownership of the mill was a major asset and source of income for manorial lords both secular and ecclesiastical, mill owners often charging freemen and villeins for the right to use the manorial mill but also being in effect service suppliers taking advantage of their local monopolistic position.[26] Studies in the 1980s and 1990s found that the major religious orders were harsher landlords than their lay counterparts. A recent comprehensive study of ecclesiastical orders and their mills suggests that many small priories and orders were more flexible and creative, even philanthropic in the way they ran their mills.[27] We do not yet know whether Thetford Priory ran their mill at Syleham in an enlightened way or not but the evidence to date suggests they were not especially generous.

Communication between Syleham and 'Brokdysshe', necessary to gain access to the ancient Kings Highway to Scole and then to Thetford was unsatisfactory for carrying flour from the water mill. The mill was too far away from the existing bridge over the Waveney near the church and probably the riverside meadows flooded regularly. The main Kings Highway in the medieval period ran through the villages of Thorpe Abbotts and Brockdish farther north than the current roads, above the flood plain and also through the now disappeared village of Thorpe Parva. We know this from documents in the Norfolk and Suffolk Record Offices.[28]

To create a better route, in 1360 the monks of Thetford purchased from Stephen and Rose Elvin of Brockdish the land on both sides of river to the east and west adjacent to Syleham Mill and on the north and south banks of the river.[29] Here a second crossing was constructed and the bridge road that is still in use today crossed the river to Brockdish. This road acquired the local name of Thetford Way and its construction along with a new bridge resulted in the gradual abandonment of the route that ran past the church. The toll charged for the use of the new bridge continued to be levied on all crossing it, save residents of Syleham, until the 1950s.

The watermill was without doubt Monks Hall manor's greatest asset and the bailiff of the manor would ensure it was kept in good running order. It would be worked by peasants of course and not by anyone from the priory.

Monks Hall manor in the late 14th century

We are exceptionally lucky in having two documents that supply a wealth of detail concerning the people who lived in Syleham and worked on the land as tenants of the Monks Hall manor during the late 14th century. Landlords kept carefully detailed records of their possessions, recording the names and holdings of all those who rented land and provided services or labour on the lord's own land.

In 1379 the Prior of Thetford, John de Fordham, ordered a valuation of all lands in Syleham owned by the monks.[30] These valuations contain a description of the arable acreage in use, meadow, pasture and woodland, as well as a list of other manor assets. The description and valuation were carried out by the most senior members of the village community and written on a roll of vellum by a trained clerk, in a form of Latin shorthand. A survey such as this is called an 'Extent'.

The extent contains no mention of a 'hall'. If there had been one it would surely have been described. So we must assume that the building of Monks Hall first took place after 1379.

The survey begins '.... This is a manor with arable land, woods, meadows, pasture, fish ponds divided as follows....' There follows a lengthy and detailed description of the manor lands from east to west; these then consisted of 171 acres of arable land, 10½ acres of hay meadow, 40 acres of pasture, 24 acres of woodland on a ten year felling rotation of trees plus 'a water mill both for fulling and grinding with a small river meadow and worth annually after deductions 56s. 8d.'

The Leet Court of the manor, that regulated such matters as maintenance of roads and ditches and dealt also with petty disputes and public nuisances, brought in an annual 20 shillings in fines. Overall the annual income from the manor was £12 14s. 4d., which in modern terms might be equated to a sum between £12,000 to £15,000 per annum although it is notoriously hard to equate modern values with old since the cost of goods and labour was so different.

The table below shows how the manor land was partitioned into plots of 12 acres, 6 acres and 3 acres, comprising a tenement (dwelling) in a messuage (land with house and garden); the name of the tenement; the current tenant/occupant; and how much annual rent the tenant paid. A separate list of the services due to the lord as a condition of the tenancy is described. Quite a number of plots are vacant in the extent, unoccupied perhaps as a result of the recurring plague and freemen moving away. Several of the plots have been part let to maintain some income. Tenements are usually identified using the name of a former family or resident tenant. Tenements often continued to be named after a long-dead tenant, sometimes for generations, until a more recent tenant's name acquired common usage. All tenants were required to cultivate the lord's demesne land and provide other services such as transport for the lord and maintenance of his mill, where the villagers were obliged to have their corn ground.

Monks Hall manor tenancies 1379–80

Acreage of holding	Tenement Name	Tenant in 1379	Annual rent paid to Priory
12	Wygenot's	Walter de Eastgate	2s. 2d.
12	Malbusshe	Vacant	2s. 0d.
12	Goneld's	Vacant	2s. 2d.
12	Turnehand's	John Turnehand	2s. 2d.
12	Rolve's	Robert Rolve	2s. 2d.
6	William Patrich's	Simon and Beatrix Wygenot	13d.
6	Page's	Vacant but 2 acres rented by Roger Godard	
6	William Hynke	Vacant but John Wygenot rents messuage and 3 acres	
6	Unnamed tenement	Services commuted	
6	Walter Kempe	Vacant but Alice Bakon rents messuage and 4 acres	
6	John Knave's	John Knave	13d.
6	Johanna Atte Cross	Johanna atta Cross	13d.
6	Robert Chykerynge	Robert Chykerynge	18d.
6	Katerina Mayhew	Katerina Mayhew rents messuage and 2acres	No rent mentioned Services commuted

6	Robert Pynchyn	Vacant. Part rented by John Plumbe and William Hynke	
6	John[undecipherable]	Vacant	13d.
3	Richard Goodnesse	Richard Goodnesse	2½d + 2 sheep
3	Simon Aleyn	Robert Aleyn	2½d
3	Bernard Egge	John Plumbe and William Sagher	2½d
3	Julian Bernard	Vacant	2½d
3	Pikkebarlit	Vacant	2½d
3	Adam Boles	Adam Boles	2½d
3	Lumer	Robert Carter	2½d
3	Osshys	Vacant meadow rented by Robert Carter	2½d
3	Wygenot	Simon Wygenot rents ¾ acre only	1¼d

Each listed tenancy is accompanied by a detailed schedule of services and given below, as an example, are the rent and services required of **Walter de Eastgate** for his twelve acres:

> .... Annual rent 2s. 2d. payable at 6½d. on each of the four Quarter Days: Lady Day March 25th, Michaelmas September 29th, Christmas December 25th. Midsummers Day, July 6th.
>
> **Item.** He shall give 2 Hens at Christmas [and] at Easter 12 eggs.
>
> **Item.** He shall give customary service between Michaelmas and Lammas [1st August] for forty weeks once a week except for 2 weeks at Christmastide, 1 week at Easter and one week at Whitsuntide in which he shall not have to give customary service.
>
> **Item.** He shall plough with his own plough for one day before Christmas and shall have nothing.[31]
>
> **Item.** In the same way at the time of the Oat harvest [he shall plough] 40 rows for one day and receive the Lord's food for one day.
>
> **Item.** He shall plough at Corn Harvest 1½ acres whether measured or not and shall have nothing.

Item. He shall plough on the Thursday of every alternate week from the Feast of the Purification (*of the Blessed Virgin Mary, 2nd February*) up to Pentecost [*the seventh Sunday after Easter Sunday*] and shall have nothing except on one day on which he shall provide his food but once in the day viz breakfast and shall have two courses and service (*see note above*).

Item. He shall make his horse do carrying service six times for the Lord's food or shall give the Lord 1d. for each carrying and shall carry at each carrying 3 Bushels Corn weight [*about 2½ cwt.*], 4 Bushels Barley weight or Oat weight [*about 3 cwt.*] as far as Thetford or elsewhere, a journey of that length for each carrying.

Item. He shall give feudal aid with his cart [*a service the lord could call on at any time but limited by the 'custom' of the manor*] and his own pair [*of horses*] for carting away manure outside the manor for the same time and shall have his own food for one meal each day and shall be allotted one task for each day or shall give to the Lord for all the cartage 8d.

Item. He shall weed without [*the lord's*] food ½ a day.

Item. He shall give at Lammas [*1st August*] 1d. for buying salt.

Item. Whenever it shall be necessary to transport a new grindstone for grinding he shall give 1d. to the same.

Item. He shall reap, bind and stack 8 acres of standing crops of various kinds and shall have nothing.

Item. He shall find two reapers for one day in Autumn to reap the Lord's corn for one meal in the day viz. Bread, two courses, and service and for each man's dinner 1 loaf of Bread which should be quartered? Two Herrings or sufficient Cheese.

Item. He shall find two reapers for one day for reaping the Lord's crops without food.

Item. If he has a cart he shall yoke it with his own pair and shall cart the Lord's corn for one day in autumn for the Lord's food till nones [*about 3pm.*]

Item. He shall mow for one day with two men or shall give 12d. [And there shall be a third part of all services etc. and of 3 acres of the best which are allowed into the Lord's hands 6½d. from the rent 6 hens 3 eggs 10 days winter maintenance service, plough service as fixed at the times of the corn and oat harvest equally.

Item. A fourth part of the said weeding.

Item. ¼d. for buying salt.

Item. carrying grindstones as necessary.

Item. 2 acres of reaped corn, one precary [¼ *bushel*] for reaping in the autumn of which half is for food.

Item. for manure carting 2d. half the mowing and carrying service....". [*the meaning of these conditions is not clear but they appear to be easements, adjustments or reductions of the services required*].

Similar schedules are drawn up for the other tenants. Walter de Eastgate, John Turnehand and Robert Rolve were by 14th century standards middling farmers with enough land to support their families. The list of services owed to the lord, the prior, is onerous and extensive. They also had to lend a hand at the mill with the grindstones and carting grain to Thetford when required.

In addition to the small tenements there are some thirty-five other rentals listed under the heading 'molland', a term used to describe land for which rent was paid instead of services. Many of the manor's tenants took advantage of the molland, which produced cash allowing them to purchase exemption from manorial services. Although some of the smaller holdings were vacant it seems that other tenants were prepared to augment the land they cultivated by renting the more productive pieces in each holding or those portions of it that suited their particular purposes.

Small pieces of evidence like this give an indication of the difficulties confronting the prior and other lords of manors at this time. The steady reduction in the population brought about by the periodic outbreaks of plague was slowly eroding the feudal system that had forced people to remain in their villages for life. Labour was at a premium and this fact alone was causing the manorial system to break down. People were less prepared to be tied to the land on a particular manor or tolerate their daily activities and lives being regulated by the 'custom' of the manor on which they lived. Landlords found increasingly that farming the manorial demesne on their own account was becoming both troublesome and increasingly unprofitable. As a result the lords of the manors were more prepared to rent out their land, thereby securing an annual income without the necessity of administering their holdings. This trend in turn provided the local peasantry with a means of improving their standard of living and lifting themselves out of servitude.

There are no fewer than 106 male and 10 female names listed in the extent document; forty-seven of these were former tenants who either were dead or had left Syleham. Around 20 per cent appear to be resident in Chickering, Hoxne, Wingfield or Syleham Comitis. Thirty-five of the thirty-eight remaining names listed are male but there is no way of knowing whether these men were married or had children. Any calculation of the population of Monks Hall manor in 1379/80 can never be more than highly speculative but there are some forty-eight messuages (houses with gardens) and three cottages listed, of which five appear to have been unoccupied.

The one man who stands out from the crowd here is **Walter de Eastgate**, who has one of the larger tenements and whose services owed to the lord are mentioned almost by way of exemplars. He may have been the reeve of the manor during this period. Maintaining the manor as a profitable endeavour was the responsibility of the manor bailiff, **John Baneringhale**. Miraculously the Bailiff's accounts for 1396–97 have been preserved in the Suffolk Record Office but while the lists are long and the details minute, it is not possible to deduce whether the manor was profitable.[32]

And so we leave the difficult and tragic 14th century and move on to the building of the current Monks Hall. We shall now meet the first residents.

Notes
1. Pearce, Christopher, 2016. 'Who were the Cluniacs? Monastic Wales Project'. School of Archaeology, History and Anthropology, University of Wales Trinity St David, Lampeter. http://www.monasticwales.org/article/7 (accessed 10.7.2017).
2. Barrow, Julia, 2009. 'Ideology of the Tenth century English Benedictine "Reform"'. In Skinner, Patricia. *Challenging the Boundaries of Medieval History: The Legacy of Timothy Reuter* (Turnhout, Belgium: Brepols), p. 142.
3. This brief history of the Priory of St Mary Thetford is online at 'Houses of Cluniac monks: The priory of St Mary, Thetford', in Page, William (ed), 1906. A History of the County of Norfolk, Vol 2 (London: Victoria County History), pp. 363–9. Available at British History Online http://www.british-history.ac.uk/vch/norf/vol2/pp363-369 (accessed 7.6.2017). Geoffrey Rocherio, prior of Thetford about 1350, wrote a full and interesting account of the foundation in a manuscript now at Corpus Christi College, Cambridge, transcribed in Martin, Thomas. 1779.

History of Thetford (London: J. Nichols), Appendix, pp. 29–32. An English abstract is given by Blomefield, Francis, An Essay Towards a Topographical History of Norfolk, online at http://www.british-history.ac.uk/topographical-hist-norfolk/vol2, pp. 103-5. The foundation charter of Roger Bigod and of his son William, and the confirmation charter of Henry I, as well as a long list of subsequent benefactors, are given by Martin, and also by Dugdale, from a register of the priory which was destroyed in the fire of the Cotton library in 1731. Cott. MS. Vitel, fol. iv. See also Duckett, Chart, and Rec. of Cluni, i, 60, 61.

4. English Heritage, 'History of Thetford Priory', online at http://www.english-heritage.org.uk/visit/places/thetford-priory/history/ (accessed 9.4.2018)
5. Chaucer, Geoffrey, c.1386. 'The Monks Tale', *Canterbury Tales*. Numerous editions online.
6. Hoppitt, Rosemary, 1992. *Suffolk's Deer Parks 11th-17th century* (unpublished PhD thesis, UEA).
7. Compotus [Accounts] of John Banerynghale, Bailiff to Prior of Thetford, for manor of Sylham Monachorum [Monk's Hall alias Syleham Hall alias Tylney's], Michaelmas 20-Michaelmas 21 Ric.II. 29 Sept 1396-29 Sept 1397 (Phillipps MS No. 26493) SRO Ipswich HD 1538/376/2
8. Extract from the Inquisition of Ninths 1341 - Silh'm: Tithes of hay and turbary worth 13s. 4d. per annum. SYL Misc. Suffolk Heritage Explorer Record.
9. Rubin, Miri, 2005. *The Hollow Crown: A History of Britain in the Late Middle Ages* (London: Penguin), Chapter 1: 'Famine and Deposition 1307- 1330', pp 17-56.
10. Dymond, D. 1995. *The Register of Thetford Priory, Part 1: 1482–1517*. Norfolk Record Society. Introduction, p 2.
11. Ibid p 2.
12. Suffolk Subsidy Return 1327 available in modern transcription in Sydenham, Henry Augustus Hervey 1846, published Woodbridge, G. Booth, 1906. Original ref. M. Jurkowski, C. L. Smith and D. Crook, Lay Taxes in England and Wales, 1188-1688. Quoting Parliamentary Close Rolls TNA: PRO SC 9 Special Collections: Parliament Rolls, Exchequer Series C54C. See Given-Wilson, C. 'General Introduction', in Given-Wilson et al. (eds), *The Parliament Rolls of Medieval England*, available online at http://www.sd-editions.com/PROME (accessed 14.7.2017), (Scholarly Digital Editions, Leicester, 2005)
13. Karakacili, Eona, 2004. *The Journal of Economic History* 64, pp. 24–60.
14. Bailey, Mark, 2007. *Medieval Suffolk: An economic and social history 1200-1500* (Woodbridge: Boydell and Brewer), Chapter 8: 'Pestilence, Rebellion and the Decline of Villeinage, 1349–1500', pp. 176–93.
15. Reduction of Feudal Aid in wake of black death. Lee, John S. 'Tracing Regional and Local Changes in Population and Wealth during the later Middle Ages using Taxation Records, Cambridgeshire 1334-1563' online at http://www.localpopulationstudies.org.uk/PDF/LPS69/LPS69_2002_32-50.pdf (accessed 9.4.2018).
16. Quoted by Gray, A. F. 1995. 'Syleham: A village history', p3.
17. Poos, L. R. 1991. *A Rural Society after the Black Death* (Cambridge: Cambridge University Press), Chapter 8: 'Migration and Settlement', pp. 159–79.

18. Butcher, A. F. 1987. 'English Urban Society and the Revolt of 1381', in Hilton, R. and Alton, T. H. 1987. *The English Rising of 1381* (Cambridge: Cambridge University Press), pp. 84–111.
19. Dyer, Christopher, 1988. 'The Rising of 1381 in Suffolk: Its Origins and Participants'. *Proceedings of the Suffolk Institute of Archaeology and History* 36, pp. 274–87. Online at http://suffolkinstitute.pdfsrv.co.uk (accessed 9.4.2018).
20. Jones, Dan, 2010. *Summer of Blood: The Peasants' Revolt of 1381*. (London: Harper Press).
21. Oman, Charles. 1906. The Great Revolt of 1381 (reprinted Kitchener, Ont.: Batoche Books), Chapter 1: 'Introductory', p. 6.. Online at http://socserv2.mcmaster.ca/~econ/ugcm/3ll3/oman/revolt.pdf (accessed 4.1.2014).
22. Federico, Sylvia. 2001. 'The Imaginary Society: Women in 1381'. *Journal of British Studies* 40 (2), pp. 159–83.
23. Barker, Juliet R. V. 2014. 1381: the Year of the Peasants' Revolt. (Cambridge, Mass.:First Harvard University Press), Chapter 12: 'Ely, Huntingdon and Cambridge'. Online at https://books.google.co.uk/books (accessed 16.7.2017).
24. Prescott, Andrew, 2004. (The Hand of God: the Suppression of the Peasants' Revolt in 1381). In Morgan, Nigel. *Prophecy, Apocalypse and the Day of Doom* (Donington, UK: Shaun Tyas), pp. 317–41.
25. Clark, James G, (ed.) and Preest, David (trans.) 2009. *The Chronica Maiora of Thomas Walsingham (1376-1422)* (Woodbridge: Boydell).
26. Holt, Richard. 1988. *The Mills of Medieval England* (Oxford: Blackwell), pp 58, 61–3. Langdon, John, 2004. *Mills in the Medieval Economy: England, 1300–1540* (Oxford: Oxford University Press), pp. 431, 441.
27. Lucas, Adam. 2014. *Ecclesiastical Lordship, Seigneurial Power and the Commercialization of Milling in Medieval England* (London and New York: Routledge).
28. Murphy, E., 2017. 'A Walk along the Medieval King's Highway from Scole to Thorpe Abbotts and Brockdish.' *Mardler, Brockdish and Thorpe Abbotts Village Magazine* 210, pp. 15–17.
29. Ref to 1360 mill development in secondary sources. East Anglian Miscellany No 2529. Papers of the Rev. Edmund Farrer, Hinderclay Suffolk Record Office, Bury St Edmunds p 60. Original source not traced.
30. Monks Hall Manor Extent 1379-80. British Library Manuscript Collections. Ref Add Ch 15561. Transcribed by Andrew Gray.
31. It was customary for the lord of the manor to supply those working on his demesne or in his service with food at certain times. A loaf of bread weighing four pounds, a pound of cheese and two quarts of ale and occasionally other things such as herrings or cold meat such as pork or cooked bacon. The term 'food and service' usually means that the meals were brought to the workers in the fields.
32. Monks Hall Manor Bailiff's accounts 1396-1397. SRO Ipswich. HD1538/376/2, NRA catalogue ref NRA 39544.

6

Monks Hall in the Fifteenth Century

John Bole, the Cossey Family and the New Hall

The first Monks Hall

The hall described in the 'extent' or survey of 1433 is a recognisable version of the Monks Hall that stands today. The Prior ordered the new survey just over half a century after the earlier one of 1379. During the intervening period the tide of the war with France had turned against England, the enemy re-invigorated by the leadership of Joan of Arc and a newly crowned French King. The powerful English nobles were increasingly divided over the conduct of the war and critical of the ineffective rule of religious, unwarlike Henry VI. Divisions in the ruling class were to lead to the civil war more commonly known to us as 'The Wars of the Roses'.

Throughout this time England was still experiencing periodic visitations of epidemic plague, while typhus and influenza ensured the population remained little more than 2.2 million. The average life expectancy of an Englishman had been reduced to around nineteen years, which signifies that the mortality rate among infants and those under five years was extraordinarily high and deaths from infectious disease afflicted all ages. Trade was depressed and towns that had been industrial and mercantile centres appear to have been in decline as manufacturing stagnated. Life was hard and death an ever-present threat to the residents of Monks Hall manor.

It was against this background that the 'extent' survey of 1433 was carried out. The picture of Monks Hall manor it provides is more comprehensive than that of 1379/80.[1] It begins:

> Silham Monkhalle.
>
> Extent and Rental of the manor of the lord Prior & Convent of the monks of the church of the Blessed Mary at Thetford, renewed in the time of Nicholas Fauldon then Prior, on the tenth day of March in the eleventh year of King Henry VI, both from the old extent and rental and on the oath of John Saghwyer (Sawyer), Benedict Barker, Peter Blount, Roger Estgate, Thomas Malo (Male), Godfrey Lacy, John Orewell, John Wolrych Senior, Thomas Carter, John Halle, John Page and John Wolrych junior, who swear....

There follows an invaluable description of the manor land immediately surrounding the hall and the manor hall itself, a very different group of buildings from those we see today but recognisably containing the same basic hall building.

> ....And the garden of the said manor lies in its own ground surrounded with hedges, water meadows, pasture and roads belonging to the said manor in its own separalty and with trenches, trees, hedges, houses and walls, shut in on every side and containing in its area by estimate and according to the old extent, 5 acres. Value per annum per acre: 8d.

The Manor Hall of 1433

> On the said manor or site, one hall with upper rooms at each end, at right angles to which is a grange with fourteen doors and two main doors, a cattle shed with houses offices and the dairy of the manor, situated by the gates at the entrance of the manor towards the said grange. There is also there a watchtower with a covered room and also, on the other side of the gate of the same, a long stable with a room at the south end of the same for the plough of the manor, and also there is, at the same place, by the hall, another stable for the horses and the stud of the lord Prior and his family with a [text unclear: perhaps 'Barn'] there with rooms attached: and a bakery on the north side of the hall with a furnace and a plumbery [plumber's workshop] sufficiently repaired. And the value of the easement of the said houses after repair per annum with the garden within the site of the same manor is 6s. 8d. Total on estimate: 2 acres.

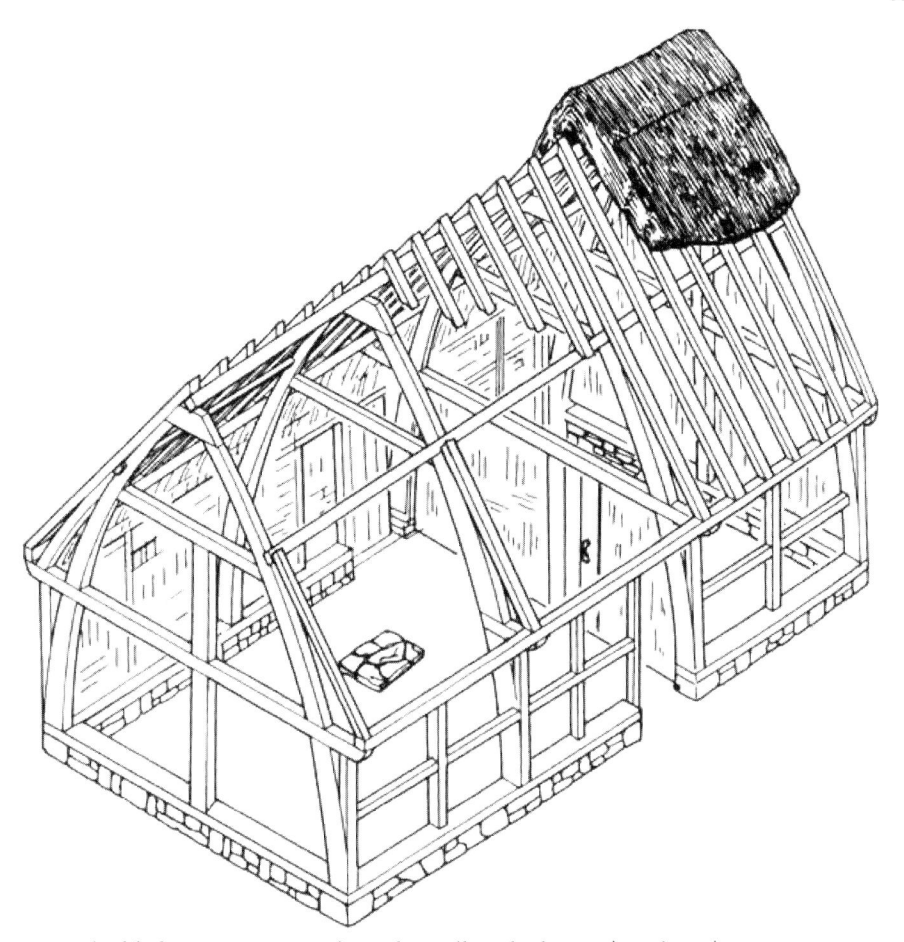

The likely construction of Monks Hall in the late 14th/early 15th century.

Illustration of a late medieval three bay hall house from Haddesley, Richard, 'English Medieval Architecture'. Online at http://www.medarch.co.uk/index.html, (accessed 4.8.2017).

The late basic three-bay timber-framed construction of the late medieval Monks Hall manor house is still broadly as described in 1433, albeit with 16th century and later alterations and embellishments. Fragments of this earlier medieval manor house are incorporated in the modern dining hall and central parlours in the western and middle parts of Monks Hall. It seems likely that the stepped gable cross wing started out as the prior's stable and stud south of the main hall. The house was much smaller than today, as the description shows, with outbuildings the dominant feature. There was a watchtower by the gates with a room above for a watchman, essential in those insecure times. The basic layout of the demesne buildings is broadly the same as now, and

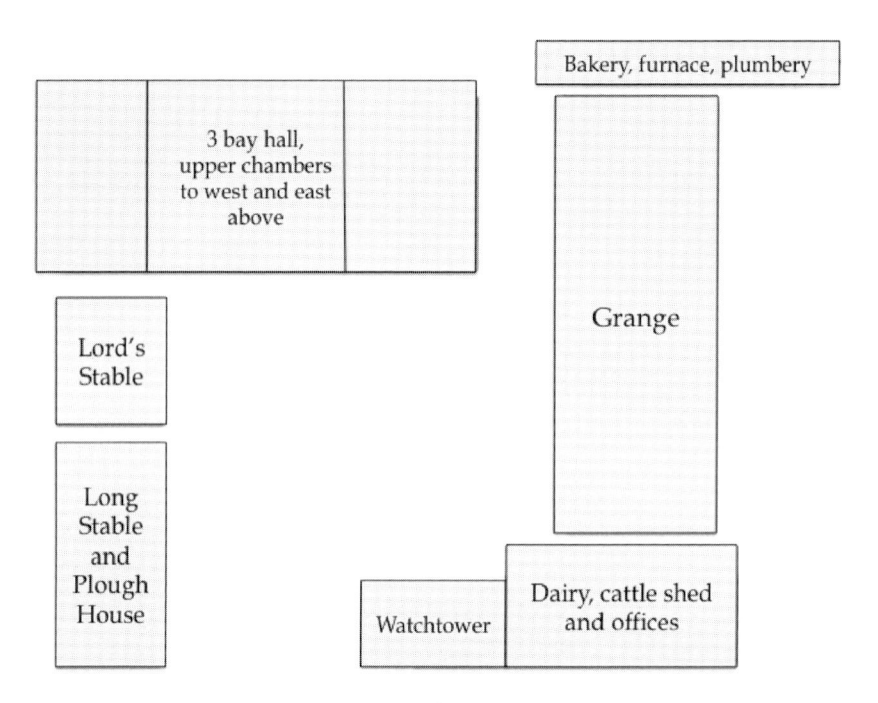

```
                    ┌──────────────────────────────────┐
                    │         Bakery, furnace, plumbery │
                    └──────────────────────────────────┘
┌─────────┬───────────────┬─────────┐   ┌──────────────┐
│         │   3 bay hall, │         │   │              │
│         │ upper chambers│         │   │              │
│         │ to west and   │         │   │              │
│         │  east above   │         │   │    Grange    │
└─────────┴───────────────┴─────────┘   │              │
┌─────────┐                             │              │
│ Lord's  │                             │              │
│ Stable  │                             │              │
└─────────┘                             │              │
┌─────────┐                             └──────────────┘
│  Long   │                      ┌──────────┬──────────────┐
│ Stable  │                      │          │ Dairy, cattle│
│  and    │                      │Watchtower│ shed and     │
│ Plough  │                      │          │   offices    │
│  House  │                      └──────────┴──────────────┘
└─────────┘
```

Plan of Monks Hall as described in the Extent of 1433.

although the current outbuildings and cottages are more recently built they were constructed on old sites.

Cattle-rearing, grain-growing and dairying were the main manorial industries but there were facilities to work lead, a furnace for smithing other metal goods and a bakery. The water mill was used for grinding grain and fulling, which assumed huge importance in the 15th century, as the production of woollen cloth became the backbone and driving force of the medieval English economy between the late 13th century and late 15th century. As the wool trade increased landowners, including priors and abbots, began to count their wealth in terms of sheep. The monasteries, including Thetford, played an active part in the trade; this pleased the King's Exchequer, which was able to levy a tax on every sack of wool that was exported.

Mechanisation of the wool finishing process in the 11th century made life much easier for the fuller, who formerly had to tread the wool in urine. Water power was used to work fulling stocks, a machine with two large wooden hammers raised on tappets. The cloth was contained in a trough, the stock, and was repeatedly beaten by the rising and falling hammers. The hammers generated heat and produced heavily felted cloth. It took several hours to get the right degree of felting. The piece shrank by about one third of its length and one quarter of its width. By the 13th century, fulling stocks were in use wherever a river provided sufficient water power.

The total acreage of Monks Hall manor in 1433 was 401½ acres, ½ rod, 10 perches and 10 feet, of which the lord's demesne land with woodland was 208 acres and other rented land over 193 acres. This was a sizeable manor. The extent contains details of every holding, the current tenant and where exactly the land lay between the Earl of Suffolk's land (Syleham Comitis), the river, the water mill and the boundary towards Hoxne. Many of the names are identical or similar to the earlier extent. Roger and Richard atte Cross presumably occupied the same land at the cross that Johanna had in 1379. There are surviving wills for some of the most prosperous manor tenants: for John Sawyer (Sagyer/ Sawer 1446), John Hall (1449), Agnes Eastgate (1461) and John Stuntley or Stuntle (1456) who tenanted a major piece of woodland in both extents that was still identifiable in the tithe map of the 1850s. There were outlying pieces of land in Denham, Chickering and Hoxne. As in 1379, a detailed schedule of services required as condition of the tenancy is listed in minute detail.

We do not know from the extent who was living in the Hall or who was acting as bailiff. It is quite possible that the Hall was reserved for visits of the prior but someone was acting as bailiff and probably resident at the Hall. I speculate that the most senior person on the manor, bailiff or reeve, was **Roger Eastgate** but this is guesswork from his holdings and the frequency his name crops up. Two generations later however we can identify some definite names of individuals who we know were working this land and almost certainly living at the Hall.

The Thetford Register

The priory kept detailed accounts for all their estates, written down by the 'Extracellarii', the monk responsible for the administration of priory affairs. The documents covering the years from 1482 to the Dissolution in 1540 were discovered among the papers of the Duke of Norfolk and are now in Cambridge University Library. These invaluable documents, known collectively as the Thetford Register, were transcribed over ten years or so by the historian David

Dymond and published by the Norfolk Record Society in 1995 and 1996.[2] Every item of expenditure, including visits to manors from the priory, all work commissioned and the costs of all activities are recorded. They are written in a mixture of Latin, English and Norman French, and it is possible with a rudimentary knowledge of these languages and the use of online translation tools to understand most of it, with help from the editor's notes.

John Bole

John Bole or Bolle (the modern equivalent would be Ball) appears in numerous entries, occasionally accompanied by Robert or William Bole. It seems possible that Bole was the reeve of Monks Hall manor. He receives payment for dozens of jobs in Syleham, including some smithing work, working in iron, repairing various items such as the watermill and bullock carts. We know there was a metal working furnace at the hall in 1433; it is tempting to think this was the same one Bole used. He is paid for organising travel and victuals for the prior on his frequent visits, although it is not entirely clear why the prior did visit this remote manor so frequently. A clue may be the iron and lead works that John Bole undertook, but we cannot be sure. The manor was assessed for tax purposes in 1498 at £17 16s. 10d. per annum. Its income from earnings was undoubtedly greater, for the monks were prepared to invest heavily in maintenance, modification and updating their assets. John Bole was paid £1 4s. 7d., in those days a considerable sum, for a range of repairs to the manor buildings.

In 1499 the monks commissioned contractors Richard Large and Edward Schylle to renovate the Bishop's mill at Hoxne and installed a new 'fulling stock' at Syleham mill for a total cost of 16s. 8d. There was clearly some collaboration between the two mills. The same year Laurence Geste was paid for collecting 'nete' beasts (cattle bred for slaughter). In 1500, Richard Reynyngham paid £1 12s. 0d., plus 4s. 0d. for 'ii magnis bovectis' (2 great oxen), 'plough beasts' that had been bred in Syleham.

The Cossey family

John Bole may have lived on the manor but there is another family with an even greater likelihood of being residents of the hall. The most important family in Syleham in the late 15th century was the Cossey family. A long line of John Cosseys, interspersed with occasional Roberts, appears in many Syleham records, including the Thetford Register. The Cosseys bought and sold cattle, managed the manorial lands, travelled widely in East Anglia and Essex, and dealt with the patron of Thetford Priory, the Duke of Norfolk. The family may originally have come from Cossey (Costessey) near Norwich. From 1370 the De La Pole family at Wingfield Castle nearby owned both the manor of Syleham Comitis next door and also the manor of Cossey, a connection of sorts that might explain why the Cosseys moved into the area.

The Cosseys acquired considerable wealth during their tenure of the bailiffry. Our first **John Cossey** made a will in 1492 although probate was not granted until 1504, when his wife Rose also died.[3] John made extensive bequests to the St Margaret's Church, Syleham and also to St Andrew's Church, Wingfield and to the chapel at Chickering. He requested and paid for masses to be sung for his soul at the Austin Friars in Orford, at the Friary at Dunwich and also at the Whitefriars at Norwich, but rather surprisingly not at Thetford. He left his tenement to his wife Rose, land to his son Robert and money to Robert's wife Beatrice. This was the will of a very successful farmer.

John's wife **Rose** was buried in 1504 with her husband in Syleham churchyard.[4] She also left everything to her son Robert and money to the churches in Syleham and Wingfield, and also some money to 'The Guild of St Margaret in Syleham' and a cow to her 'belchilde' (grandchild). The desire to have masses said for people's souls after death was popular but many could not afford it, so many individuals joined religious guilds, which were a cross between a social club and a friendly society. Members paid a fee, and often gave gifts of property to the guild. Money was also raised through feasts held in the guildhall. In return, the guild paid a chantry priest to say masses for the souls of its members, and ensured that members had proper funerals. The guild at St Margaret's seems to have been short-lived but is nevertheless an interesting social phenomenon.

John and Rose Cossey lived at Monks Hall during the Wars of the Roses, the episodic and bloody battles for supremacy between Yorkist and Lancastrian branches of the House of Plantagenet. Many Suffolk men fought with the House of York, loyal to King Richard III, under the leadership of John Howard, 1st Duke of Norfolk, and his son Thomas Howard. John Howard and many other Yorkists were killed with the king at Bosworth Field in 1485; Thomas Howard was wounded. The last battle at Stoke in 1487 more or less wiped out the Yorkist fighting force and although Thomas Howard regained royal favour some years later from Henry VII, the priory and its manors would have found these years difficult.

There is certainly no doubt that violence and lawlessness flourished during the Wars of the Roses. Soldiers brutalised in the 'Hundred Years' Wars in France behaved with a ferocity which their commanding officers were powerless to control, while some magnates were little better than sadistic ruffians. Thousands of men died horribly in battle, or were mercilessly butchered while trying to escape. Yet the wars were by no means continuous, nor did England experience many of the usual horrors of civil war, like those suffered later in the 17th century.

There were, at most, thirteen weeks of fighting in the thirty-two years of the Wars of the Roses. The problems of keeping an army fed and watered meant that individual campaigns lasted for a matter of days or weeks, not months. Some of the battles were very short, and none lasted longer than a day. Most took place in open countryside and hardly affected life in the towns and villages. None were fought in East Anglia; the nearest battle was at Empingham in Rutland. The conflict had very little effect upon the population at large and relatively few civilians suffered attack or privation. Nor did the castles, halls and manors of the aristocracy suffer greatly. Only the great defensive castles of the north became targets for military action.[5] But nevertheless John Cossey would have been keeping his watchtower in good repair in case of marauding bands of discharged soldiers.

Most of the population regarded the Wars of the Roses – our modern name for these violent civil battles, not theirs of course – as a dispute between noble factions. The majority of people managed to avoid committing themselves wholeheartedly to either party unless obligated to fight by kinship or loyalty to a lord taking sides in the dispute. The large towns of Norwich and Ipswich showed a disinclination to take sides, more concerned with maintaining their wool trade and paying taxes when required to whichever side was governing at the time.[6] But if Syleham men did join the fighting the likelihood is that they were fighting on the Yorkist side.

Bailiffs such as John Cossey were more concerned about hanging on to their own land if there were neighbouring wealthy magnates inclined to take land by force, and lawlessness was common. The Paston family, whose valuable family correspondence documents the lives and struggles of a Norfolk gentry family, reveal a family beset by litigation but also subject to the violent predations of wealthy carpetbaggers such as John de la Pole, Duke of Suffolk.[7] The richer the Pastons became, the more energy they had to invest in defending their territory in the courts and in physical battle. Life was probably less fraught in a rural Syleham manor but being so close to de la Pole estates in Wingfield, the Cosseys must have been wary of their hugely powerful neighbours.

More important to John and Rose Cossey would have been the social changes in the 15th century engendered by changes in the economy. Plague remained endemic, a recurrent unavoidable hazard. Villein labour service had largely disappeared, to be replaced by copyhold tenure (tenure by copy of the record of the manorial court). There was a well-developed land market among peasants, some of whom managed to rise above their neighbours and began to constitute a class called yeomen. John Cossey was probably the first yeoman on Monks Hall land to feel some ownership of the land he held in copyhold but he was still beholden to the priory and could be evicted at will.

Some larger landlords entirely abandoned direct management of their estates in favour of a leasehold system but the priory does not seem to have done this. Converting holdings to sheep pasture solved the labour shortage but sheep required more extensive land. It is thought that most productive arable land and huge swathes of the plateau in north Suffolk were enclosed at this time for sheep grazing.

Four hundred years of monastic ownership of Monks Hall manor was drawing to a close. Religious sentiment was changing all over Europe as the ideas of the Reformation took hold. The accession of Henry VIII in 1509 was to change the face of England forever.

Notes
1. Monks Hall Manor Extent 1433. British Library, Manuscript Collections Ref Add Ch 16562, transcribed by Andrew F. Gray, unpublished, MHA.
2. Dymond, D. 1995. The Register of Thetford Priory. Part 1: 1482–1517; Dymond, D. 1996, Part 2: 1518–1540. (Norfolk Record Society and Oxford University Press).
3. Last Will and Testament of John Cossey, 10 January 1492, SRO IC/AA1/1/2/27, probate 1504.
4. Last Will and Testament of Rose Cossey, 20 August 1504. SRO IC/AA1/1/2/18.
5. Williamson, M. 2013. 'Destruction in the Wars of the Roses'. Online at http://weaponsandwarfare.com (accessed 17.11.2013).
6. Haward, W. I. 1926. 'Economic Aspects of the Wars of the Roses in East Anglia'. English Historical Review Vol XLI/CL:XII, pp. 170–89.
7. The Paston Family Letters can now be read online at http://www.medievalhistories.com/the-paston-letters-online/ (accessed 21.7.2017).

7

The Dissolution of the Priory and a new era for Monks Hall

Robert and Beatrice Cossey

References to Robert Cossey, the bailiff or reeve of Monks Hall manor, begin to appear in the Thetford Register following his parents' death in 1504. In 1506 he was paid 8s. 0d. for leather and for the renewal of drainage ditches. In 1511, 'great' Oxen were sold for £2 9s. 0d. and in 1523, 'Pro Roberto Cossey pro le making le pownde [an enclosure where stray cattle were kept] apud Sylham', 16s. 0d. This is a good example of the cod Latin with odd bits of French and English that make up many of the entries. But matters of a more worrying kind were afoot.

In 1523 'the Lord Prior of Thetford came to Monks Hall Syleham for the Counsel of the Lord Duke of Suffolk'.[1] 'In expensis' for this one night's stay is recorded the princely sum of 4s. 3d. Robert Cossey was pulling out the stops to ensure a successful visit. The priors and monks liked entertaining and being entertained with music, singing minstrels and even drama. They did not see any conflict between their strict rule and entertainment. A substantial meal would be prepared too. It is likely that this meeting had a very serious purpose. Charles Brandon, 1st Duke of Suffolk, was Henry VIII's brother-in-law and, by 1523, his right-hand man in the field of battle, a trusted courtier and friend.[2] A perceptive and worried prior was seeking advice and influence.

William of Ixworth was appointed Prior of Thetford in 1518. In the five years since his appointment, he had witnessed the disestablishment of many small religious establishments, friaries and nunneries, mainly in East Anglia. The process was perfectly legal and had begun in the late 15th century to use the resources of impoverished, indebted or deserted religious establishments to improve or found new educational establishments. St Radegund's Priory in Cambridge was dissolved in 1496 and converted into Jesus College; the dissolution of several other friaries funded other colleges in Oxford and Cambridge. The process was approved by the vast majority of the population as being a sensible use of redundant resources.

Cardinal Wolsey, then the most powerful man in England, with Thomas Cromwell keeping accounts, speeded up the process in earnest by acquiring papal authorisation in 1518. Through the 1520s he dissolved twenty-nine smaller foundations, using the proceeds to fund Ipswich Grammar School and what is now Christ Church, Oxford. By the early 1520s insightful religious men from medium-sized establishments must have been concerned about which religious foundations would fall under the axe next. There had also been a huge imposition of taxes in 1522–3 that fell especially hard on monasteries and priories. Seeking the good will of the Duke of Suffolk was sensible politics. We do not know the outcome of this meeting at Monks Hall in 1523.

The tax burden continued to enrage the wool producers of Suffolk. A further raising of taxes led to rioting in Lavenham and Brent Eleigh in 1525, swiftly dispersed by the Dukes of Suffolk and Norfolk. While there may have been local resentment, there is no record of similar revolt in north Suffolk. For the next fifteen years or so life at Syleham continued much as before although lurking anxieties must have surfaced from time to time as Reformation fever hit local parish churches and the population agitated for a different kind of religion.

Robert Cossey and his wife Beatrice had two sons, infuriatingly for the author both called John. The habit of naming more than one child by the same name was common in medieval days when parents did not expect the majority of children to survive. The Paston family in north Norfolk also named two sons John and both survived to adulthood, as did the two John Cosseys.

During Robert's lifetime the Cosseys acquired the profitable tenancies of the majority of Monks Hall manor land and extended their holdings into Syleham Comitis and Wingfield, manors that had been seized by Henry VIII after executing the last Plantagenet Duke of Suffolk, Edmund de la Pole. Beatrice died some time before Robert but no record of her death has yet emerged.

Robert's will of 1536 donates extensive bequests to churches in the neighbourhood, to the cathedral church in Norwich, and to pay for mending various highways, to Brockdish, Brome and Hoxne and from Brockdish to Needham.[3] This is an unusual, insightful bequest that his son repeated by making a similar bequest years later. Robert gives silver marks to the church to the value of about nine months of a working man's annual income, a not insubstantial sum. He carefully divides his wealth between the two Johns, the property mostly to his younger son John and his wife Alice, money and furniture mainly to the older John. He leaves the valuable plough and horses to the younger John and also silver spoons, sophisticated and valuable possessions at a time when cutlery was seldom used. It seems Robert and Beatrice had aspirations to a gentlemanly life style. The watermill was temporarily out of commission when the will was drawn up but Robert leaves instructions for its repair.

There is one other unusual bequest in widower Robert's will. Beatrice had died before Robert but there is a major bequest, which is written before any other gifts to his children or grandchildren, to **'Katherine Basse'** of "my bed that I laye in", that is the mattress, coverlet, hangings and bed linen, and also 20 shillings in money. Beds were valuable items and their hangings and linen a cherished item. It is likely that Katherine was Robert's mistress. It was common enough for wealthy men to take mistresses in late medieval days and then, as now, men who did not want to complicate their existing children's inheritance would provide for the mistress in their wills. Let us hope that relations were good between Katherine and Robert's two Johns. In 1544, Katherine married Ralph Wright from a local yeoman family.

John and Alice Cossey

John Cossey the elder son took up farming in Brockdish over the river, as is clear from his brother's will of 1544.[4] It seems that it was Robert's younger son John who took on the bailiff role of Syleham from his father. Robert may have been in failing health for some time before he died because in 1524 John Cossey is formally named as Bailiff of Monks Hall manor by the prior at Thetford and receives a stipend of £1 2s. 8d. per annum. John supplies the priory with linen at 8d. per yard, which would have been woven on the manor from flax grown there. John also receives regular payments for the upkeep of a 'Shodcart' (believed to be a special cart capable of carrying heavy loads) indicating a regular demand for transport of considerable capacity.

THE DISSOLUTION OF THE PRIORY AND A NEW ERA FOR MONKS HALL

John Cossey's wife, mentioned in the Thetford Register, is paid for work she has done for the priory. She is named as 'Frances' but I think this may be a simple clerical error as John's wife at that date was called Alice and she died only the year before he did in 1543.[5] John and Alice had three sons, John, Robert and Thomas. There was also a daughter called Katherine. Was she named after John's father's Katherine?

As well as paying rent to the priory the bailiff also had to pay his tithes to support the rector, along with every other tenant in the manors. A copy of the Syleham Tithes from the early 16th century still exists, certified by John Cossey, John Kiss and Richard Stratford as:

> A most certayne and true accompt of ye Tythes and Herbages wch were to have bene accustomarye payed yn Sileh'm for ye space of three score yeris and more as ys provid by ye testymonye of these menne who names are below written wy others.[6]

There follows a list of money equivalents for the tithes due on cows, calves, lambs, pigs, geese, hens, wood, corn, hemp, hay and a fixed charge on orchards, which seems to indicate that the rector received his tithes in cash. The rector also got paid tuppence for "For eache communion on fyrst rec'vynge" and tuppence "For eache oone baptized".

In addition to tithes the parish priest was supported by the produce of a grant of land owned directly by the church called 'the glebe'. In Syleham the glebe was five acres in extent that the parish priest could either cultivate himself or lease for a cash return. The Syleham glebe was located to the west of the road running north down the hill to Cross cottages, that is, behind the Old Vicarage.

I think we can say with some certainty that John and Alice and their children lived at Monks Hall and it was probably not much changed until everything changed after 1540. At John's death in 1544 the land they tenanted was divided equally between their three sons, unusual for East Anglia where the eldest son usually inherited the bulk of the estate. John also leaves bequests to his married daughter and to her son, his grandson Richard, and 6s. 8d. to the newly married Katherine Wright, his father's beneficiary. John's will describes several new closes on the greens and increasing arable land, indicating greater wealth creation. But by the time John Cossey died, the lord of the manor was no longer the prior at Thetford. After years of uncertainty the Dissolution had transferred the ownership of the manor to Thomas Howard, Duke of Norfolk.

John Cossey and Alice really belong to the pre-Dissolution manor. Can we say anything else about them before leaving them? Recently early 16th century Suffolk wills have been analysed for content that indicates changing religious sympathies.[7] John Cossey and another prosperous local yeoman, John Spalding, have been identified as likely protestant dissenters; they gave no donation to the church high altar, and made no references to saints or to postmortem prayers and masses. So it may be that John Cossey was sympathetic to the dissolution of the foundation that had governed the manor for so long.

It is easy to gloss over the profound implications of being a dissenting protestant in the early 16th century before the Dissolution. This was a period when ordinary men were at risk of being hauled up to appear before consistory (religious) courts for saying or doing the wrong thing. An incident at St Peter's South Elmham Hall in 1538 landed a 'Frenchman', a mason Peter

St Peter's Hall, St Peter South Elmham, now the headquarters of St Peter's Brewery.

THE DISSOLUTION OF THE PRIORY AND A NEW ERA FOR MONKS HALL

Vyknell of Pockthorp (he was probably Flemish), in the Norwich court. The hall was being extended in grand style from the valuable Caen stone bought from nearby Flixton Priory, recently dissolved by Wolsey and sold off to a wealthy local landowner called Tasburgh. The masons were celebrating their work with a midsummer party, no doubt with copious ale, when Richard Doubleday and 'Adams' began to sing a song 'against the Bishop of Rome'.[8] Vyknell 'said he would he were with the said bishop, to show him what good hearts and good willers he hath in England' or as another deponent said, 'that he might show him how Englishmen rail and jest on him.' John Collett, another mason, reportedly replied 'Is not this a bold word for a Frenchman, for if an Englishman should so have spoken such words, he should immediately be hanged at his own door.' Joking about the Pope was a blasphemous offence. The end of the court case is not reported and it is possible that the masons were saved by Henry's break with Rome. The vicissitudes of official religion made men wary of expressing any view that was at odds with the official line of the day. When John Cossey made his will he was following the tide of change sweeping through England that would not be reversed until Catholic Mary I came to the throne in 1553.

Impression from the Seal of John Cossey.

Courtesy of Salisbury and South Wiltshire Museum.

There exists a medieval seal in the British Museum of one John Cossey, found in a field near Swindon but thought to be from East Anglia, from the 15th or 16th century. It is a pointed oval shape often associated with priests, made of copper-alloy, a flat seal matrix depicting the hand of God above a chalice. The inscription around is set between beaded borders, and reads + S'IOHANNIS. kOSSEI (Seal of John Cossey).[9] It seems likely that the bailiffs of Monks Hall manor would have used a symbol indicating their allegiance to the priory in their personal seal and they were wealthy enough to need one. We cannot be sure, it is probably unlikely, but it could have belonged to one of our John Cosseys.

The dissolution of the Thetford Priory[10]

The process of dissolution took longer at Thetford than most other religious foundations because of the influence and negotiating skills of the powerful priory patron Thomas Howard, 3rd Duke of Norfolk (1473-1554), an uncle of two of Henry VIII's wives, Ann Boleyn and Catherine Howard. The machinations around these marriages were to lead to his later difficulties. He narrowly escaped execution, in spite of having wielded considerable influence during the period 1530-40. He was in large part responsible for the downfall of both Cardinal Wolsey and later Thomas Cromwell, and although closely involved in the king's desire to divorce Catherine of Aragon to remarry Ann Boleyn, he was not sympathetic to the changes in the religious foundations.

Thomas Cromwell initiated a series of visitations in the summer of 1535, chiefly by four people, Richard Layton, Thomas Legh (or Leigh), John ap Rice and John London. The first two were doctors of the University of Cambridge, London was from Oxford. Doctors Layton and Legh were an infamous twosome renowned for their surprise tactics, pompous manner and rigorous questioning. They carried with them two documents, one a long questionnaire to be administered to each of the monks and the second a set of injunctions to be issued at the end of the visitations. They found exactly what they were looking for of course, laziness, corruption, ignorance of the Rule and general decay everywhere.

Legh and Leyton reached Thetford early in 1536, and alleged that they obtained confession of theft from one monk, and of 'uncleanness' from another, adding that they suspected the seventeen monks had concocted a good story before they got there, as so little evil had been confessed. Prior William had his monks well rehearsed. In other places they painted a sordid picture of the lifestyle in some of the monasteries and no doubt some of the accounts of whoring and drinking were true. The Abbot of Fountains Abbey, for example, 'notoriously keeping six whores, defamed here by all people... Six days before our access to his monastery he committed theft and sacrilege, confessing the same...'

Parliament passed the Act Suppressing Smaller Religious Houses in 1536 and a further act the same year to extend the legislation. In its final shape the first measure of suppression merely enacted that all the religious houses not possessed of an income of more than £200 a year should be given to the Crown. The heads of such houses were to receive pensions and the incumbents, despite the alleged depravity of some, were to be admitted to the larger and more observant monasteries or be licensed to act as secular priests. The measure of turpitude fixed by the Act was thus a pecuniary one.

The Dissolution, and other government intervention in ecclesiastical affairs, met with opposition in a series of uprisings in Lincolnshire and Yorkshire and other northern counties between October 1536 and February 1537. The Pilgrimage of Grace took its name from the most serious uprising in Yorkshire, which the participants called 'this pilgrimage of grace for the commonwealth'. On Henry's orders, over 200 people were hanged in connection with the uprisings.

The autumn of 1537 saw the beginning of the fall of the friaries in England. Prior William was sufficiently confident of his protection by Norfolk to refuse a favour to Cromwell, who in March that year had requested the preferment of Cromwell's servant, John Myllsent, to the priory farm of Lynford. William wrote back that they could not do it on the grounds that their patron, the Duke of Norfolk, had the custody of their seal, which must have seemed to Cromwell a lame excuse.

But the prior's optimism did not last. In 1538 and 1539 some 150 monasteries signed away their corporate existence and their property by a formal deed that handed over all rights to the king. Ironically, the uprising that had been intended to preserve the monastic institutions of England hastened their destruction. It had cost anywhere from £100,000 to £200,000 to suppress the uprising. As a result Cromwell turned immediately to arrange the confiscation of the rest of the monastic properties to pay for it. A new Act of Dissolution was passed in 1539 and Henry's triumph was completed by the hanging, drawing and quartering for constructive treason of three great abbots, Richard Whiting of Glastonbury, Thomas Marshall of Colchester and Hugh Cook Faringdon of Reading.

Thomas Howard looked with dismay upon the approaching destruction of Thetford priory and of the church, where not only his remote but also his more immediate ancestors had been interred. His father, Sir Thomas Howard, Earl of Surrey and 2nd Duke of Norfolk, had been buried before the high altar of the priory church in 1524, where a costly monument to him and Agnes his wife had been erected. Still more recently, in 1536, Henry Fitzroy, Duke of Richmond, bastard son of the king, had been buried in the same place. As the Thetford Register makes clear, the Duke and Duchess used the priory for entertaining and were frequent visitors. Their main home was at Kenninghall Place, a grand mansion just 12 miles away from Thetford, but in 1527 for example, one 'elaborate' dinner at the priory included 'big' and 'small' eels, dates, figs, almonds and raisins, 2 pounds of prunes and wine, the whole cost being £22 9s. 8d., an enormous sum for the period. On one occasion the Duchess left some jewellery behind and Prior William writes for instructions as to what to do with it! It appears that while the Duke was building his grand new house at Kenninghall in 1527-28 he frequently lodged at the nearby priory.[11] William often expressed his anxieties about Dissolution to the Duke in letters and almost certainly in person too. In the 1530s it is clear that both Howard and his wife thought they could protect the priory.

As a means of preserving the church and establishment, the Duke proposed to convert the priory into a church of secular canons, with a dean and chapter. In 1539 he petitioned the king to that effect, setting out a list of all the important people buried there. At first the king appeared to be interested and Thetford was included in a list with five others, of 'collegiate churches newly to be made and erected by the king.' A detailed scheme was drawn up for insertion in the expected letters patent, whereby the monastery was to be translated into a dean and chapter. The dean was to be Prior William and the six prebendaries and eight secular canons were to be the monks of the former house. The nomination of the dean was to rest with the Duke and his heirs.

It was a clever scheme but the king changed his mind and insisted on the absolute dissolution of the priory. The Duke found that further resistance was hopeless and on 16 February 1540, Prior William and thirteen monks signed a deed of surrender. It is hard to know how this news was taken by the Cossey family, presumably with some trepidation. Two months later, however, the priory site and the whole possessions of the priory, including all the manors, were sold to the Duke of Norfolk himself for £1,000 and an annual rental of £59 5s. 1d. Cossey had dealt with Norfolk regularly as patron of the priory and the Duke's 'takeover' may have come as a relief.[12]

The remains of Henry's natural son and those of the late Duke's father, with their tombs, were removed to the newly erected chancel in Framlingham, where they remain. We do not learn what became of Prior William but he had been close to the Howards and it seems likely that they would have found him a preferment somewhere. The monks and nuns of disestablished foundations were treated quite well as a rule. Only a few who resisted were summarily executed. The others, including 5000 monks, 1600 friars and 2000 nuns, were given pensions, for the most part reasonable and better than nothing. The average pension of an ordinary monk or regular canon stood at the figure of five or six pounds per annum, and in the case of heads of houses it was even larger. Many monks and friars went into regular church office and, being literate and educated, soon rose to bishoprics, deaneries and substantial livings.

Norfolk's ownership of Monks Hall manor did not last long. In 1545, the year after John Cossey died, the Duke sold the manor to a close relative, Thomas Tilney, who clearly bought it with the intention it should become the home of his second son Emery Tilney. The Tilneys are an entertaining family who will become the subject of the next chapter. It was the Tilneys who rebuilt Monks Hall as we see it today.

Notes
1. Dymond, D (ed). 1996. *The Register of Thetford Priory*, (Norfolk Record Society and Oxford, Oxford University Press) Part 2: 1518-1540 p. 449 and n. 775.
2. 'Henry VIII: August 1523, 21-31', in Letters and Papers, Foreign and Domestic, Henry VIII, Vol. 3, 1519–1523, ed. J S Brewer, 1867 London, pp. 1353–72. Online at British History Online http://www.british-history.ac.uk/letters-papers-hen8/vol3/pp1353-1372 (accessed 22.7.2017).
3. Last will and testament of Robert Cossey 13 July 1535. SRO IC/AA1/9/218. There was a second 'Robert Cossey Senior' buried in Syleham 8 October 1541 who was probably an uncle of Robert Cossey the bailiff. Parish Register of Syleham. SRO, Ipswich.
4. Last will and testament of John Cossey. 20 April 1544 SRO Ref IC/AA1/13/147.
5. Alicia Cossey sepulti fuit primo die Julii anno dm/iu super. 1543. Syleham parish register SRO, Ipswich.
6. Exemplification of decree of Court of Augmentations, ratifying lease for 99 years by Robert Budde, Master of Wingfield College, and his brothers, to Richard Freston of Mendham, esq., of church and tithes of Syleham. 9 February 1543. SRO Ipswich HD 1538/428/5.
7. Wickins, Peter L. 2012. *Victorian Protestantism and Bloody Mary: The Legacy of Religious Persecution in England*. (Bury St Edmunds: Arena Books), Appendix 14: Wills of the Hundred of Hoxne p. 317.
8. Words about the Pope 25 Dec R O. 'Letters and Papers: December 1539, 21-25', in Letters and Papers, Foreign and Domestic, Henry VIII, Vol. 14 Part 2, August-December 1539, ed. James Gairdner and R H Brodie 1895 London, pp. 262–74. Online at British History Online http://www.british-history.ac.uk/letters-papers-hen8/vol14/no2/pp262-274 (accessed 23.7.2017).
9. Seal of John Cossey. British Museum. Unique ID: WILT-D81E23
10. The story of the dissolution of Thetford Priory given here is from a number of sources and sites. Particularly useful are 'Houses of Cluniac monks: The Priory of St Mary, Thetford', in Page, W, (ed.) 1906. *A History of the County of Norfolk*: Vol. 2, pp. 363–9. Online at British History Online http://www.british-history.ac.uk/

vch/norf/vol2/pp363-369 (accessed 22.7.2017) and D. M. Head, 1995. *The Ebbs and Flows of Fortune: The Life of Thomas Howard, Third Duke of Norfolk*. (Athens, Ga: University of Georgia Press).
11. Ibid. 1 p. 522.
12. The grant to Norfolk is also reported in papers of Henry VIII, see Copy from Patent Roll of royal grant, 'In consideration of good services, to Thomas, Lord Howard of Walden and Henry Howard, brother of Thomas, late Duke of Norfolk, and son of Henry, late Earl of Surrey.' Howard of Castle Rising Collection, Settlements and Cognate Papers NRO. HOW 152, 342 x 6.

7

Emery Tilney, Protestant and Poet, 1545–1606

Monks Hall and manor were owned by Emery Tilney throughout the last half of the 17th century. He and his family were the occupants for a goodly part of his adult life. He was an unusual man, deeply religious as a young man, in the manner of his intolerant times, but he was also in some ways unworldly and possibly not completely honest. He was embroiled in almost continuous family litigation and ended up the beneficiary. Some of his decisions seem ill thought through, confusing future generations about the fate of Monks Hall manor. His grandfather, Sir Philip Tilney, left us one of the finest 16th century gardens. Emery's first cousin Edmund Tilney was Master of the Queen's Revels and censor of Shakespeare's work. Another cousin entertained Queen Elizabeth I at his home. His nephew Charles was executed for treason following the Catholic Babington conspiracy, and his son married the sister of one of the most celebrated of New England settlers.

More important for this story than any of these family connections is that the house we know as Monks Hall was almost certainly built specifically for Emery by his father **Thomas Tilney**, who had the money and the motives to do so, some time between the years 1545 and 1557. The next chapter will focus on the building and its 16th century development, but let me introduce the remarkable Tilney family first. A family tree is below.[1]

The Tilney family (often spelt Tylney) were at the heart of political and court life in the reigns of Henry VIII, Edward VI, Mary Tudor and Elizabeth I, sometimes too close for comfort to the most powerful men in England.

The Tilney Family of Shelley, Suffolk 1530-1620

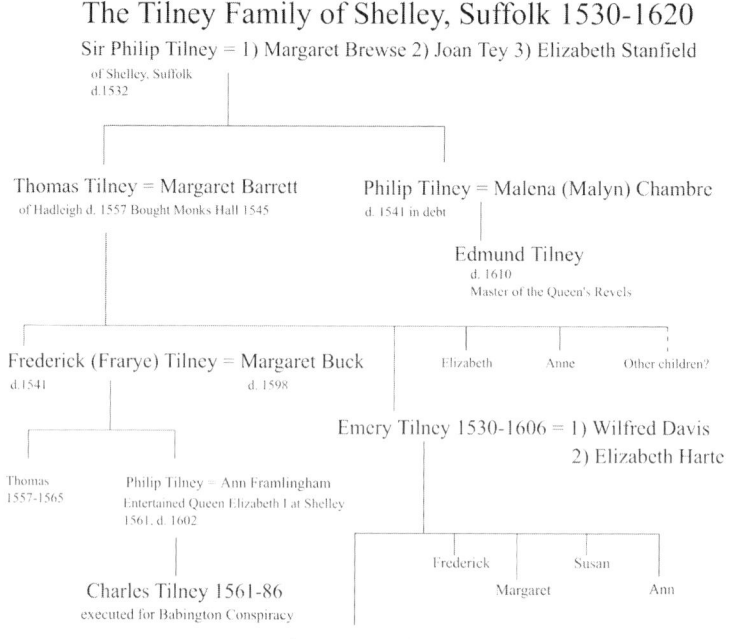

Sir Philip Tilney = 1) Margaret Brewse 2) Joan Tey 3) Elizabeth Stanfield
of Shelley, Suffolk
d.1532

- Thomas Tilney = Margaret Barrett
  of Hadleigh d. 1557 Bought Monks Hall 1545
  - Frederick (Frarye) Tilney = Margaret Buck
    d.1541   d. 1598
    - Thomas 1557-1565
    - Philip Tilney = Ann Framlingham
      Entertained Queen Elizabeth I at Shelley
      1561, d. 1602
      - Charles Tilney 1561-86
        executed for Babington Conspiracy

- Philip Tilney = Malena (Malyn) Chambre
  d. 1541 in debt
  - Edmund Tilney
    d. 1610
    Master of the Queen's Revels
  - Elizabeth
  - Anne
  - Other children?
  - Emery Tilney 1530-1606 = 1) Wilfred Davis
                             2) Elizabeth Harte
    - Frederick
    - Susan
    - Margaret
    - Ann

Thomas Tilney b. 1543 d. 1620 = Elizabeth Gosnold
(New England connections)

Sir Philip Tilney, Emery's grandfather, was courtier and treasurer to Thomas Howard, 2nd Duke of Norfolk, responsible for the exchequer during Henry VIII's prosecution of the Scottish war.

Sir Philip bought the manor of Shelley in Suffolk in 1517, having risen to good fortune through the marriages of his cousin Elizabeth Tilney, the grandmother of Anne Boleyn, and his sister Agnes, godmother of Mary Tudor and Elizabeth I. Agnes succeeded Elizabeth as the wife of Thomas Howard, 2nd Duke of Norfolk. Philip served as Norfolk's steward at Framlingham Castle, was 'knight of the sword' at the marriage of Prince Arthur to Catherine of Aragon in 1501, and treasurer under Norfolk of Henry VIII's expedition to Scotland in 1513, being present at the Battle of Flodden. The 3rd Duke of Norfolk, who acquired Monks Hall from the exchequer after the Dissolution, was the son of the 2nd Duke and Elizabeth Tilney.

Sir Philip Tilney came from a long line of knights of the same name, who had already acquired extensive lands around Boston in Lincolnshire and Suffolk. In 1519 he built a splendid new brick house in the manor of Shelley, in Dedham Vale, Suffolk, where he created a moated garden that is now considered to be one of the most interesting early 16th century gardens.² Most of the huge house was demolished after the Tilneys abandoned it in about 1627 but the restored gardens can still be visited and parts of the old hall survive.³

Sir Philip's older son **Thomas Tilney**, who lived in nearby Hadleigh until he inherited Shelley Hall in 1532, made the decision to buy the manor of Monks Hall from the 3rd Duke of Norfolk in 1545.⁴ Thomas Tilney was a prosperous JP in Hadleigh and inherited extensive lands from his father in Hadleigh, Shelley, Layham, Reydon, Holton, Stoke, Polstead and Edwardstone in Suffolk, and in Wyberton, Skirbeck and Boston, Lincolnshire.⁵ Thomas and his wife Margaret, *nee* Barrett, had five children who survived to adulthood. Their eldest son Frederick, called 'Frarye' by the family, was born about 1515, the second son Emery after a gap of some fifteen years in 1530. Daughters Elizabeth and Anne may have come in between and there may well have been other children who did not survive infancy.

Emery's older brother Frederick/Frarye Tilney married Margaret Buck and they had two children, Thomas and Philip. But then Frarye died young in 1541, leaving Margaret to survive him by fifty years. Her tomb, topped with the startlingly life-like effigy of Margaret, stands in Shelley Church.⁶ Margaret's sons were due to inherit Shelley, so when Thomas bought Monks Hall specifically for Emery's use, Thomas was clearly trying to do something for his younger son, who would not inherit Shelley Hall manor. Frarye's will was the focus of endless legal wrangling between his widow Margaret and her nephew Thomas, Emery's son, and his heirs.

Emery Tilney was only fifteen years old when Monks Hall was bought in 1545 and had several years ahead of him at Cambridge and training in the law at the Inner Temple. He probably did not take up residence in Monks Hall manor until after he married. One authority says he moved in in 1565 but I can find no evidence of this. While it may have taken some years to complete the building of Monks Hall, it would seem likely that Emery and his family probably moved there in the late 1550s. When he did eventually settle, Emery seems to have used the house until he inherited Shelley Hall in 1603. Like all Suffolk Tilneys his spiritual home was Shelley and it is likely that he was buried there in the family chapel. Neither his birth, nor his first marriage nor his death can be found in the usual English registers, although this is not uncommon.

Thomas Segges, the tenant in between

Thomas Tilney began to rebuild Monks Hall from about 1546, but while Emery was still away studying he needed a good tenant to keep the manor hall in good repair and the demesne lands productive. Thomas Segges of Syleham was that tenant. The Segges (or sometimes Syggs) family were successful tradesmen in Syleham but young Thomas Segges, who was probably a carpenter by trade, had a tragically short life and died in 1558, leaving three orphaned children. His will gives a very good description of the Hall and his hopes that the tenancy will continue for his children. Sadly this did not happen; and probably it was after Thomas Segges's death that Emery Tilney decided to use Monks Hall as his family home. Thomas Segges's will is accompanied by an inventory of all his goods, which gives us valuable insight into how he lived at the Hall.[7] Post-mortem inventories were compiled in order to ensure that the heirs could be sure of acquiring their goods, to discourage thefts from the property until the bequests were dispersed and also sometimes as an aid to tax calculations.

Thomas describes the hall in his will:

> I give unto Thomas my son my house called The Hall, the buttery and the chamber in the west end of the said house and the shop in the yard and one half of the barn, finding half the reparations of it. I do give the said Thomas my son the premises on the west side of the house leading from the hedge and the ditch at the barns end right down to the river Waveney and the said Thomas to enter into the said Hall and all other premises given to him at the feast of St Michael the Archangel which shall be in the sixth year after my decease. I will that my executors or the executors of him shall occupy or lease the said hall and all other premises before given…" "I will that my executors or the executors of him shall therewith pay the rent [out of the income of the land] find the reparations and bring up my daughter Agnes. I do give unto William my son all my houses on the back side of the Hall chimney towards the east with all the premises leading from the said hedge and ditch to the barn's end to the 'kynne' [?] on the east side of the said house… [The executors are asked to bring up William for 8 years before he takes up his bequest.]

This is followed by a division of the 'ort yard', that is a garden for vegetables, to be divided between his sons Thomas and William. His household goods are to be divided between the three children as described in the inventory, his daughter Agnes is also to receive 5 marks.

The description of the Hall, barns, River Waveney, garden and barns are recognisably similar to the extent of 1433 but now there is a 'chimney', workshops and houses north east of the hall, which we know existed where the main farm buildings are now sited.

The executor named to oversee this will is one William Fuller alias Alen of Syleham. He was responsible for ensuring the children inherited their goods and land but he also had the responsibility to look after the land and the children. Neither young Thomas nor William survived childhood. William died in 1561 and there is no record in Syleham of the marriage of Agnes Segges (baptised in 1545).[8] It is likely that Thomas had no surviving issue. Probate took eight years after Thomas's death, not especially unusual in Elizabethan times.

The inventory of Monks Hall 1558, appended to Thomas Segges' will:[9]

> I do give to Thomas my son,
> Table in the Hall
> Two long forms
> A posted bedstead in the chamber
> A flock bed and bolster of like
> A bedcovering of red
> A blanket
> A pair of sheets
> A pillow and a 'pillow bere'
> All the hangings in the chamber and the shelves
> All the tools that be in my shop
> All my timber
> Beside all lying in my shop and yard a spit and andiron
> A great brass pot
> A sort pan
> 2 pewter dishes
> 3 penetrated platters
> A salting trough
> A cheese press
> A swill tub, a [chown] and all apparel in the Hall

A roasting iron, a pair of tongs
The chair with the back
A hay thick and a grate

For William my son
The trundle bed in the Chamber
Three posted bedstead in the shop
A cupboard
A flock bed
A transom
A pair of sheets
Two blankets
A coverlet of blue and white
A pillow and a pillow bere
A new table with a seat in it
A red coffer
A new coffer
A pewter dish
A new salt
A pewter saucer
A platter penetrated
A spit and andiron
A great kettle with two '[cares]', a start pan
A boiling tub and a hake

I do give to Agnes my daughter
A posted bedstead
[Another] bedstead
A long coffer
A new table with a seat in it
A great pewter dish
A pewter salt and a pewter saucer
A treen, penetrated platter of wood
The middle brass kettle
A pair of fine sheets
A burying sheet

A table cloth
A pillow of [unclear] and a pillow bere
Two white women's caps and all such linen as was her mother's.

This comprehensive valuable list allows us to walk around Monks Hall and see Thomas Segges's family home as it was then. The furniture is sparse but he had two tables that converted into seats, a fairly recent invention, and a number of beds that indicated he was prosperous. The pewter also indicates a degree of middle class comfort but if we compare it with a modern home it looks spartan indeed.

Deaths in the upper Waveney Valley in the late 16th century

It seems quite possible that Thomas Segges's family simply never survived long enough to inherit all the inventory goods, in which case they probably went to the Fullers, whom we will meet again. Before leaving Thomas Segges to the eternal peace of Syleham churchyard, it may be worth adding that the death of almost all the family within the space of a few years was not rare at this time in the Waveney Valley. Andrew Gray studied the crises of mortality in the villages of the valley between 1539 and 1603 and found that there were waves of increased numbers of deaths in several villages that probably reflected recurrences of epidemic infectious disease.[10] But early death was then common enough; we do not know for sure what happened to the Segges, so we must leave this sad family here and turn back to the freehold owners, the Tilneys.

Tilney family disputes

Emery Tilney was born in 1530 and grew up in first Hadleigh and then Shelley. His father Thomas Tilney was for many years embroiled in a family dispute over his claim to Shelley Hall. He claimed the manor of Shelley was his by inheritance from his father Sir Philip's will, but in 1544 Thomas' second stepmother, Elizabeth, later married to Francis Framlingham, challenged Thomas' ownership in court, saying that her husband Sir Philip had left the Shelley property to her for her use in her lifetime.[11] The contested point was how long Elizabeth should have use of Shelley after her husband's death. The case dragged on for three years and although it was apparently settled in Elizabeth's favour in 1545, she did not benefit. Thomas was already ensconced at Shelley. The properties eventually passed to Thomas's son Frarye's children. Elizabeth, who we must assume was none too fond of her pushy stepson, appears never to have repossessed Shelley but was as recompense given various Lincolnshire properties. Again, these never left Thomas Tilney's control either. The Lincolnshire lands figure in his will, so some kind of settlement must have been reached between him and his stepmother or quite possibly he ignored the judgment against him.[12]

The Wyberton, Skirbeck and Boston properties in Lincolnshire are significant in the Monks Hall story because in 1567, and clearly for some years before that, they were tenanted by a John Cossey, who may have been a relative of the former bailiff of Monks Hall manor.[13] It seems possible that when Thomas Tilney decided to renovate Monks Hall and make it suitably grand for his son, he offered the sitting tenant John Cossey an alternative tenancy in Lincolnshire. This is admittedly a hypothetical and as yet unproven explanation. Branches of the Cossey family remained in Syleham for many years, but one at least became a resident of Tilney's Lincolnshire manor.

Emery finds Protestantism

Emery Tilney was sent to Corpus Christi College Cambridge in 1543, when he was thirteen years old.[14] This was the usual age to go to Cambridge in the 16th century, but more unusually he was referred to in the register as 'sizar', meaning he was receiving financial assistance from the college and may have been expected to do some menial work in return for the grant. One is tempted to think this is a mistake in the college records since he came from a family of very substantial wealth. In the 17th century, however, Isaac Newton, son of a manor owner, was also admitted as 'sizar' to Cambridge, so clearly there was some flexibility in the status.

Although spared the worst of the religious tumult that the Reformation brought to England, Corpus Christi College produced adherents to both Catholic and Protestant fanaticisms. Impressionable Emery fell under the influence of George Wishart or Wiseheart, who went to Cambridge to preach in 1542 and remained for just a year, the year Emery arrived.

Protestantism defined Emery as a consequence of his experience at Cambridge. George Wishart was born in Scotland in 1513, educated at university in Louvain, France and then became a priest. By 1538 he was back in Scotland as a schoolteacher in Montrose, where he taught his students the New Testament in Greek, illegally. Wishart was forced to flee Scotland for Bristol, where he got into more trouble for his preaching. He then retreated abroad and spent the next three years in Switzerland and Germany absorbing Reformation Protestant ideas, some quite eccentric. He returned in 1542–43 to teach for a year at Cambridge. After he left he returned to Scotland but alienated Cardinal Beaton and was eventually martyred by burning at the stake in 1546.[15]

Wishart was important in the early period of Scottish Protestantism, the first proponent of Swiss reformed theology and a central figure around whom scattered evangelicals could unite, particularly after his martyrdom. To contemporaries, Wishart was personally gentle and generous, austere but forgiving. His vehemence from the pulpit, though, portrayed him as harsh and vindictive to non-adherents of his fanaticism. He attracted both close friends and bitter enemies.

Emery Tilney wrote a paean of devoted praise about George Wishart in John Foxe's 1563 *Actes and Monuments of these Latter and Perillous Days, Touching Matters of the Church*, known popularly as *Foxe's Book of Martyrs*, a polemical account of the sufferings of Protestants under the Catholic Church. John Foxe writes in the 1583 edition:[16]

> Of late came to my handes, certified in wryting by a certaine scholler of hys, sometime named Emerey Tylney, whose wordes of testimoniall as he wrote them to me, here folow. About ...[George Wiseheart, Protestant Martyr]

Emery's contribution was widely circulated and remains his major claim to fame.[17] The book was highly influential and helped shape lasting negative popular notions of Catholicism. The book went through four editions in Foxe's lifetime and a number of later editions and abridgements.

This year at Cambridge was to fix Protestantism of an inflexible kind into Emery Tilney's soul. The accession of Edward VI in 1547, which had ushered in a wave of further anti-Popish reforms to the liturgy was consistent with Emery's personal enthusiasms. Round about 1550 he published his own lengthy piece of religious poetry, an anti-Papist, pro-Protestant tract called 'Here beginneth a song of the Lordes supper'.[18]

Nearly 500 lines long, Emery's poem is a tirade supporting the ideas of

Edward VI, or perhaps more accurately those espoused by the boy king's advisors. The tediously discursive and intolerant poem does not make easy reading. Perhaps it is not surprising that Emery published no other works. He was only twenty years old when this work was published, the age of youthful callous extremism. His ideas may have moderated over the coming years and it is unfair to exercise 21st century liberal judgments on a 16th century mind. East Anglia was the natural home of Protestantism, where the largely rural but prosperous, and therefore increasingly educated, wool trade community were sympathetic to the notion of a more personal relationship with God and resented the Catholic Church's imposition of a fixed liturgy that seemed to have little relevance to people yearning for a personal understanding of faith. Emery's choice of faith was that of the majority in East Anglia.

Emery's religion can be better understood if we appreciate that Hadleigh, the prosperous town where he grew up, was then preoccupied by social division and conflict between religious groups. A series of active Protestant preachers led John Foxe to describe the town as a 'university of the learned', meaning fervent Protestants. Between 1530 and 1560 Hadleigh was first marked by the recantation of Protestant leader Nicholas Shaxton in 1546 and then the eventual martyrdom of their Protestant rector, Dr Rowland Taylor, shortly after the accession of Mary I. John Craig, a historian who teased out the details of ordinary people's faith in Hadleigh at this time, found that many people of all social classes were aware of the finer points of theology, that they took principled positions in contemporary debates, and that these religious divisions were carried over into local political disputes.[19] Young Emery Tilney would have absorbed religious ideas even before he went to Cambridge.

Emery's nephew, another Philip Tilney, who inherited Shelley Hall early as a result of his father Frarye's early death, was not swept up by the tide of Protestantism. A religious conservative with Catholic sympathies, he was one of only two Suffolk gentlemen, the other being Sir William Waldegrave, to retain their influence in local government in the 1570s.[20] William Cardinall complained about young Philip Tilney's reluctance to embrace the Protestant faith during a court case, but Philip must have been good at smoothing over his views since it did not stop him from entertaining his cousin the Queen at Shelley in August 1561.[21]

Philip's only son, though, Charles Tilney (1521–1586), was a more active recusant Catholic who was a conspirator in 1586 in the Babington plot against Queen Elizabeth to place Catholic Mary Queen of Scots on the throne of

England. He died a horrific death by execution, being briefly hanged then dismembered while still alive. His death left his father with no heir.

Emery Tilney becomes a lawyer

Young graduates who were not drawn to the clerical life went from Cambridge and Oxford to be trained as lawyers and Emery was no exception. Round about 1546–1548 he was admitted to the Inner Temple, where his father had studied and his own son Thomas would also attend. Emery still had rooms there by the time his father made his will in 1557, and appears in cases recorded in The National Archives. One case in particular suggests his continuing sympathies with the Protestant cause. The case was heard in the Court of Chancery about 1563.[22] Emery acted for John Fenner of Amberley, Sussex (1509–1566), who had just been elected to Parliament as Member for Midhurst, against a claim by Robert Burlage for an annuity from Fenner's lands. The electoral patron at Midhurst had returned Catholics to the first two Elizabethan Parliaments but the Act passed in the first session of the 1563 Parliament made it mandatory for newly elected MPs to take the oath of supremacy, to accept the Queen as head of the Church. John Fenner was described as a 'favourer of godly proceedings', meaning passionate Protestant.[23] Emery was a suitably godly advocate for him.

Most legal work was in London and while Emery kept rooms in the Inner Temple it is likely that he would have returned home regularly to Syleham. Throughout his tenure of the Hall, Monks Hall was called 'Tylneys' and the Manor too became known by that name. Emery Tilney probably would not have wanted to be reminded of 'Monks' or the connection to the Catholic Thetford Priory.

Emery's marriage and family

At some unrecorded point Emery Tilney married Winifred Davis of Cranbrook in Kent, the daughter of John Davis. They had five children, none of whom were baptised in Syleham. We know nothing about Winifred (or Winefrede) at all, except that she was born about 1535 and died, it is thought, in the 1570s. The family would have employed a bailiff to look after the estate demesne lands and most of the manor would have been held copyhold by tenants. It seems likely that William Fuller, who supervised Thomas Segges's will, was tenanting some of the land at least.

Emery Tilney raises some cash

Emery Tilney decided, perhaps with the idea of raising ready cash, to divest himself of the manorial lands that he personally was not occupying.[24] He therefore sold off several 1000 year leases to tenants working the manorial land via a mechanism called 'mortgage by demise', not to be confused with our notion of modern mortgages. The 'mortgage by demise' method of conveyancing leases was uncommon in eastern England at that time but was common enough in the west of England as a way of raising funds from tenants by the 'entry fine' they paid to secure the right to pass on their copyhold land to heirs. A good example of this is the 1000 year lease:

> …made 15 January, 6 Elizabeth I (1563/4) between Emery Tylney Lord of the manor of Monks Hall in Syleham, on the one hand, and William Fisher of Stradbroke, yeoman, on the other: Witnesseth, that where the said William Fysher hath the day of the making hereof and holdeth to him and to his heirs of the said Emery as of the said manor, one acre and half of land lying in Wygnotts Croft in Syleham aforesaid".[25] " Mr. Tylney leased, for the sum of £9 3s. 4d., the above said lands for one thousand years to William Fisher, for the yearly rent of 6½d."

But as many chroniclers have noted, selling long leases does not actually release the tenants from obligations to the manor. The uncommon nature of the agreement and perhaps the unusual drafting led to many years of litigation from Syleham folk, their children and grandchildren, who had invested in their property in good faith but then discovered they were no better off than any other copyhold tenant. Certainly the manor was not 'extinguished' as Tilney had claimed. Was Tilney dishonest or simply carelessly naïve? The evidence does not look good. In fact it looks like downright sharp practice designed to produce ready cash.

Richard Stratforde was one of the Syleham tenants who had taken advantage of the offer of land on a long lease. His grandson Nicholas Stratforde decided to sue Emery Tilney for his claim to the house and land that had been granted to his family many years earlier.[26] Tilney's counterclaim was that the lease had been forfeited by Nicholas' father, another Richard, as a result of a lease made to Agnes, Nicholas' grandmother. The complex arguments are nigh impossible to follow. Tilney summoned several of his tenants to speak on his side, including

Richard Stratforde, Nicholas' father, Thomas Algar and Thomas Teder. We do not know the outcome. Some years later, after 1603, another tenant, Thomas Herryng, also sued Emery Tilney over his land in Syleham but again we do not learn of the result.[27]

More litigation

In 1601 Emery Tilney, by now seventy-one years old, was still living at Monks Hall when he was mentioned in a tenant's will, indicating that he was still resident there.[28] In 1602, however, his nephew Philip Tilney died and, being without an heir as a result of the execution of his son Charles, Philip left his entire estate to Emery; this included Shelley Hall, all the lands that went with that manor and also the Suffolk manor of Aldham, which Philip had only recently purchased. What wonderful good fortune! Too good to be true? The circumstances of Philip's death and revealing of the will are highly suspicious.

Emery was the executor of Philip's 'will'. On the day of his death, Philip had not yet made a will and was advised to do so quickly by his legal agent Philip Coleman, his physician Thomas Mosell and the local rector Dr George Meriton. Philip however refused and four hours later he was dead.[29] Thomas Tilney, Emery's eldest son, who was acting in a legal capacity for Emery on this occasion, then 'found' some scribbled notes in Philip's house that appeared to be a will leaving everything to Emery. Afterwards of course, everything inherited by Emery would pass to his heir, this same Thomas. The 'discovery' of these scribblings naturally raised everyone's suspicions but Emery Tilney quickly took possession of Shelley Hall.

The dodgy will was almost immediately challenged by Sir George Buck, the nephew of Margaret Tilney, the widow of Emery's older brother Fraye and mother of recently deceased Philip. Buck was trying to extract what he saw as his rightful property in Skidbrooke, Lincolnshire, belonging to his now dead aunt. He believed, probably correctly, that the Lincolnshire property had been wrongly appropriated by Emery's father Thomas.[30] Coincidentally Buck worked closely with Emery's other cousin Edmund Tilney, the Master of the Queen's Revels.[31] Buck eventually followed Edmund Tilney as Master of the Revels but this old family legal wrangle poisoned their relationship. Buck lost his case and Emery therefore inherited Shelley Hall and all the lands in Suffolk and Lincolnshire.

Emery Tilney remarries

Emery was by now ageing but he was wealthy and therefore still a good catch. We do not know when his first wife Winifred died, quite possibly in the late 1570s. His children were grown up and his son Thomas was his right hand man. After 1603 Emery made Shelley Hall his main home. He married Elizabeth Harte in London on 18 June 1602 in the Church of St Mary Aldermary in the City of London but died only three years later in 1605.[32]

Emery Tilney's post-mortem survey of his possessions (Inquisition Post Mortem or IPM) still survives in The National Archives.[33] Translated from the Latin, it includes a confirmation that at his death he still owned 'Tylneys', Monks Hall Syleham, confusingly referred to as 'Syleham Hall'.

> Inquisition indented taken at Ipswich in Suffolk on 5th October, 3 James I [1605] before George Skarpe Esquire the King's Escheator in Suffolk by virtue of the King's writ *de diem clausit extremum* after the death of Emery Tylney Esquire:
>
> The jurors say on oath that Emery Tylney, before he died, was seized of the manor of Shelley otherwise called Shelley hall, otherwise called Markes, with appurtenances, and of 12 messuages, 600 acres of land, 100 acres of meadow, 1000 acres of pasture, 200 acres of wood, 300 acres of heath, £.....[illegible] of rent with appurtenances in Shelley, Layham, Polstead, Roydon, Stoke & Edwardstone in Suffolk, **and in the manor of Syleham Monks otherwise called Syleham Hall with appurtenances in Syleham in Suffolk & Norfolk, and of various other lands, tenements & hereditaments in Syleham appertaining to the same manor or appurtenances &c in Suffolk & Norfolk**; and of the manor of Aldham with appurtenances in Aldham in Suffolk.

The Tilney family connection with Monks Hall ended after Emery's death in 1605, when his son Thomas Tilney sold the manor to **William Fuller**.

There is an addendum to the Tilney story that connects Emery's son Thomas, who grew up at Monks Hall, with the founding of the United States of America. Young Thomas Tilney married a local Suffolk girl, Elizabeth Gosnold, sister of Captain Bartholomew Gosnold, one of the founding fathers of Virginia. In 2003 an archaeological dig at Jamestown discovered the likely location of Gosnold's grave. In June 2005 researchers sought permission to take DNA samples from the remains of Thomas's sister, Elizabeth Gosnold

Tilney, buried in the church of All Saints, Shelley. The first DNA samples taken were probably those of the wrong body but a further sample taken in 2010 appeared to be hopeful. There are reports on the web that the samples from the possible Gosnold grave and Tilney body matched, but there has been no official confirmation. There is however a plaque in All Saints Church to commemorate the connection between Emery's daughter-in-law and Bartholomew Gosnold.

Notes

1. Tilney family pedigrees from multiple history sites and from 'The Visitations of Suffolk made by Hervey, Clarenceux, 1561, Cooke, Clarenceux, 1577 and Raven, Richmond herald, 1612, with notes and an appendix of additional Suffolk pedigrees', pp. 73–4, 170, Harvey, William (d. 1567). British Museum. MSS (Harleian 1103); Cook, Robert (d. 1593); Raven, John Earle and Metcalfe, Walter Charles (Exeter: privately printed, 1882).
2. Moated site and remains of demolished parts of Shelley Hall, a post-medieval great house. Historic England listing number 1019815.
3. Martin, Edward 2005. 'The archaeology and history of the designed landscape and moated garden at Shelley Hall', Suffolk Archaeological Service Suffolk County Council, published in *Proceedings of the Cambridge Antiquarian Society* XCIV, pp. 241–4.
4. Transfer in 1545 (36 Henry VIII) of Syleham Monachorum Manor from Thomas Duke of Norfolk Great Treasurer and Earl Marshall of England to Thomas Tilney, to the use of Thomas and his wife Elizabeth and son Emery and their heirs and assigns... Brewer, John Sherren. 1862. 'Letters and Papers, Foreign and Domestic, of the Reign of Henry VIII' preserved in the Public Record Office, the British Museum and Elsewhere in England, Vol. 10, p 671.
5. McIntosh, Marjorie K. 2013. *Poor Relief and Community in Hadleigh, Suffolk 1547–1600* (Hatfield: University of Hertfordshire Press), p. 38.
6. Margaret Tylney's tomb bears the following inscription. 'This tombe was made by Philip Tylney esquire in remembrance of his duty to his dear mother Dame Margrett, the wife of Frederick Tylney esquire who had issue by her, Thomas Tylney who died without issue & the above named Philip Tylney who by Ann ye daughter of Framlingham of Debenham had issue Charles ++ yet died without issue, his father living 1598'.
7. Thomas Segges of Syleham, will 1558, probate granted 1565 Norwich Consistory Court Probate Records NRO NCC administration act book 1563–1570, fo. 159.
8. William Segges Will 1561, Probate 1565 NRO. NCC administration act book 1563–1570, fo. 159.
9. See note 7, inventory transcribed by Andrew F Gray 2005 and rendered into modern English by the author.
10. Gray, Andrew F. 1998. 'Mortality Crises in the Upper Waveney Valley 1539–1603: A preliminary study'. Unpublished paper courtesy of Mary Lewis, Syleham Parochial Church Council.
11. Short title: Tylney v Tylney. Plaintiffs: Elizabeth, late the wife of Philip Tylney,

knight, and afterwards the wife of Francis Framlyngham, esquire, and daughter of Robert Jeffrey, deceased. Defendants: Thomas Tylney, son and heir of the said Sir Philip. Subject: Manor of Shelley Hall, with appurtenances (described), and lands in Shelley, Layham, Reydon, Holton, Stoke, Polstead, and Edwardstone, settled on complainant conditionally on a release of her rights in manors, lands, rents, and services in Wyberton, Skirbeck and Boston. Suffolk, Lincolnshire. TNA C 1/1164/62 1544 22 April 1547 Feb 15. And Tilney v Tilney 1545 TNA C 78/1/39.

12. Thomas Tilney's will 1567. Probate Record TNA PROB 11-42B-299.
13. John Cossey's tenancy mentioned in Thomas Tilney's will 1567. Probate Record TNA PROB 11-42B-299.
14. Database of Cambridge Alumni by Venn. http://venn.lib.cam.ac.uk (accessed 10.4.2018).
15. George Wishart. Dotterweich, Martin Holt, 1895 Oxford Dictionary of National Biography, online at http://www.wishartconnections.org/index.php/notablewisharts/george-wishart (accessed 9.8.2018).
16. Foxe, John, 1563. Actes and Monuments of these Latter and Perillous Days, Touching Matters of the Church. Numerous later editions. Online at https://www.johnfoxe.org (accessed 11.4.2018), called 'Foxe's Book of Martyrs'. In 1583 ed'n Emery Tilney's description of Wishart is at Book 8 p. 1291.
17. Emery Tylney. Dogmata eiusdem Georgij. (translation, The dogmas of the same George).
18. Tilney, Emery, 1550. Here beginneth a song of the Lordes supper (London: printed by W. Copland, sold by R. Stoughton), online at http://www.otago.ac.nz/english-linguistics/tudor/song_lordes_sup24078.html (accessed 27.7.2017).
19. Craig, John. 2005. *Reformation, Politics and Polemics: The Growth of Protestantism in East Anglian Market Towns, 1500–1610* (Aldershot: Ashgate), xiv, p. 267. Hadleigh study in greater depth in Craig, J. 1999. 'Reformers, Conflict, and Revisionism: The Reformation in Sixteenth century Hadleigh'. *The Historical Journal*, 42 (1), pp. 1–23.
20. MacCulloch, Diarmaid. 1975. 'Radulph Agas, Virtue Unrewarded'. *Suffolk Archaeology and History*, Vol XXXIII part 3 p. 283.
21. Cardinall v Tilney, Horner. 1591 Records of the Court of Star Chamber 33 Eliz. TNA STAC5/C20/33. Cardinall (c 1510–1568) was a quarrelsome Protestant lawyer who was a close associate of the Earl of Oxford.
22. Short title: Burlage v Tilney. Pleadings, Court of Chancery: Six Clerks Office: Pleadings, TNA C 3/16/36 1558-1579
23. Fenner, John (MP Midhurst) c. 1563, published in Hasler, P. W. (ed.) 1981. The History of Parliament: The House of Commons 1558–1603 (Woodbridge: Boydell and Brewer), online at http://www.historyofparliamentonline.org/volume/1558-1603/member/fenner-john (accessed 9.8.2018).
24. Manor of Syleham, Monk's Hall or Tylney's or Syleham Hall in Copinger, W. A. 1909. The Manors of Suffolk: Notes on their history and devolution, with some illustrations of the old manor houses. Vol. 4. (Manchester: Taylor, Garnett, Evans and Co). https://archive.org/stream/cu31924092579576/cu31924092579576_

djvu.txt (accessed 9.8.2018).
25. The arrangement between William Fisher and Emery Tilney was noted in the will of William's father, Robert Fisher, who died 1563. Referred to in Hyde, M. S. and Plummer, J. 1997. 'English Ancestry of New England Settlers, Joshua and Anthony Fisher'. *New England Historical and Genealogy Register* 151.
26. Stratford v Tylney. Claim by descent and for relief against pretended forfeiture. TNA C2/Eliz/S23/44.
27. Herryng v Tylney. 1603-1606 Lands in the manor of Munkshall alias Tylney Hall in Sylham, Suffolk. TNA C 2/JasI/H14/16
28. Will of Thomas Howard made September 1601. SRO R39/184.
29. Streitberger, W. R. 1978. 'On Edmund Tilney's Biography'. *The Review of English Studies* 29 (113) p. 18.
30. 1603 legal action by Sir George Buck esq., eldest son of Robert Buck, brother of Margaret Tilney decd, wife of Frederick Tilney, dec'd, whose son was Phillip Tilney v Emery Tilney esq., uncle of Phillip Tilney and Thomas Tilney. Inheritance of the manor of Skidbrooke [Skidbrooke cum Saltfleet], Lincs and other lands, late of Margaret Tilney dec'd. TNA C78/103, no. 20. The case is described at some length in a number of academic studies. Sisson, C. J. (ed) 1933. *Thomas Lodge and Other Elizabethans* (Cambridge, Mass.: Harvard University Press) p. 478; Finkelpearl, P. J. 1980. 'The Comedian's Liberty: Censorship of the Jacobean Stage Reconsidered', in Kinney A. F. and Collins, D. S. *Renaissance Historicism. Selections from English Literary Renaissance* (Amherst: University of Massachusetts Press), pp. 191–206, and online. Streitberger, W. R. 1978. 'On Edmund Tilney's Biography'.
31. For the history of larger than life character Edmund Tilney, Master of the Queens Revels and censor of Shakespeare's plays, see Dutton, Richard, 2008. 'Tilney, Edmund (1535/6–1610), courtier'. Oxford Dictionary of National Biography.
32. Marriage of Emery Tilney and Elizabeth Harte. London Metropolitan Archives, St Mary Aldermary, Composite register: baptisms, marriages and burials 1558-1653, P69/MRY3/A/001/MS08990, Item 001.
33. IPM of Emery Tylney Esq. TNA TilneyWARD 7/29/17/002.

8

Tilney's Hall

Monks Hall today is essentially Thomas Tilney's building and Emery and Winifred Tilney's home, in spite of many alterations since the mid 16th century. If they were to return today they would recognise it instantly. What we see now is a house that was extensively renovated in the early 20th century, with 'Tudor' diamond shaped leaded lights in old mullion frames, 18th and 19th century windows, the timber frame exposed to reveal studding and the method of construction. It looks exactly how we think an ancient timber-framed house ought to look. But essentially the house remains unchanged from the mid 16th century.

In 1995, Colonel and Mrs J. T. B. Leader, who had done much of the modern renovation fifty years earlier, commissioned 'a vernacular survey' of the hall from Andrew F. Gray, local historian and architectural enthusiast. Gray's immaculate drawings, plans, detailed description and interpretation survive in unpublished form in the Hall archives.[1] I have drawn extensively on Gray's work for this chapter and all the drawings of the house are his. An architect, Matthew Poray-Swinarski, drew the floor plans in 1945.

Monks Hall falls into the vernacular tradition of manor houses found in the south-east of England. Both manor hall and church were of major importance to village communities throughout the medieval period. They were in many respects the heart of the village, the manorial hall acting as an administrative centre where management of the land was determined and minor disputes resolved. Like the church, the manor hall was a substantial building. When

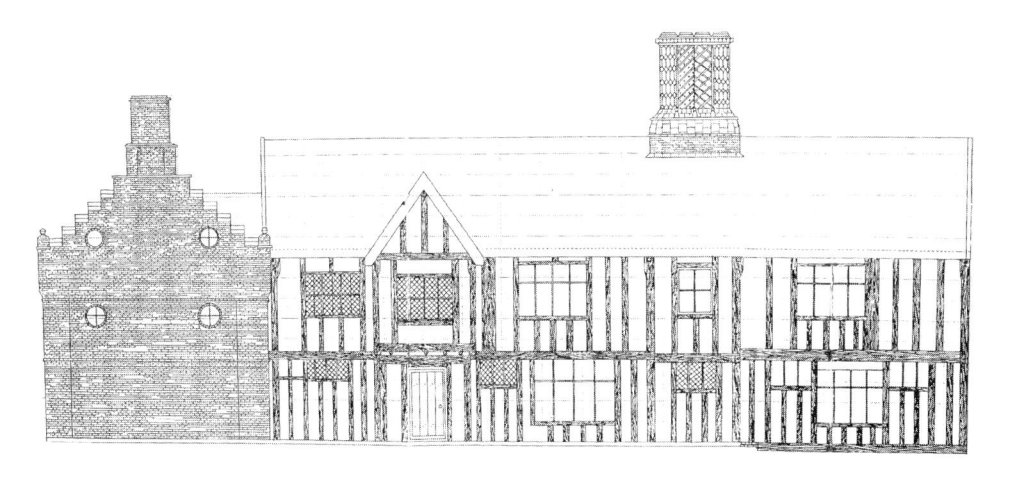

Drawing of South Elevation, Monks Hall, by Andrew F Gray 1995.

most peasant dwellings were transitory, rarely lasting beyond a generation, the hall imparted a sense of continuity and stability that was both visual and enduring.

Written before Gray's detailed investigation of Monks Hall, Pevsner's Buildings of England gives a cursory description that was expanded a little in the most recent 2015 edition:

> Fine timber-framed house with a projecting wing end in a stepped gable with four small circular windows. This is the oldest part of the house, perhaps c15, remodelled in the c17. Main range c1600, with exposed timbers and gabled and jettied porch. Chimneystack with four circular decorated chimneys. Good panelled interiors, including one with an early c17 overmantel from Ufford Place (demolished 1956).[2]

Pevsner described what he saw, a timber-framed Tudor building. When the building was listed grade II* in July 1955, a similar description was given but in greater detail.[3]

> Manor farmhouse. Main range c.1600; earlier wing set forward to left, remodelled probably early C17, forming L-shape plan to house. Timber-framed and plastered, the main range with exposed studding at the front. Roofs mainly plaintiled. 2 storeys and attics. 3-cell main range with cross-passage entry. Some original ovolo-moulded mullioned

windows, diamond-leaded, and a good C17 mullion and transom window to first floor; other windows at front are late C18/early C19 casements with large panes. Good original porch, the upper floor jettied on 3 sides; mutilated balustrading to side openings. Inside the porch the original studded plank entrance door. Very fine stack with 4 enriched circular shafts complete with caps and bases. The projecting wing has a crow-stepped brick gable end with circular windows to the upper floors, corbelled eaves, pinnacles with ball finials and a stack with an inset panel in the base. One side-wall of this wing has a C17 splayed first floor window.

Interior. The hall has complete oak panelling, much of it original; over the fireplace part of an elaborate early C17 overmantel brought from Ufford Place near Woodbridge c.1940. At lower end of hall a plank and muntin screen with a painted overdoor depicting Solomon's Judgement (said to be late C17). Ovolo-moulded beam and joists to hall ceiling. Parlour has complete pine panelling of early C18 and a contemporary bolection-moulded fireplace with painted overmantel. Parlour chamber has fireplace of similar date, flanked by pilasters, with painted overmantel; good C19 cast iron grate with tiled surround. On both chimney breasts there are remains of fresco paintings (normally concealed and not seen during survey). Earlier wing probably has C15 core: evidence of sooting on some members and also of diamond-mullioned windows. Good first floor stuccoed fireplace with 4-centre arch and quoined surround. There is a small gap between the 2 wings and at first floor level is the remains of C16 incised geometric pargetting on the former outside wall of the earlier range.

Neither Pevsner nor the Listed Building description take account of the Extent survey of 1433, which gives a much earlier date of the end of the 14th or early 15th century for the core of the main three-bay south range and the crosswing, although the crosswing probably started life as a stable and was incorporated and embellished in the mid 16th century.

Monks Hall is a building of considerable complexity. Plainly the fabric has undergone a number of phases and remodelling which must reflect the social and practical demands of its owners. The internal arrangements reflect a period earlier than the conventional 16th century Tudor house. The 1433 Extent describes a three-bay house. Dating to the early 15th century was borne out by a metal detector survey in the late 20th century by Mr Mischa Sakanovic, which produced evidence of the location of the 'plumbery' mentioned in the

1433 Extent, some 10m or so to the north-east of the present building in what is now a vegetable garden.[4] Further evidence is provided by the quantity and quality of pottery shards and artefacts discovered in the whole grounds, which included a wide range of medieval material, including the fine silver penny of Henry III (reigned 1216–1272).

The early 15th century hall

The Extents of 1379 and 1433 suggest that day-to-day running of the lord's demesne was in the hands of the chief or principal tenants/bailiffs who would no doubt have been answerable to the Lord Prior. The extent of 1433 makes clear mention of 'One hall with upper room at each end' establishing the existence of the hall itself and suggests that the building of 1433 was of the open hall type. Open hall houses were timber-framed and could consist of one or more bays depending upon the wealth, status or whim of the potential owner. Timber box frames were prefabricated in the builders' yard, and then transported to the construction site to be assembled and re-erected. Gaps between timbers were then filled in with wattle and daub, brick or some combination of other materials available locally.

In this early 15th century hall, one bay was taken up by the formal centre of the house, the main 'hall'. Here the manorial court was held, visitors were received and entertained and it was usually open to the rafters. Visitors would have seen the substantial, elaborate and finely finished timberwork supporting the roof. There was usually a central hearth, sometimes equipped with a smoke hood channelling smoke up to wooden louvred vents in the roof's ridge. Doors on either side at one end of the hall reached family rooms, parlour and stairs to two bedrooms above.

The process of putting in a ceiling over the open hall and inserting chimneys during the mid 16th century brought about alterations that often make it difficult to locate evidence for any venting system in the roof.[5] It is hard to see how the vents would have functioned, in removing smoke from the main hall, because the walls at either end of the hall appear to have always been sealed up to the rafters by a wattle and daub panel, thus making a barrier between the hall and the little gable. As the open hearth is always accompanied by a cross-passage, it has been suggested that if the house were filling with smoke while the wood tried to kindle, opening the cross-passage doors would cause a through draft, encouraging the smoke to dissipate, thus forcing the wood to catch fire more quickly and produce less smoke. Lighting these fires seems to have been a smelly business. It is likely the fire would have been kept going for hot water, cooking and warmth most of the time.

In the early 1990s, Matthew Johnson studied the construction and function of medieval hall houses of Suffolk. He points out that while we are used to thinking that the form and construction of houses indicated how the residents used the spaces, it is also true that the way they lived socially in the spaces was in part determined by the partitions, the hall and the passage.[6]

The furniture in the early house would have been the simplest possible, a trestle table, a few stools, wooden and pottery bowls, plates and cutlery.[7] In the hall there would almost certainly have stood a spinning wheel. But we know that the Cossey family were acquiring wealth and material goods and undoubtedly early Monks Hall would have been one of the grandest in Syleham alongside the hall of the other manor.

Tilney's Hall: The mid 16th century reconstruction

The simple early hall house was not going to be grand enough for the Tilney family. A new public statement of position and status was required. House architecture changed of course as family members sought more and larger private spaces and acquired 'things' and furniture. Over the period of 1500 to 1600 Suffolk's agrarian economy shifted in ownership from a few exceedingly wealthy landowners to a large body of country gentry and yeomen. Houses of this new gentry and yeoman class became grander; houses of the mid to late 1500s shout 'I own this' to neighbours and workers on the manor land who now thought of themselves as proper tenants with rights and privileges but also needed reminding of their station. Monks Hall was the vision of someone with a keen eye for what was in fashion and what would impress. It is in part a matter of informed guesswork as to how the house has developed, but Gray's likely sequence of development is shown below.

Tilney's Hall was a timber-framed two-storey manor house with a late 14th or early 15th westerly cross wing incorporated into the main hall probably in the mid 16th century. Joining these two buildings together gives an eccentric discontinuity in floor levels and it is clear where the wall was removed to sandwich the buildings together.

Exposed timber framing on the **southern façade** reflects a three-bay box construction with concealed bracing. Only in the east bay can the timber soleplate be seen, elsewhere it has been replaced with brick of flint mortar set in rubble. Substantial jowl headed wall posts carry horizontal tie beams; the bracing is internal and concealed. Wall studs are set vertically, their spacing closer on the ground floor than on the upper. Intervals between the studs are mortar rendered.

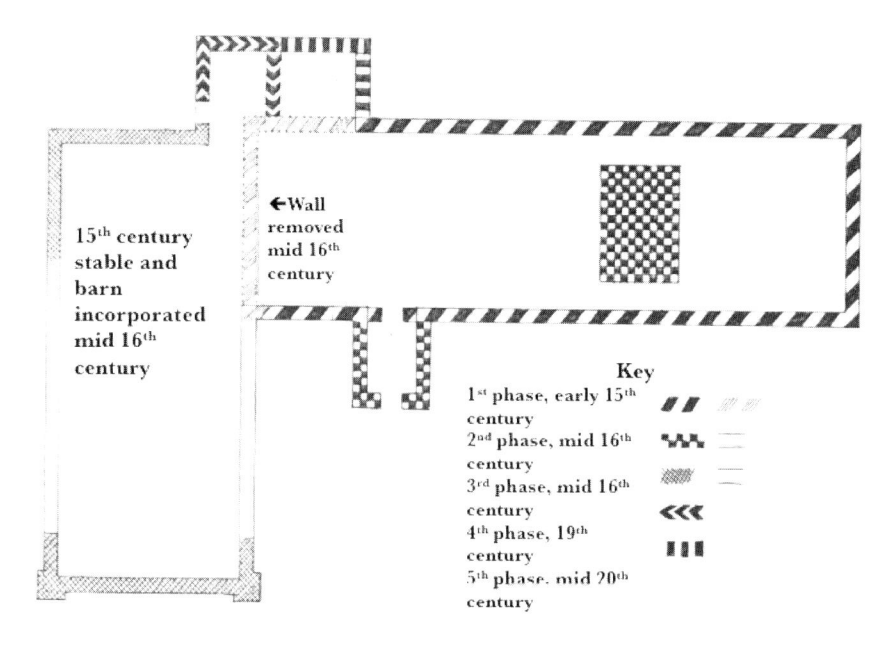

15th century stable and barn incorporated mid 16th century

←Wall removed mid 16th century

Key
1st phase, early 15th century
2nd phase, mid 16th century
3rd phase, mid 16th century
4th phase, 19th century
5th phase, mid 20th century

Monks Hall development sequence by Andrew Gray.

The Porch and Central Bay. The south-facing porch is of box frame construction providing a two-storey structure with an entrance hall and a jettied upper room with a steeply pitched roof. Two large windows, one on either side, probably started life as mullions. The heavy oak door looks authentic but is probably of a much later period.

The **north face** of the house is fully rendered and it is quite possible that the house was rendered all over in the 16th century. We know that it was fully rendered and lime-washed in Victorian times (see photo taken at the turn of the 19th/20th century in later chapter on the Read family). Close ornamental studding is usually an indicator that the beams were meant to be exposed and

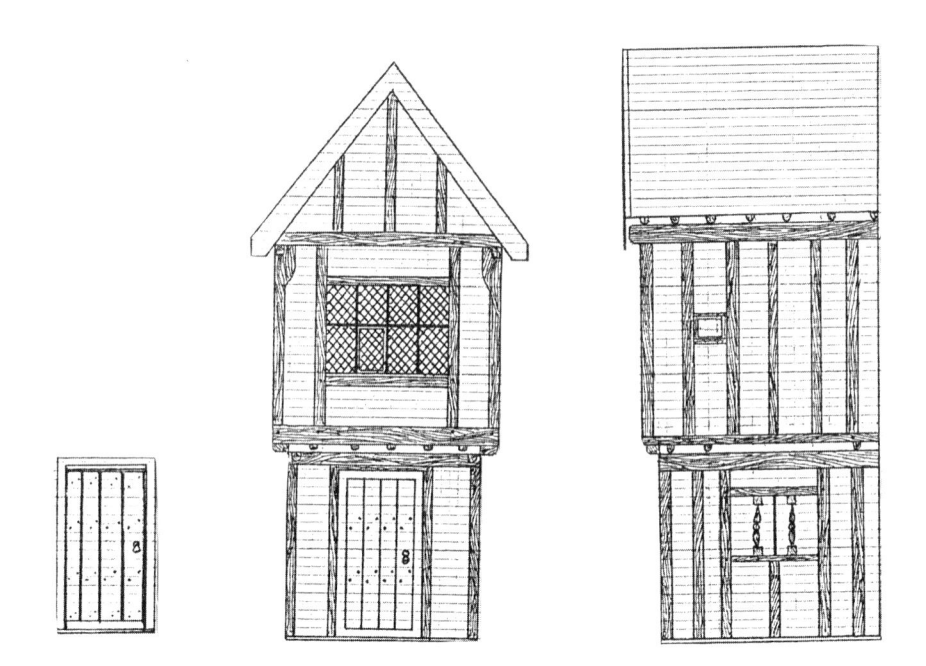

The outer door, porch and jettied room above, south and east elevation, drawn by Andrew Gray, 1995.

the narrow studding on the ground floor suggests that possibly the studding on the façade and porch were visible, although we cannot be sure. There is a modern oriel window inserted on the ground floor and the one-storey later kitchen range is sited at the west end of the north face. Until this additional facility was added it seems likely that the owners used the crosswing fireplace

North Elevation, with kitchen building on right.

for cooking, which shows evidence of where spits and hanging pots would have been hung.

The façade of the western **crosswing** is of mellow red brick in an ornate style but at the core is a timber-framed building, the façade added on later at an angle and with some random type of brick bonding that suggests a degree of structural 'botching' to create the desired effect. The striking **crow-stepped gable** was possibly added in the 16th century. Centuries of East Anglian trade with the low countries, Germany and Scotland had exposed wealthy men to elaborate crow-stepped brick gables on Hanseatic league buildings and although gables of this kind are often 17th century or later, reflecting a later Dutch influence, it seems most likely that the crow-stepped gable on Monks Hall was added as a decorative feature to soften the utilitarian structure it hides when it was joined to the rest of the house. The brickwork is typical of the period, a mixture of irregular bond on the west and east sides but English cross-bond on the southerly façade.

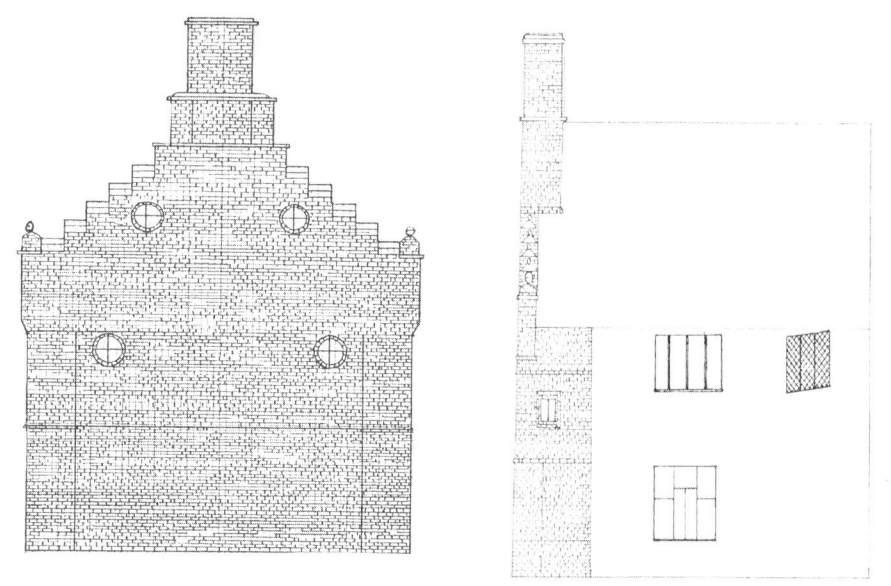

Westerly crosswing. East elevation crosswing.

The only feature not consistent with the mid 16th century date for the crosswing are the four round windows, which strike a later note and may have been put in to add further light in the 17th or 18th century. There is a chimney stack drawing from a huge open fireplace at the southern end of the crosswing.

The chimneys

The other mid 16th century feature is the central group of chimneys in ornate brick sitting atop the tiled roof. The bass plinth is a plain rectangle brick capped with a drip sill, which terminates at the roof ridge. Above this, a line of four highly decorative stacks, which at first sight seem to be aligned running east to west but are in fact a shallow arc. This creates something of an optical illusion because the centre stacks are larger when viewed from the rear, indicating that they house more than one flue.

Outer stacks are separated from the central pair by small moulded triangular ornaments topped with terracotta balls and constructed of moulded bricks as shown in the illustrations. Those in the centre display different decorative patterns. Each stack is topped by a number of projecting brick courses, one of which is arranged in a zigzag pattern.

Photograph of Monks Hall chimneys 1934.

The Queen 14 August 1934.

The chimney stack has always been regarded as a fine one by commentators and the stack looks more complicated than it is. Girling wrote in the 1930s:

> Patterns which appear to be highly complicated are remarkable because they were achieved by simple means. In some cases all the bricks in the shaft were cast in the same mould, the pattern being obtained by correct placing of the bricks, one towards the other. The four shafts of the stack at Monks Hall Syleham are built thus, as are two of the shafts at Framlingham Castle. The spiral and its variants such as zigzags and lattice patterns were popular motifs.[8]

The fashion for elaborate stacks of this kind was relatively short-lived, making it reasonably easy to be sure of the construction date of 16th century.

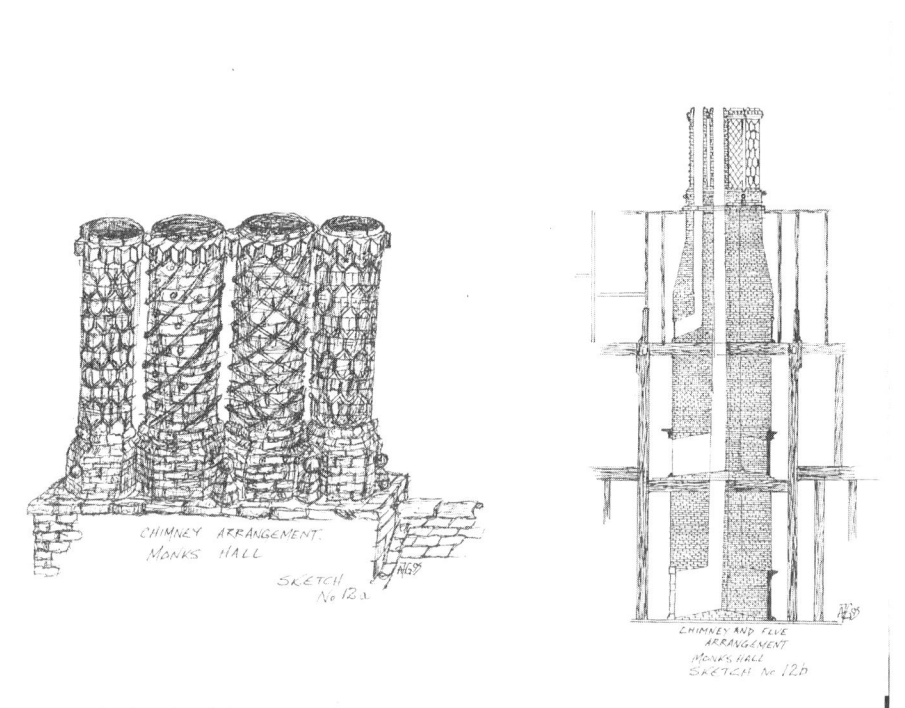

Andrew Gray's sketch of the chimney stack in 1995 and the flue arrangement allowing the smoke to escape from four fires inside the house.

In the **easternmost bay**, three light mullion windows with diamond lattice glazing and rounded mouldings flank a large four-light wooden-framed casement window on the ground floor. Shortened studs below this window and a large mortar slab above indicate that studding here has been massively cut away to facilitate the insertion of this window. An unusual feature of the first floor bay above is an overly large vertical stud that appears to carry a tie beam. The window here is similar in pattern to that below, though slightly shorter in height. The windows are later than the 16th century, probably 18th century; much older, probably 16th century, mullion windows have been made to look 'Tudor' by lattice glazing in the early 20th century.

There are numerous additional features that have been added in later centuries: a modern oriel window on the north face, a new kitchen range on the north possibly in the 19th century, many later windows to bring more light into the old hall.

Interior

The first thing that strikes a visitor is the pleasant dimensions of rooms that are not huge but impressively designed to reflect the way 16th century family life was conducted. But the interiors we see now are largely 20th century embellishments designed to add a richness of quality that the house may not originally have had. The details of these will be covered in the chapter on the 20th century owners, Colonel and Mrs J.T.B. Leader. The internal embellishments dating from the 17th, 18th and 19th centuries will be mentioned as we reach those periods.

Monks Hall floor plans

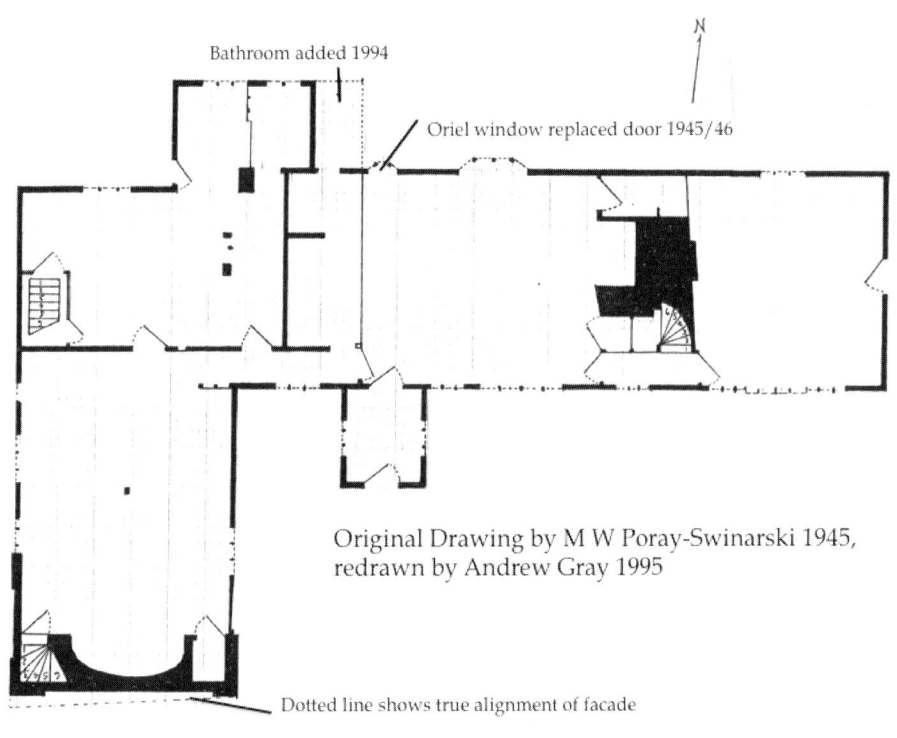

Bathroom added 1994

Oriel window replaced door 1945/46

Original Drawing by M W Poray-Swinarski 1945, redrawn by Andrew Gray 1995

Dotted line shows true alignment of facade

Ground Floor Plan.

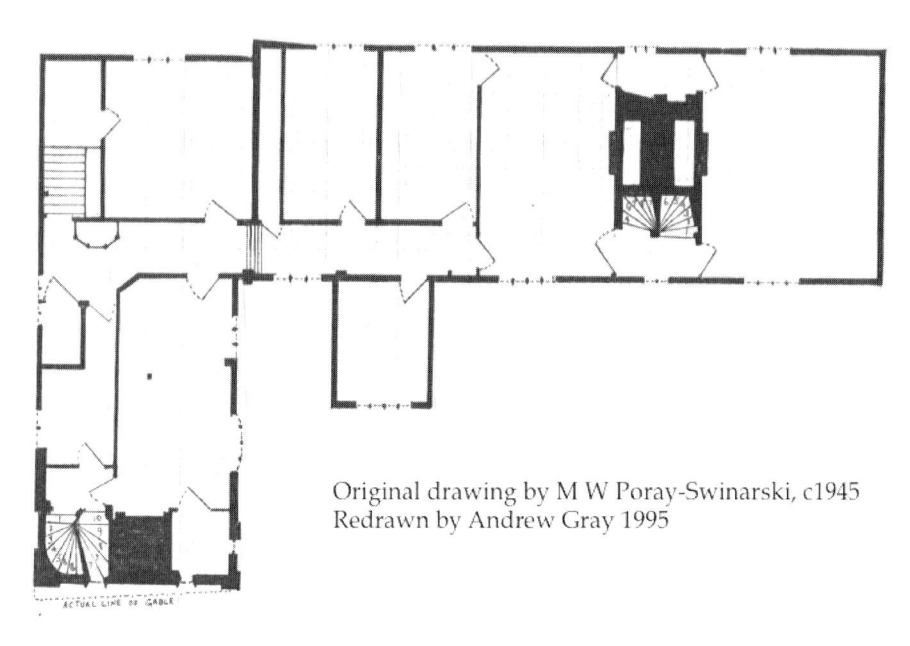

Upper Floor Plan.

Original drawing by M W Poray-Swinarski, c1945
Redrawn by Andrew Gray 1995

Notes
1. Gray, Andrew F., 1995. 'Monks Hall Syleham. A Vernacular Survey'. Unpublished paper Monks Hall Archive.
2. Pevsner, N. 1961 (2nd edition 1974, revised by Enid Radcliffe 2015). *Buildings of England: Suffolk* (Harmondsworth: Penguin Books), p. 459.
3. British Listed Buildings 5/116 Monk's Hall Listing NGR: TM2016178470.
4. Gray 1995 mentions but gives no reference for Mischa Sakanobic's metal detection, silver penny or pottery finds.
5. Lewis, E. 1988. 'Medieval Hall Houses of the Winchester Area'. Winchester City Museum, p. 11.
6. Johnson, Matthew, 1993. *Housing Culture: Traditional Architecture in an English Landscape* (London: UCL Press), pp. 136–56.
7. For a good description of the inside of early local medieval houses, see Sandon, E. 1977. *Suffolk Houses. A Study in Domestic Architecture* (Woodbridge: Baron Publishing), Section 3 'Commoditie, the planning of houses', pp. 33-63.
8. Girling, F. A. 1934. 'Suffolk Chimneys of the 16th Century'. *Proceedings of the Suffolk Institute 22*, part 1, p. 104–7. Also article by Frank Girling, *Chimneys of the Sixteenth Century* in The Queen August 14th, 1935 p37, Monks Hall Archive.

9

The Fuller Family 1605–1722

The Fuller family owned Monks Hall manor for over a century, a very turbulent century too. They were prosperous yeomen farmers, characteristic of a landed class hovering below the gentry, probably well known locally but invisible on the wider stage. From the scraps of information they left, they were typical of East Anglian Puritans, natural parliamentarians during the Civil War and yet relieved when the austere age was over and the monarchy restored. William and Anna Fuller and their descendants farmed during a century where some gains were made in agricultural productivity but economic hardships generated by Civil War and poor access to knowledge about improved methods in farming led to less striking developments in agriculture than in the following century. Turnips, however, were grown in increasing quantities for winter fodder and enclosures of groups of fields and commons continued apace, providing more economical units for ploughing and grazing.

Farming at Monks Hall in the 17th century

The lack of written references to the Fullers suggests they concentrated on their farming and their family. The manor still existed, tenants on their land would have paid their rents and looked to the Fullers to be fair and just landlords. The Waveney Valley and the plateau above were largely a pastoral area. The most important livestock were dairying herds producing milk for cheese but with some bullock-rearing for meat and arable fields of wheat grown alongside. The decline in sheep-rearing was in part substituted locally by flax and hemp production.

Large areas of the eastern region were still occupied by farmers engaged in traditional subsistence agriculture, effectively quite isolated, but the middling estate farmers of north Suffolk, near the Kings Highway from Norwich to Ipswich, looked to London and other markets to sell their produce. This may be why the dairy farmers of north Suffolk felt so connected to matters going on in Westminster and Parliament as the prodromal years before the Civil War focused their sympathies on the religious struggle that was at the heart of political differences.

The Suffolk cheese trade

Suffolk cheese was shipped off to London by cart for consumption there. The original Suffolk cheese was then one of the most famous cheeses in England. Cheese is best made from the rich milk of West Country cows fed on long lush grass. The dry Suffolk climate produced a very hard cows' milk cheese, possibly similar to Parmesan, the unique rockiness and durability celebrated, or decried as 'flinty' in poems, songs and jokes. The most economical sort was called 'bang'. 'Hunger will break through stone walls and anything except a Suffolk cheese,' Samuel Pepys remarked. 'I found my wife vexed at her people for grumbling to eat Suffolk cheese'.[1] Daniel Defoe thought Suffolk had 'the best butter and the worst cheese'.[2] It became the official cheese of the early 17th century Navy because it was the cheapest available.

Linen and hemp production

Small-scale flax production was once widespread throughout the eastern counties, but by Tudor times it had become concentrated in the Waveney Valley on the borders of Norfolk and Suffolk, following a line ten miles wide along the Waveney Valley, running from Eye to Beccles.[3] Acts of Parliament of 1533 and 1563 stipulated that farms of sixty or more acres should grow a quarter of an acre of hemp or flax. Fields and properties nearby might be called 'Hemplands' or 'Hempfield', such as Little Hemplands, the Syleham parish clerk's house, which still holds that name, and Great Hemplands, clearly visible on the tithe map of Syleham drawn in 1839. In 1859 there were still eight hemplands listed on Syleham Green and a 'retting pit pightle', where hemp was softened in water before being further refined.[4]

By the 17th century the Hoxne Hundred was noted for its linen and hemp weavers. This was a lucrative trade. By 1674, the tax returns reported only 14 per cent of the population of Syleham was so poor they were exempt from taxes, whereas in the Hartismere Hundred in general about a third were too poor to pay taxes.[5] It is not surprising then that drabbet, linen and hemp milling and weaving continued into the early 20th century in Syleham.

Hempen linen was noted for its hardwearing qualities. Both hemp and flax were used in the process of making linen but the climate and soil in Suffolk seemed to suit hemp rather than flax, and flax needs much more labour to grow and harvest. Hemp grown for making ship cables and canvas or for sacking needs a well manured and damp soil, yet a poorer soil is good for fine and slender linen fibres. In the 17th century Diss became the centre for the collection and distribution of Suffolk Hempen Cloth at its Cloth Hall, or Weavers' Hall, which was at The Saracen's Head Inn, where William Fuller may have sold some of his cloth.

The Fuller family

Fuller is one of the commonest names in East Anglia. This is hardly surprising because in the medieval period fulling wool was a very common occupation. In the north of England fullers were called walkers, hence Walker in Yorkshire is as common as Fuller in Suffolk. But by the late 15th century the name Fuller is found across all ranks of society and provides no clue as to the origin of individuals.

Sorting out one Fuller family from another is apt to drive the genealogist to despair. This is particularly so in the Waveney Valley, as every amateur American genealogist called Fuller is anxious to trace his ancestry back to the famous Redenhall Fullers, Edward and Samuel, Puritan signatories of the Mayflower Compact, who sailed on the Mayflower in September 1620 with Edward's wife and young son Samuel to find religious freedom and a new land. Edward and his wife died soon after landing at Plymouth, New England, in the first harsh winter that killed half the pilgrims, but their son Samuel survived and went on to have four sons of his own, who have now thousands of direct descendants.

We can be grateful though for the literally dozens of Fuller websites, although some have an eccentric understanding of the local geography of the Waveney

Valley, some frankly delusional. There is one optimistic site that traces a 14th century John Fuller mentioned as a freeholder serving on a jury in Harleston right down to Buckminster Fuller! It is so easy to convince oneself of an association where none existed and yet one cannot help but be sympathetic to this urge to make connections with adventurous ancestors. Fortunately many sites do contain painstaking investigations, with checkable references, into various branches of Fullers, and the author has been helped immensely by these assiduous American researchers.

William and Anna Fuller, owners of Monks Hall 1605–1634

Best to say right from the outset that while it is possible there is a common ancestral connection between the Mayflower Fullers of Redenhall and William Fuller of Syleham, who bought Monks Hall manorial estate in 1605, records were simply inadequate in the early 16th century before parish records were kept with any regularity.

If Fuller is a common name, so is William; there are pages of William Fullers in the Suffolk probate records and some five pages listing wills of relevant William Fullers in the Norfolk Record Office. We could be researching Fullers for a long time and still not sort out one from the other. Fortunately there are some obviously relevant records and close connections with one branch of Redenhall Fullers, although not necessarily the Pilgrim Fathers' branch.

To distinguish one Redenhall Fuller family from another, one branch was referred to as 'Fuller alias Alen [or Allen]'. The use of an 'alias' in 15th and 16th century wills is surprisingly common; no clear reason for this has been detected by those who have studied the phenomenon.[6] In our case Alen or Allen was probably used to identify the descendants of a William Fuller (died 1574) who had married Agnes or Anne Allen, a minor heiress who had inherited some property in Mendham and Harleston. But the addition of 'alias Alen' to some Redenhall and Syleham Fullers in wills and parish register entries has been especially useful in tracking down our Monks Hall William.

The best place to start the hunt is inside St Margaret's Church, Syleham, where William and Anna lie buried in the chancel beneath a solid stone slab right near the altar, just below the piscina, in a dark corner and obscured by a table.

The plain brass plaque on the gravestone is inscribed in Latin and

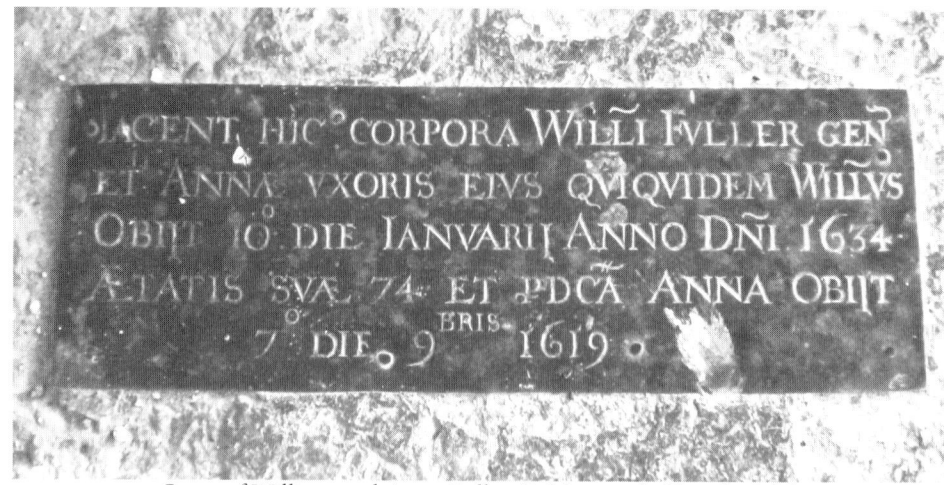

Grave of William and Anna Fuller, St Margaret's Church, Syleham.

Translation from the Latin: 'Here lie the bodies of William Fuller, Gentleman and Anna his wife, that is William died 10th day of January in the Year of Our Lord 1634 aged 74 and Anna died 7th Day of September 1619'.

commemorates William, giving his age as 74, a burial date of 1634, and his wife Anna who died in 1619. This simple but elegant form of memorial may give us a clue to the Fullers. It is in stark contrast to the huge slate tombs of the Lamb and Barry family that occupy the rest of the floor space in the chancel, grander memorials to the owners of Syleham Hall manor. On the other hand there is an almost identical brass plaque and stone grave on the opposite side of the chancel to Antony Barry (Snr) of Syleham Hall, who died in 1638. The two graves and brass plaques are clearly by the same hand. Presumably there was a brass engraver locally who was well thought of at the time and whose plain style was agreeable to the 'Godly' Protestant ethic that both Fuller and Barry families espoused.

William Fuller's 1634 will (written in 1628) survives in the Suffolk Record Office.[7] It is long and handwritten by a scribe whose spelling is wonderfully phonetic, eccentric even for the mid 17th century. After Anna's death, William remarried, a woman called 'Cleere', which I think we can guess was pronounced 'Clare'. Happily for us he lists many relatives and friends in his will and we can therefore trace his children and grandchildren. He provides generously for Clare after his demise but

> I will that my Executor shall bury me neere and by my Laste wyfe [Anna] in Syleham Chanselle and Laye a desente stone or stones over oure gravses withe in one yeare after the daye of my buryall

Part of the first page of the Will of William Fuller of Syleham, d. 1634.

as indeed was done.

William gives generous benefactions to the 'pore people of Saint Andrewes in Illkellshall, Silleham, Brodishe, Hoxton, Nedeham, Harlsstone and Mendhan Ende, Waibred and Winkefelld' and also to the local preachers 'Master Thomas Daines fourty shillings and Master Briant Witherell of Sileham twentie shillings'. It would be usual to leave money to the poor in parishes where the yeoman owned land and the number of parishes gives some idea of the extent of William Fuller's widespread agricultural empire.

William's first wife Anna Puckell was a widow when they married, with two children, Richard and Mary. William was clearly fond of them, leaving them money and rings. William and Anna then had three children of their own, Benjamin, Lydia and Judith. After Anna's death, when he married Clare, he acquired more stepchildren. All his children and stepchildren were generously provided for in a complicated will, with four pages of detail, but son Benjamin inherits the main property of Monks Hall.

William, Anna and Clare Fuller unfortunately do not feature in any local accounts of Syleham except as names in lists. Research has been hampered by the lack of surviving parish records of Syleham for this period. The registers of births, marriages and deaths are well documented but there are no vestry records or churchwardens accounts. Unusually there were no parish charities recorded for the 17th century.[8] The Fullers were yeomen farmers with educational aspirations for their son but if they participated in local affairs, as is likely for a yeoman family, we cannot tell.

Where did William Fuller come from?

While their deaths are listed on all the usual genealogical websites, there are no births recorded in Norfolk or Suffolk in 1560–65 that can clearly be identified as our William. The following clues may be helpful but are not conclusive.

Firstly, there was a William Fuller born in 1553 to William and Sybill Fuller (*nee* Spalding) in Bradwell, Suffolk. We know from the register at the University of Cambridge that at least one Fuller described himself as of both Syleham and Bradwell, but this turns out to be a miscopying of Bardwell rather than Bradwell.[9] It was only after several weeks search that it dawned on the author that many transcription errors had confused a suburb of Yarmouth with the village in mid-Suffolk. It seems that both villages are involved in our story. William Fuller of BRADWELL, near Yarmouth, married Sybill Spalding in Syleham in 1551. Sybill was almost certainly the daughter of John Spalding of Syleham, whom we know had a daughter called Sybill of the right age.[10]

Secondly, William and Sybill had more than one son called William. There were extensive connections between branches of the Fuller and Spalding families in Syleham and both families were wealthy landowners.[11] The 16th century William Fuller of BRADwell was wealthy enough to acquire a coat of arms, recorded in the official record as 'Arg, 2 bars and a canton Gu', which is two red bars across a white/silver field with a red square quarter in the upper left corner.[12] Three generations later, in 1664, William Fuller of Syleham and BARDwell had a coat of arms recorded as 'Arg, 3 bars and a canton Gu', a clear derivative of the earlier one. This is a strong pointer to the close link between these families. These arms have been copied indiscriminately by unrelated Fuller families elsewhere down many generations but these are recorded clearly in official heraldries for the men who used them in the 16th and 17th centuries.

THE FULLER FAMILY 1605-1722

Turning now to the obvious question of whether William Fuller alias Alen of Syleham, the executor named to oversee Monks Hall tenant Thomas Segges's will in 1565, was related to the William Fuller who bought Monks Hall. The executor had been responsible for ensuring Thomas' children inherited their goods and land but he also had the responsibility to look after the land and the children until they reached their majority. We know that neither young Thomas nor William Segges survived to adulthood. This William Fuller must have been a well-respected figure locally to be chosen as executor by Thomas Segges. It seems likely that these two William Fullers were related.

Executor William Fuller, alias Alen/Allen of Syleham, was surely linked to the Redenhall family of that name and we know one William Fuller alias Alen of Redenhall and his wife Agnes or Anne (nee Allen) had substantial property in Mendham and Harleston and also had a son named William.[13] This William is referred to as a 'shearman', a calling that sounds like a sheep shearer but in fact could also mean someone who traded in wool or arranged the shearing of sheep. The most likely explanation of the clues we have to date

The Fuller Family of Syleham 1551-1722

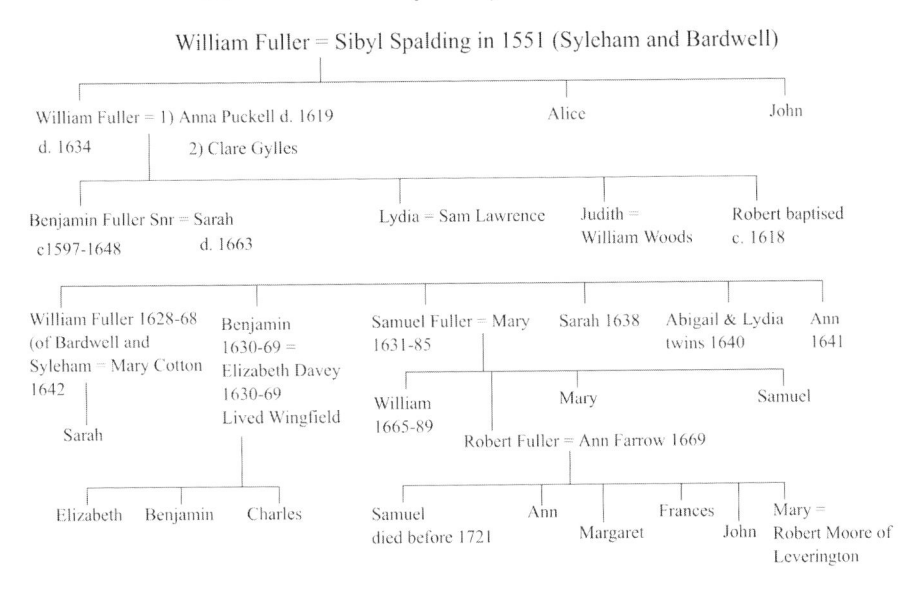

Possible Family Tree of the Fullers of Syleham 1551-1722.

is that William Fuller who bought Monks Hall was one and the same as the son of the Segges executor. There is a will written by William Fuller alias Alen of Redenhall in Harleston in 1575, but this at this point it is not possible to say whether he was related to the man who had property in Bradwell.[14]

The tentative tree above has been drawn from the parish registers of Syleham, Harleston and Redenhall, some wills, the brief biographies of Cambridge University Alumni and some litigation and property documents in The National Archives and in Norfolk and Suffolk Record Offices. The later years are accurate; the early ones are on rather unsure ground.[15]

A key document is the will of John Spalding of Syleham made in September 1544.[16] This sets out the extensive property and land Spalding owned in Syleham, Brockdish, Needham, Rushall, Dickleburgh, Billingford, Hoxne and Wingfield. He lived with his wife Agnes and at least five children, all girls, in a house in Syleham parish with a direct road to the 'Hall Place'. Possibly this is the property now called 'Syleham Manor', which seems to be in the right geographical location. At the time of his death Spalding had a grandson called John Fuller, who must have been the son of his daughter Margaret Spalding, who had married one Thomas Fuller of Redenhall in 1540.

Nine years after John Spalding's death, in 1553, his widow Agnes, who had been left almost all of her husband's extensive property, remarried in middle age one William Fuller of Redenhall. Since Thomas Fuller's father was named William it is very tempting to guess that Agnes married her son-in law's father.

These intimate connections between wealthy local yeoman families consolidated their extensive holdings for future generations. John Spalding of Syleham's considerable wealth devolved in due course to his widow's second husband's family, to William Fuller, possibly born in Bradwell, and it is likely that he is the one who married Anna and bought Monks Hall manor from Thomas Tilney. However this is guesswork informed by experience and may be quite wrong.

William and Anna's three children (they may have had more) were baptised in St Margaret's, Syleham: Benjamin (born c1600), Lydia, baptised in 1602, and Judith, who was born later than Lydia according to William's will. In the baptismal register in 1618 there is also Robert Fuller, 'son of William'. It appears that William's first wife Anna died in the immediate aftermath of Robert's birth. This Robert did not survive childhood as he is not mentioned in William's will. It would be quite usual for a widower with young children to remarry quickly and William's second wife Clare Gylles was a widow herself, in need of a father for her children.

Life in Syleham in the early 17th century

We know that the Fullers and the Spaldings both had Puritan leanings, as did most of the East Anglian population. They sympathised with the Protestant side of the seismic religious movements that ruptured the country in the late 16th and early 17th centuries. Some members of these families, perhaps most, were Puritans. Several young people from these families eventually made their way to New England in the exodus from the persecution by the established church and state in the time of Charles I. But there is no evidence that William or his wives were directly involved in the turmoil between differing practices of religious observance. Anna had died and William was nearing the end of his life when Archbishop Laud instigated the reinstatement of what were suspected as 'papist' symbols, conventional altars, altar steps and altar rails in chancels, implemented with enthusiasm by detested local Bishop Wren of Norwich.

17th Century woodcut of a Puritan family meal.

The first half of the 17th century was a time Puritan influence was extending deep into Suffolk, permeating from towns into villages and engaging local gentry families as well as the labouring and tradesmen communities in rural areas. There has been much debate about why the adoption of 'Godly beliefs' was so widespread in Suffolk, in contrast to Norfolk and Essex, where the landed gentry and prosperous yeoman were more split in their adherence to the traditional church and Puritan dissent was largely focused on towns.[17] It may have had to do with the high level of prosperity in the dairying regions of Suffolk, and the widespread mercantile connection between the wool, linen and dairy areas of Suffolk and the Low Countries, where religious dissent was taking hold, and also the trade with London, where all kinds of dissenting ideas were being explored and the city folk were overwhelmingly parliamentarian. While the woollen cloth industry in south Suffolk was in serious decline, the north Suffolk agricultural areas were booming and yeomen farming families were doing well, at least until the Civil War started.[18]

From the late 16th century the weaving of sacking and sailcloth was an attempt to offset the decline in the wool trade. This decline was due to the falling demand for Suffolk dyed cloth in Europe, to export restrictions and to the outbreak of war with Spain. So by 1622 clothiers in south Suffolk are reported to have had thousands of unsaleable cloths in their warehouses and many were in debt 'much decayed in their estates by reason of the great losses they have received'.[19] The farmers of north Suffolk were rescued by the hemp and dairying industries so the Fullers may not have done badly.

Christopher and Anthony Barry's survey and tithe records

William Fuller was a tenant on land on the next-door manor of Syleham Hall, as well as owning Monks Hall manor, on manor land formerly tenanted by the Spaldings. He appears in a list of tenants compiled for a survey, called a 'terrier', of the hall manor made by Christopher Barry, the owner of Syleham Hall. William had 'live sheep', producing finished wool and also hemp on these rented plateau lands.

Christopher Barry kept a handwritten account of the extent of his own lands but also a detailed account of annual tithes owed throughout the parish, including Monks Hall lands.[20] This valuable little vellum-bound document gave Barry a record of his 'impropriated tithes', that is income he was due on all the titheable lands in the parish that he had acquired, or his forebears had.

He was responsible for the maintenance and support of the parish priest out of the tithes, who in Syleham's case was a 'perpetual curate', subordinate to the Rector of Wingfield.[21] This little document is the best evidence we have for what crops and livestock were important to the parish in the 17th and early 18th century and how much they produced. Barry was meticulous in his annual recording.

Benjamin Fuller was in his mid to late 30s when he inherited Monks Hall manor from his father William in 1634. His father may have been ailing for some time because his first will was made in 1628 and he added several codicils in 1632. Benjamin was almost certainly the second son since it was this family's custom to name the oldest son William. The author can find no record of an infant death; quite often there would be no official record of a perinatal death. Benjamin and his wife Sarah reverted to this family custom of naming their own first son William when their first child was born in 1628.

Yeomen with ambitions like William and Anna Fuller wanted their children to be well educated, in order to enter those lucrative professions that were the only real alternatives to becoming a farmer, the church or the law. So Benjamin was sent to Emmanuel College, Cambridge, where he was admitted on 14 June 1614, and then graduated BA in 1617 and MA in 1621. This means he would have been at Cambridge when his mother died in 1619. Emmanuel College had been founded only twenty years earlier by the Puritan Sir Walter Mildmay, who intended his college to educate Protestant preachers. Benjamin's admission there confirms the Fuller family's Puritan leanings.

Emmanuel grew rapidly, so that by the 1620s it was the largest college in Cambridge. Perhaps surprisingly, given the nonconformists' reputation for joylessness, the fellows knew how to relax too, and outraged Lancelot Andrews, the future Master of Pembroke College, by playing bowls in the fellows' garden on Sundays. Twenty years later that would be unthinkable as puritanical ideals hardened. But the college had a reputation for sound scholarship and later still, five fellows and members of the College were involved in the new translation of the Authorised Version of the Bible.

Benjamin would have met many other East Anglian students whose families were Puritan. Within ten years of his graduating, in the 1630s, many Puritan clergy went into exile to avoid persecution. Of the first one hundred graduates who migrated to New England fully one third were Emmanuel men. Cambridge in Massachusetts was named in honour of an Emmanuel preacher Thomas Shepherd. Another, John Harvard, emigrated in 1637, dying the following year and leaving his books and half his estate to the new college that was to bear his name.

But Benjamin did not enter the church nor, it seems, involve himself in politics. He returned home to Syleham to help his father look after his estate. The storm clouds were gathering against the king, who disbanded Parliament in 1629 and ruled for eleven years without Parliament at all. By then Syleham gentry and yeomen were solidly parliamentarian.

The Fullers' neighbours at Syleham Hall manor produced at least one son who joined the parliamentarian army, Captain Anthony Barry Jnr, but there is no record of any of the Fuller children doing so.[22] This may be because of the paucity of records. Neither Fuller nor Barry families are listed in a 4000 strong list of serving parliamentarian officers recently collated by the Cromwell Association.[23]

Benjamin appears in Barry's tithe list in 1636, replacing his father William as Anthony Barry had replaced his father Christopher. In subsequent years Benjamin appears as Ben Fuller, so he was probably called Ben by family and friends.[24] We do not know anything about Ben's wife Sarah, their marriage does not appear in the English parish records or non-conformist records, although it is highly unlikely that a family of this social standing would have attended any worship other than the parish church.

Benjamin and Sarah had at least six children, so Monks Hall would have been nicely full of children's laughter, although Puritan parents were usually strict and expected children to behave with adult-like decorum. Their oldest child William was educated at schools in Wingfield and then Hoxne with Mr Hall. Benjamin Jnr, the second son, was educated at Hoxne under Mr Hall for 4 years then at Yoxford with Mr Eachard, a conventional cleric who was to become Rector of Wingfield and Syleham after the Civil War.[25] These were not large schools but an educated man would take some local pupils to prepare them for university.

When Benjamin came to send his own sons to Cambridge in 1646 and 1647, towards the end of the Civil War, he chose Caius College (later Gonville and Caius), which had a more even balance of religious opinion than Emmanuel, which suggests that as early as the end of the Civil War, Benjamin was not overly committed to the Puritan way of life. Benjamin and Sarah's children recorded in the Syleham parish registers were William, baptised 1626, Benjamin 1630, Sarah 1638, twins Abigail and Lydia 1640, and Ann 1641.

Civil War and religious turmoil

In the 1630s life in Suffolk generally became more precarious and turbulent as the depression in the woollen industry continued and outbreaks of plague recurred. Wealthier and more articulate members of society such as Benjamin Fuller protested vigorously about the king's Ship Money tax imposed annually from 1635. By 1640 the resentful yeomen and gentry of Suffolk had managed to raise only £200 out of the £8000 demanded. The High Sheriff, Sir Symonds D'Ewes of Stowlangtoft, was expected to make this up himself, which he claimed was ruining him, possibly with some justification. The only useful records of individuals' religious and political affiliation for this period did not survive for Suffolk.[26]

The war against Scotland was also highly unpopular. Soldiers mutinied at Bungay and Bishop Wren's continuing attempts to impose religious uniformity were resented. The new Puritan 'lecturers', who had brought welcome religious discussion to Suffolk churches in contrast to the hide-bound traditional clergy, were hounded out of office, some excommunicated. After the war however, when the episcopacy was abolished, many traditional local clergy in their turn were persecuted and ejected from their livings by 'The Suffolk Committee for Scandalous Ministers', a persecutory machine that ejected 150 unpopular traditionalists on the testimony of parishioners with a grudge.[27] Hoxne Vicar Thomas Sayer was brought before the committee sitting at Diss in June 1644 and on the flimsiest evidence was thrown out of his living after forty-eight years of service, the main complaint being he did not do a lot of preaching.

In Syleham the curate Brian Witherell, appointed in 1624 and a beneficiary of William Fuller Snr's will, was promoted to Rector in Brockdish in 1636 and the Barry family at Syleham Hall, who held the advowson (the gift of the living), decided to defy the Bishop and not appoint a traditional curate.[28] The parish made do with unofficial 'lecturers'. These included from 1646 the agreeable Samuel Habergham, a priest with Puritan leanings, called 'pastor', who remained a popular fixture of Syleham for the next thirty-one years.[29] He does not appear in the official Church of England record at all.[30] Hence the curious gap in the list of priests hanging in St Margaret's Church.

Suffolk was probably less disturbed by Civil War events than many other counties although local villages did raise troops and sent volunteers, and paid for training soldiers, repairing arms and armour, and relieving sick and injured soldiers. The local churchwardens' accounts from the parish of Cratfield for this period record for example:[31]

> Item: Layd out to two towne souldiers when they went to Burry the 28th of March 1644 £1 5s. 0d..
>
> Item: layd out for two knapsacks for two towne souldiers, 3s. 0d.
>
> Item: payd for 2 horses for them 6s. 0d.

The local population was overwhelmingly parliamentarian and the few Royalist sympathisers either left or kept very quiet indeed. The few gentry who supported the king never organised themselves in Suffolk, only 10 per cent of large estates were 'sequestered' (confiscated) but they raised £40,000 for the exchequer, more than any other county.[32] But these wealthy Royalist sympathisers were in a minority, overwhelmed by the organised parliamentarians.

The Eastern Association military machine ensured that there were few battles on East Anglian soil. The ports of Lowestoft and Kings Lynn initially had strong Royalist support and in March 1643 there was an attempt to raise insurrections for the king and take the ports. The local gentry were quickly surprised by Cromwell, who took them as prisoners to Cambridge and held them until they agreed to help Parliament. Similarly, though the majority of Cambridge College masters were traditionalists for the king, Cromwell's swift intervention 'persuaded' them to comply.

The county was run efficiently through the two civil wars by a committee of parliamentarian gentry but there is no record of a Fuller being a member. In total ninety-nine families served on the committee but they tended to be more prominent gentry than the Fullers.[33]

One of the least attractive features of this period was the persecution of 'witches'. During the first Civil War, Matthew Hopkins assumed the title of Witchfinder General, touring the county extorting confessions from mainly isolated eccentric old women. In Suffolk over one hundred individuals were accused and at least sixty were executed by hanging. The parliamentarian county committee remained disappointingly silent about the activities of the witchfinders. The superstitious hunting down of unpopular or eccentric old people continued for the next century but the pace slowed down as protest against the abhorrent process grew.

Nor can we gloss over the activities of William Dowsing, from nearby Laxfield, who was provost-marshal of the armies of the Eastern Association responsible for supplies and administration. In 1643 he was appointed as 'Commissioner for the destruction of monuments of idolatry and superstition' to carry out an ordinance that 'all Monuments of Superstition and idolatry should be removed and abolished', specifying: 'fixed altars, altar rails, chancel steps, crucifixes, crosses, images of the Virgin Mary and pictures of saints or superstitious inscriptions.' In May 1644 the scope of the ordinance was widened to include representations of angels – a particular obsession of Dowsing's – rood lofts, holy water stoups and images in stone, wood, glass and on plate. Dowsing carried out his work in 1643–44 by visiting over 250 churches in Cambridgeshire and Suffolk, removing or defacing items that he judged fitted the requirements outlined in the ordinance.[34]

There were other iconoclasts but Dowsing is unique because he left a journal recording much of what he did. Syleham Church seems to have escaped his vandalism, although he smashed his way destructively through the churches of Hoxne, Eye, Occold, Rishangles and Metfield, destroying stained glass, brasses, levelling steps and removing images as he went. The Fullers probably would not have opposed the iconoclasts in any case, although moderates were offended by the wanton destruction.

The Civil War's aftermath affected rural areas badly. It is thought that 85,000 people, mostly men but also women camp followers, died in combat. Up to 130,000 people were killed indirectly, primarily as a result of disease.[35] Fighting went on elsewhere but everyone was affected by recruitment of troops and troop movements, which brought disease and compulsory boarding, usually without payment. National taxation was heavier than ever before, perhaps ten times pre-war rates, and it reached down the social scale. An excise on many consumer goods had an effect on even those people too poor to pay taxes based on land or goods. Parish administration was affected in many areas, too, which meant poor relief was disrupted. The birth rate was 10 per cent lower in the 1650s than it had been twenty years earlier and the population stagnated. Disruption of trade and bad harvests meant the late 1640s were some of the hardest on record for ordinary people.

Benjamin Fuller Snr died in 1648 having seen Cromwell established as leader of the parliamentarian commonwealth. By the end of the Civil War and the execution of King Charles II, the enthusiasm for the dour and joyless regime of the Puritans was waning and after Cromwell's death and the failure of his son to provide leadership, the country became in effect a military dictatorship. The astonishingly rapid Restoration of the monarchy in 1660 was a relief to most people. Agricultural wages and conditions seem to have improved slightly during the Republic but this was not sustained after the Restoration. Estates like Monks Hall ploughed on regardless.

Benjamin Fuller was followed by his eldest son, yet another **William Fuller (1628–1668)**, who chose to live in both Bardwell and Syleham but seems to have been mainly resident in Bardwell Hall manor.[36] He took on the tenancy of Bardwell from about 1658.[37] There are no memorials to the Fullers in the parish church of St Peter and St Paul, Bardwell.[38] This William was also educated at Caius College, Cambridge, from 1646, after school in Wingfield and Hoxne.

Part of the Will of William Fuller of Bardwell and Syleham 1668, showing the legacy to his brother Samuel of Monks Hall estate Syleham.

Will of William Fuller of Bardwell 1668. SRO Ipswich BRO. IC 500.1.120.93

His mother Sarah, who did not die until 1663, probably continued to live at Monks Hall.[39] William too returned to the life of the landed gentleman after Cambridge and first appears in Barry's tithe list in 1649.

William married Mary Cotton at Hoxne in 1642 and they had just one surviving child, a daughter Sarah born about 1650. Mary died in 1658 during the epidemic that devastated Bardwell parish that year, two weeks after giving birth to an unnamed child who also died. They are both buried in Bardwell.[40] It is clear from William's will that he was understandably close to his only daughter Sarah and provides generously for her in his will. We know that William bore arms and his extensive property holdings suggest he was a significantly wealthy man. His will includes gold, silver, 'rings' and many other expensive items, all for Sarah.

William died when he was just 40 years old, and bequeathed Monks Hall and all the property and land there and 'in Broadish' (Brockdish) to his younger brother **Samuel** in 1668. The second son Benjamin was settled with his wife Elizabeth Davey on substantial property in Wingfield but in any case he survived his brother William only by one year.

Samuel (1631–1685) and Mary Fuller

Samuel Fuller married Mary Bullman in Withersdale on 29 November 1664.[41] Four years later he inherited Monks Hall. 'Mr Fuller' is mentioned in the Hearth Tax Records of 1674, when Monks Hall apparently had eight hearths. The only Syleham owner with more hearths was of course 'Mr Barry Jnr', Anthony Barry at Syleham Hall, who had nine hearths.[42]

Apart from this tax record and the register entries for their children, Sam and Mary are as invisible in the records as the rest of the family but we do have his will of 1685.[43] He leaves his wife Mary an annuity of £50 per year to be funded out of the income from Monks Hall manor estate, together with the income from his land in Brockdish. All his property is for her use in her lifetime; after her death the property is to be divided between their three sons, William, Robert and Samuel, and his daughter Mary. Young William was appointed executor but was only twenty years old when his father died, so his mother was asked to 'supervise.' The other children were even younger when Sam died and would not inherit their portion until they came of age. To his oldest son William were given:

lands and tenements [in Syleham between] the common of pasture of the Highway and Syleham brook and the highways leading from the said brook to Chickering on the most north-east side in part and the lands of William Balls, John Howard and Mr Green (magister) on the east, south and north sides.

Second son Robert Fuller was bequeathed a portion of land when twenty-one, to the west of William's larger portion. Third son Samuel received lands in Hoxne. Daughter Mary was given land in 'Broomhills', an area in Syleham, and land adjoining Broomhills called Sanson's pightle and Sanson's meadow on the west of the land down to the River Waveney and east of the property of the Hartes and the hill. These were formerly 'Mr Barry's and Stuntley lands' and 'Mr Green's lands on the south and meadows in the east.' 'Stuntley' lands were mentioned in medieval manorial documents and later became 'Stuntle' wood. The land called Broomhills in Syleham has not been identified. Mary also received an annuity from William of £15 until she was twenty-one, when she would receive an additional £300. Nephews Benjamin, Charles and Elizabeth (children of Samuel's brother Benjamin) were to have £10 each.

The will was witnessed by Christopher Barry from Syleham Hall, John Aldous, a yeoman farmer in Syleham and two women, Elizabeth Glover and Rose Browning, who were probably servants as they made a mark instead of a signature. Sam provided well for his daughter and though the lion's share of his property went to young William, his other sons would have enough land to live on comfortably. There is no mention in Samuel's will of land in Bardwell and it seems probable that Samuel's niece Sarah had married and the Bardwell property passed to her and her husband.

A probate inventory was attached to Sam's will, compiled by his neighbours and probably also friends, Christopher Barry and John Aldous. One can imagine the two of them solemnly walking around Monks Hall compiling the obligatory list.[44] It reveals the family lived quite simply, without ornament. The furniture was basic. In the Hall for example, there are 'One long table, a form and two joint stools, 8 great chairs'. Clearly this was the formal dining room but there is no buffet, cupboard or lowboy nor other ornament.

There is neither silver nor pewter listed and only a few brass pots although there is apparel and books, though not itemised. In addition to the 'Hall and Parlour', three bedrooms are mentioned: the Parlour Chamber (the bedroom above the parlour), a Buttery Chamber (bedroom above the buttery), Entry

Chamber (bedroom over the main entrance), and a Back House, a common feature of houses of this period, a separate building outside with latrine and washing boiler, with a second floor providing a Back House Chamber, in effect a further bedroom. There was a range of utility rooms: a small buttery and scullery, a dairy, a pantry. Finally the livestock are listed: 107(?) [number smudged] cows and heifers and 1 bull, 6 horses, 1 colt and 3 hogs. The value of the total inventory was £365, which included £85 from other sites owned by Samuel. This is the will of a relatively wealthy yeoman but one who lived according to older Puritan simplicity.

William Fuller (1665–1689)

Sam and Mary's oldest son did not long survive his father, dying at the young age of twenty-four. He never married. His estate passed to his brother Robert, the last of the Fullers to live at Monks Hall. After William's death, the estate in Syleham was once more united into a larger 300–400 acre estate.

Robert and Ann Fuller (lived at Monks Hall 1689–1722)

Robert, baptised 1669, was just twenty when his older brother died. We have no burial date for his mother Mary, and Robert was probably still living with his mother at Monks Hall in 1689. He may have lived there all his life. Robert did not go to Cambridge, possibly because he was needed at home to run the estate.

On 4 May 1691, two years after his brother died, Robert married Ann Farrow from a Redgrave family at St Mary's Church in Botesdale.[45] In September that year Ann received £25 from a legacy from her grandfather, Gregory Fisher of Redgrave.[46] The Fishers were long established in Redgrave and indeed are still there. They are thought by some to be related to the Fisher family of Syleham from whom one of the earliest New England settlers, Anthony Fisher, migrated in 1637, although this supposition is mainly based on their common use of armigerous elements such as a dolphin.[47]

Robert and Ann had six children but their eldest son Samuel died sometime before 1721. Their daughter Mary married a gentleman, Robert Moore of Leverington in Cambridgeshire, leaving Ann, Margaret, Frances and John unmarried. There is one archival record referring to Robert and Ann Fuller's property dealings in Kersey, Suffolk, in 1694, but no other clues as to their activities outside of farming.[48]

Syleham glebe terriers

Robert's land is mentioned in the 'glebe terriers' of Syleham that have survived from 1705 and 1706.[49] The glebe land belonging to the parish church, which supported the rector and curate, should have been surveyed in detail every year to ensure that no neighbouring landowners were encroaching on church land. The Archdeacon of Suffolk, on behalf of the Bishop of Norwich, commissioned a survey to be carried out by the 'principal inhabitants of the parish'. Their task was to describe in detail what acreage the glebe land comprised and where the glebeland abutted on other owners' or occupiers' lands.

In common with most parishes, Syleham got round to surveying the glebe less assiduously than every year, usually every two or three or sometimes five years. The glebe terriers are a useful source of information about the glebe neighbours. In 1705 Syleham glebe occupied several acres of land behind the vicarage, also west of the road up to the upper village, land around the church and 'causeway' and along towards the mill and land west of the church 'up unto Mr Robert Fuller's land'. Oddly though, Robert Fuller is not named as one of the 'principal inhabitants of the parish.' Anthony Barry, the owner of the glebe and tithes, signed the terrier declaration with John Roberts 'churchwarden', Henry Rix 'curate' and John Gowing, 'schoolmaster'. Either Robert Fuller was not regarded as a principal inhabitant or there was some reason why he did not participate. Over the river in Brockdish at a similar period anyone with substantial land in the parish was always listed on the terrier.[50]

Up until 1709 Robert Fuller is mentioned in the terrier but some time between 1709 and the next record of 1716, the glebe land identified as abutting on Monks Hall manor ceased to be glebe and was taken back into Anthony Barry's direct ownership.[51] At this point we lose a valuable source of confirmation of ownership of Monks Hall estate. The series goes on however and in 1725 the principal inhabitants are named as Anthony Barry, John Cotton and Richard Molly [or Mully?].

The mystery of Ann Fuller's death

Ann Fuller died in 1721. Very unusually, there is a record in the Syleham parish register of her burial, but in a different parish. 'Ann Fuller wife of Robert

Fuller on 22 January 1721 in Redgrave.' She returned to her home parish perhaps to the family grave. But there is another record of Ann's death in Barry's tithe book. In the tithe records, Robert Fuller appears in the tithe list of 1717, his tithes having been substituted by a cash sum, or 'compounded', of £6 10s. 0d. The same is recorded in 1718 and 1719. Most of the other farmers are still paying in kind, in lambs, wheat, pears, milk, barley, hemp and 'herbage'. A handful have their tithes recorded in cash sums, although for much less than Robert, for about £1 or £2. In 1720 Robert's tithes were 'Not compounded', the tithe book entry reads, for the first time in years, for unexplained reasons. Was that at his request? Was it because he had difficulties in producing the cash sum? Then follows a curious note for the next year, which does not refer to tithes at all but says 'Robt. Dcsed Jny 22 1721' against Robert's name, *the date Ann was buried in Redgrave*. So Robert appears to have died the day his wife Ann was buried. I went back to check this entry several times in case I had the note wrongly copied. It is important to be sure to which year these dates referred as they were using the old Julian calendar but all the dates are consistent. However we know that Robert did not die then. He sold Monks Hall in 1722. So I have come to the conclusion that Barry's note of the death refers to Ann, not Robert, a slip of the pen or shorthand for 'Robert's wife dcsd'? Except that she did not die that day, but was buried.

Why did Christopher Barry record Ann's death in this private way in a tithe list? One is tempted to think the death had some special significance for him. Barry's journal was a personal one although there are actually very few personal entries. He left instructions on the inside cover, 'NB this book is to be buried with Mr Barry after my death as it was only for me During my lifetime.' He did not want these notes revealed. Fortunately for us, posterity ignored his wishes.

Robert decided to sell Monks Hall after his wife's death. The children were all grown and he was fifty-two, an age when men were then considered elderly. But one cannot help wonder whether Robert had been doing badly and needed to sell or was it because he wanted to leave Syleham for other reasons? There is one other archival source about what happened later. Robert also owned property in Mellis, at Whitmore Farm, which Robert gave to his eldest daughter Ann, a spinster, after the Syleham sale.[52] She sold at least part of that estate in a complicated set of arrangements, to her three younger sisters, unmarried Margaret and Frances and married Mary Moore. By 1724 Robert and his unmarried daughters had all moved away from Syleham to live in Wisbech, Cambridgeshire, perhaps to be near sister Mary and her family.[53] Robert was buried on 25 October 1727 at St Peter's Church Wisbech.[54]

After more than a century the Fuller family ownership of Monks Hall ended. In 1722 Monks Hall estate was sold to a wealthy investor, William Wollaston.[55]

Improvements to the house, late 17th century

The joyous optimism of the Restoration of the monarchy led to major building works and renovation of property all over East Anglia. It was suddenly all right again to add pictures and decorate the home. We do not know exactly which of the Fullers commissioned the four round windows in the crosswing or decorated the inside but it was likely to have been Samuel and Mary Fuller, shortly after the Restoration, perhaps as a celebration.

It has to be said though that Sam and Mary seem to have lived pretty simple lives and it may therefore have been a different member of the family or a later family who put in renovations and decorations. The majority of the panelling in the hall was put in much later in the 20th century but the pine panelling in the parlour is typical of the late 17th century period and appears to be made for the room.

The cross passage plank and muntin screen is original although it has been moved slightly in a later century. Over the parlour door in the screen is a late 16th century Flemish painting, *The Judgement of Solomon*, painted in oil on a wooden panel 59 x 80cm (23 x 31in).[56] The panel is formed out of three boards in horizontal alignment, cut down at the upper edge. In 2018 the painting was professionally restored by Sidney Sykes, who writes, "The panel was badly split horizontally. Many years of dirt, smoke and heat and layers of heavy varnish had discoloured and damaged it. There were holes and knife marks and cuts to several of the faces. Some new figures appeared; there are now 18 in all, as well as two babies and a black dog. The landscape and the throne canopy in the background have been revealed." Recently, art historian Stephen Calloway has traced the image back to an original painting by the 16th century Antwerp artist Frans Floris 1517-1570. However, the anonymous, probably provincial and not greatly skilled painter has copied his image directly from an engraving made in 1556 by the Dutch engraver Dirk Volkertsz Coornhert, who was a friend of Floris. The subject was very popular in the 17th and early 18th

The Judgement of Solomon, late 16th century Flemish, Monks Hall.

centuries, telling the biblical story in 1 Kings 3:16–28 of two mothers living in the same house, each the mother of an infant son, who came to Solomon. One of the babies had died and each claimed the remaining boy as her own. Calling for a sword, Solomon declared his judgment: the baby would be cut in two, each woman to receive half. One mother did not contest the ruling, declaring that if she could not have the baby then neither of them could, but the other begged Solomon, 'Give the baby to her, just don't kill him!' The king declared the second woman the true mother, as a mother would give up her baby to save its life.

The painting was very nearly lost in the 21st century when it was taken out of the screen and put in an auction with the rest of the furniture and paintings in 2016. Fortunately it was spotted in the catalogue by Stephen Calloway as an integral part of the house heritage listing and was returned before the sale. It is very difficult to be sure when the painting was inserted into the screen. Stephen Calloway writes, 'Whilst the subject and composition was a product of the confident Catholic culture of Antwerp, one could imagine the subject being equally acceptable to either a Catholic or a Protestant purchaser - the subject is not at all idolatrous and the strong emphasis on justice and morality based on intellectual rigour rather than unthinking piety, would have exerted as strong an appeal to a English audience informed by Reformation principles as to the members of an old Catholic family.' 'The panel could have been incorporated into the interior at Monks Hall at almost any time - perhaps even in the earlier part of the twentieth century, at a time when many owners were actively re-vamping old manor houses to enhance their olde-worlde charm'[57]. There are no records of purchase, no indication yet of when it became part of the fabric, although it must have been before the heritage listing of 1955.

If the yeomen Fullers are a little invisible, perhaps because they were a retiring sort of family, the next owners were all highly visible and well known. The Wollastons have so much written about them it is quite difficult to decide how much to include here and we must give space to the tenants who lived and worked at Monks Hall. But the author cannot resist the erudite Wollastons so the next chapter must talk about them.

Notes
1. Pepys, S. *The Diary of Samuel Pepys* 4 October 1661.
2. Defoe, Daniel Defoe, 1722-–24. Tour through the Eastern Counties of England. (London). Online at http://www.buildinghistory.org/primary/defoe/suffolk.shtml (accessed 10.4.2018).
3. Evans, N E. 1985. *The East Anglian Linen Industry* (Aldershot: Gower). References to Syleham pp. 68, 90, 139.
4. Tithe map of Syleham, Suffolk. 1839 SRO (Ipswich) Ref IR30/33/402; Award in the matter of Syleham Greens in the County of Suffolk 1854. Hemplands listed in pieces of land numbers 82, 113, 155, 163 (Great Hempland) retting pit pightle 160 and 169, 368 and 364. SRO Ipswich. FC 84/n2/1.
5. Evans, p. 90.
6. Rootsweb. Michael Russell 2013 Index of Terms used in 17th & 18th Century Wills, Inventories and other Documents. http://freepages.genealogy.rootsweb.ancestry.com/~fordingtondorset/Files/Glossary.html (accessed 24.12.2014) and Some Devon Surname Aliases by Mike Brown http://genuki.cs.ncl.ac.uk/DEV/DevonMisc/Aliases.html (accessed 24.12.2014).
7. Will of William Fuller 1634 SRO Ipswich. ZC/AA1/70/47.
8. The records of Wingfield parish were also checked in case Syleham's documents had been retained with the later joint parish but there are no relevant surviving records. Parish Charity Records SRO Ipswich. Ref FC84.
9. Venn J. (ed). 1924. *Alumni Cantabrigienses: A Biographical List of All Known Students, Graduates and Holders of Office at the University of Cambridge from the earliest times to 1900*. Vol. 1. (Cambridge: Cambridge University Press).
10. Will of John Spalding of Syleham 11 September 1544. SRO Ipswich R15/218.
11. Murphy E. 2015. *The Moated Grange: A history of south Norfolk through the story of one home 1300-2000* (Hove: Book Guild), Chapter 4: 'The Early Spaldings c1460–1625', pp. 43–72.

12. Corder, Joan. 1965. 'A Dictionary of Suffolk Arms'. *Suffolk Record Society*, Vol VII. Wm Fuller of Bradwell, Ipswich columns 7 and 8. 1644 Fuller of Bardwell and Syleham column 17.

13. Until the 19th century, a large part of Mendham parish was north of the river in what is now part of Harleston. Will of William Fuller alias Alen 1574 NRO. William's mother, called Agnes Allen alias Fuller, (sic) widowed by 1562 had a property called Mendham Pightle. The same piece of land was the subject of litigation in 1618. NRO NNAS G2/1/4 and 1650 NNAS G2/1/12.

14. The Will of William Fuller alias Alen of Redenhall with Harleston, St. Mary Yeoman. Archdeaconry Court of Sudbury. Written 1573, probate 1575.

15. Venn J. *Alumni Cantabrigienses*.

16. Will of John Spalding of Syleham made 11 September 1544. SRO Ipswich. R15/218.

17. Holmes, Clive 1974. *The Eastern Association in the English Civil War* (Cambridge: Cambridge University Press), Chapter 1: 'Social Organization in East Anglia', pp. 7–15.

18. Dymond D. and Northeast, P. 1995. *A History of Suffolk* (Chichester: Phillimore). Chapter 5: 'Reformation and Division' 1530–1630, pp. 58–71.

19. Suffolk industry at http://www.historicalsuffolk.com/suffolk-industries.php (accessed 16.9.2017).

20. Terrier by Christopher Barry, started in 1605. Also contains Anthony Barry's tithe book, from 1642, compiled by Anthony Barry Snr and Jnr. SRO Ipswich Ref HA226/1378/46a.

21. Impropriated tithes owned by Christopher Barry mentioned in Syleham section of Lewis, Samuel, 1840. *A Topographical Dictionary of England: Comprising the Several Counties* (4th edn, London), p. 214.

22. Page, Augustine 1841 *A Supplement to the Suffolk Traveller, Or, Topographical and Genealogical Collections Concerning that County Hundred of Hoxne, Syleham or Seilam*.(Ipswich and London, Joshua Page.) Mention of Captain Anthony Barry in 1642 in Syleham, p.422.

23. The Cromwell Association, 2017. 'Online Directory of Parliamentarian Army Officers', ed. Stephen K Roberts, online at British History Online http://www.british-history.ac.uk/no-series/cromwell-army-officers (accessed 5.9.2017).

24. Terrier and Tithes, Barry. 1636. Benjamin Fuller listed on Syleham manor rentals until 1648.

25. Venn, J. A. and Venn, J. 1952-4. Alumni cantabrigienses; a biographical list of all known students, graduates and holders of office at the University of Cambridge. Fuller entries in Vol 2, pp. 183–4. Online at https://archive.org/details/alumnicantabrigipt1vol2univiala. Laurence Eachard was a strong Laudian and ceremonialist who was expelled from his post during the Civil War but was restored after. See Elmer, p. 2016. 'East Anglia and the Hopkins Trials, 1645-1647: a County Guide', Yoxford, online at http://practitioners.exeter.ac.uk/wp-content/uploads/2014/11/Eastanglianwitchtrialappendix2.pdf (accessed 11.4.2018).

26. In 1642, during the Civil War a number of lists concerning the religious

persuasion and loyalty of subjects was drawn up by parliament. The first and largest of these was the Protestation Return, in effect an oath of loyalty to the new Protestant Parliament although ostensibly to King Charles I. Ministers, churchwardens, constables and overseers of the poor took the oath before justices of the peace. These officials were then to ensure that every male over 18 (and some women) took the oath and had their names recorded. One of the principal objects was to discover resistance to the Protestant religion, primarily by identifying and listing recusants (Roman Catholics) who refused to swear the oath and who were thereby barred from holding any public office. These lists are the nearest thing the researcher can get to a complete census of adult males for the next two centuries. BUT frustratingly all the lists for Suffolk have been lost so we cannot trace the Fullers that way. Protestation Returns 1642. Parliamentary Archive. Online at http://archivesmapsearch.labs.parliament.uk (accessed 10.4.2018).

27. Holmes, Clive (ed) 1970. 'The Suffolk Committee for Scandalous Ministers 1644-46'. *Suffolk Record Society* Vol XIII. Hoxne reference pp. 74–8.
28. The Clergy of the Church of England Database 1540–1835 (CCEd), online at http://theclergydatabase.org.uk (accessed 9.8.2018).
29. Sam Habergham was spoken of highly in a letter to Oliver Cromwell from Anthony Barry and James Hobart of Syleham during the commonwealth period in response to enquiries about the state of the churches. Original Letters and Papers of State: Addressed to Oliver Cromwell found in collection of John Milton. Published by John Nickells 1743.
30. Ibid. 28.
31. Botelho, L A (ed) 1999. 'Churchwardens Accounts of Cratfield 1640-1660'. *Suffolk Record Society*, Vol XLII. (Woodbridge: Boydell Press), p. 59.
32. Everitt, Alan M. 1985. Landscape and Community in England (London: Hambledon), Chapter 7: 'Suffolk and the Great Rebellion 1640-1660', pp. 129-154.
33. Everitt 1985 contains a list of families who served on the Suffolk Parliamentary Committee.
34. The Journal of William Dowsing 1643-44, online at http://www.williamdowsing.org/journalnoindex.htm (accessed 10.4.2018).
35. Hughes, Ann 1998. The Causes of the English Civil War (2nd edn, Basingstoke: Palgrave Macmillan), here Chapter 10: 'Great Misconceptions of the Civil War'. http://www.historyextra.com/article/premium/great-misconceptions-civil-war (accessed 9.8.2018).
36. William Fuller's residences documented in Venn, p71.
37. William Fuller's occupation of Bardwell Hall can be identified from four years' Hearth Tax entries, and from his Post Mortem Inventory, compared with others for the same house. The date he first took on the tenancy is surmised from the fact that the previous tenant, Edmund Craske, was holding Bardwell Hall in 1655, as mentioned in the will of Robert Rushbrooke, the owner of the house, and Edmund Craske can be shown to be in Bardwell in the early part of 1658, but then disappears. The burial of William Fuller's wife proves he was in Bardwell by December 1658. Information courtesy Ruth Stokes.

38. Suckling, A I. 1846–48. *The History and Antiquities of the County of Suffolk*, Vol. 1, Bradwell pp. 321–3.
39. Will of Sarah Fuller, widow, Syleham. NRO, NCC 1663 no 134.
40. William Fuller & Mary Cotten, w. 27 May 1642 Hoxne. Marriages at Hoxne 1548-1837. Suffolk Registers Various Parishes. Ancestry.co.uk. Burial of Mrs Fuller, wife of Mr Fuller Bardwell parish records 23 December 1658, infant Fuller buried 7 December 1658.
41. Marriage of Samuell Fuller of Syleham and Mary Bullman of Withersdale. Ancestry.com. Suffolk, England, Extracted Church of England Parish Records 1538-1837.
42. Suffolk Hearth Tax Records 1674, Syleham in Hoxne Hundred. Transcript SRO Ipswich FB6/A2/2
43. The Will of Samuel Fuller of Syleham 1685. SRO Ipswich ZC/AA1/115/70.
44. Probate inventory Samuel Fuller 1685. SRO Ipswich Ref FE1/3/95.
45. Marriages extracted for Redgrave, St. Mary with Botesdale, Suffolk Robert Fuller married, by Licence, Ann Farrow. 'Husband: Of Syleham, St. Mary. Gentleman. Wife: Of Redgrave, St. Mary with Botesdale. Of Botesdale.' Folger MS.L.f.1-1058. The Hale family of King's Walden and other papers, Folger Shakespeare Library, Washington, DC.
46. Acquittance from Robert Fuller and Anne Fuller of Syleham, Suffolk, to Edmund Fisher of Redgrave, Suffolk, 1691 September 26 For receipt of £25, full payment of a legacy from Gregory Fisher, grandfather of Anne Fuller. Edmund Fisher was the executor of the last will and testament of Gregory Fisher, late of Redgrave. Folger manuscripts MS. L.f.830. Folger Shakespeare Library, Washington DC.
47. See discussion in Ancestors of Kenneth Schmehl & Linda Herring. Online at http://wc.rootsweb.ancestry.com (accessed 9.8.2018).
48. Short title: Fuller v How. Plaintiffs: Robert Fuller and Anne Fuller his wife. Court of Chancery: Six Clerks Office: Pleadings before 1714, Mitford TNA C 8/540/121694.
49. 'Glebe terriers of Sileham. Gleabs in Suffolk.' SRO Ipswich FA569/S50/1 for 1705 and FA569/S50/2 for 1706.
50. Glebe terriers Brockdish ref. NRO. DN/TER series.
51. Terrier Ref SRO Ipswich for 1709 FF569/S50/3, for 1716 FF569/S50/4.
52. SRO Ipswich HA116/4/1/62/2-13 Whitmore farm Mellis property transfers. 1722 Ann Fuller, Robert Fuller's daughter by wife Ann deceased, spinster to Margaret Fuller spinster and Frances Fuller, spinster. 1724 part of property to sister Mary wife of Robert Moore the younger of Leverington Cambridgeshire.
53. SRO Ipswich HA116/4/1/62/2-13 Whitmore farm Mellis property transfers. 1722 Ann Fuller, Robert Fuller's daughter by wife Ann deceased, spinster to Margaret Fuller spinster and Frances Fuller, spinster. 1724: Part of property to sister Mary, wife of Robert Moore the younger of Leverington, Cambridgeshire.
54. Burial of Robert Fuller 15 October 1727 England, Select Deaths and Burials 1538-1991. Ancestry.com.
55. Sale of Monks Hall Estate mentioned in only one source, an unpublished book by S. W. H. Aldwell, Vicar of Wingfield and Syleham. 'A Short History of Syleham,

its Manors and Church c 1936' SSF124 - SRO, Ipswich PRC 644, p. 2. Aldwell writes, 'I have since found that it was purchased by William Wollaston in 1722'. There is a second copy of Aldwell in the Monks Hall Archive.
56. Cheffins Fine Art, Cambridge, identified the oil painting as Flemish school, 2013 but it is now though to be late 16th century.
57. Personal Communication Stephen Calloway, August 2018.

10

The Brainy Wollaston Family 1723–1867

Successful 18th century men invested in land with a passion. When London-based William Wollaston added Monks Hall estate to his property 'portfolio' he was making a sound investment. Land represented secure, solid achievement and was becoming more valuable as the quiet revolution in farm productivity took hold in the richer areas of Norfolk and Suffolk. Vast tracts of land and manor houses were sold as investments to absentee owners.

For the management of their rarely visited properties the new landlords depended on land agents who found suitable tenants, negotiated rents, drew up contracts, collected rents and ensured adherence to any stipulations as to how the land was to be farmed. Monks Hall estate was rented out to resident tenants, probably at fairly modest rents, in order for the landlord to possess an ever-increasing capital investment. Rents were generally set annually, called tenancy-at-will, but there was usually continuity of tenancy for many years and a passing down from father to son unless the estate was sold.[1] We do not know the names of the land agents who supervised Monks Hall contracts but they would have played an important part in the tenants' lives.

At present, though the Wollaston owners figure in various property lists, we have no idea whether any of them visited Monks Hall regularly. Since they had several properties, an agent no doubt collected rents and dealt with tenants' problems. We know that one of the Wollaston family regularly took out a licence for a gamekeeper at Monks Hall and therefore probably hunted there himself with the tenant, James Walne, who also had a game licence for

The Wollaston Family by William Hogarth 1730.

The Wollaston Family by William Hogarth 1730. This celebrated early 'conversation piece' showed William Wollaston MP, Francis Wollaston's brother and his family. Barely seen lurking at the back left is their black servant, a status symbol of the time. Hogarth later parodied this early work in his 'Marriage a la Mode' and other works. Now in New Walk Museum & Art Gallery, Leicester Arts and Museums Service Accession No. L.F40.1982.0.0.

the estate. They may have been occasional visitors but none of the Wollastons ever lived in Syleham.

Absentee landlords do not generally modernise a property in the way that resident owners do. It is easy today to identify immediately which council house has been sold off to eligible owner-occupiers by the new front door and replacement windows and which have been left in their original rented state. Monks Hall estate remained broadly unchanged and untouched because it had owners with their heads in their books or looking at the stars. Their lives were London ones. There was no great incentive to change the hall as long as the land continued to generate profits and while profits were poor through the depression of the 1730s and 1740s, rents could be adjusted and the land in any case continued to rise in value. Monks Hall remained blessedly neglected, while Suffolk gentry nearby were everywhere busy fashioning new Georgian facades on to old houses and expanding their houses to accommodate a more social lifestyle. The neighbours, the Mann family down the road at Syleham Manor, did just that, leaving the ancient buildings as utilitarian apartments at the back.

Monks Hall was sold as an investment to the vastly wealthy William Wollaston some time before he died in 1724. There are only two references to this event that I can find; one is a throwaway line in a little book written about Syleham by the Vicar, Revd Aldwell, in 1936 but no sources are quoted. The other mention is in William Wollaston's will of 1724.[2]

William Wollaston (1659–1724), owner of Monks Hall 1722–1724

Wollaston fathered one of the most extraordinary families in Britain, certainly one of the brainiest, which during the 18th and 19th centuries produced no fewer than seven Fellows of the Royal Society and one President.[3] They were gifted scientists, thinkers, philosophers, priests and prolific breeders. The line of succession of Monks Hall estate ownership passed down from William Wollaston to his son William, Member of Parliament for Ipswich, and eventually in the mid 19th century to Reverend Charles Buchanan Wollaston, who sold it after his father's death to the sitting tenant James Read.

Wollaston was a schoolteacher in Birmingham, a Church of England priest, a scholar of Latin, Greek and Hebrew, a theologian and a major Enlightenment era English philosopher.[4] He is remembered today for one book, which he completed only two years before his death: *The Religion of Nature Delineated*.[5] Yet despite his cloistered life and his single book, he is considered by some, because of his influence on 18th century philosophy, as one of the great British Enlightenment philosophers, along with Locke, Berkeley and Hume. His work contributed to the development of two important intellectual schools: British Deism, and 'the pursuit of happiness by the practice of reason and truth', a moral philosophy that has some similarities to that expressed in the United States Declaration of Independence.[6] Locke thought Wollaston's philosophy decidedly 'odd' and 'strange' and David Hume spent a good deal of time disparaging Wollaston's notions. More recently academics have rescued Wollaston a little from these attacks but more erudite men have undoubtedly eclipsed him.

William came from quite a poor family but had the great good fortune to be named as heir by his wealthy cousin, also William Wollaston, of Shenton,

Leicestershire, who died in 1688, leaving a fortune that his family had made in the wool trade a century earlier. This astonishing bequest, that William had not expected, allowed him to give up teaching and in 1689 he acquired a wife, Catherine, daughter of a prosperous London draper. They settled in Charterhouse Square, London, just north of Smithfield, in those days a fashionable spot, and William devoted himself to literary work. He was said never to have passed a night out of the house there until his death, so we can be pretty certain he never set foot in Syleham.[7] Two of his sons, Francis and William, married daughters of John Fauquier, Governor of the Bank of England, and became brothers-in-law to Francis Fauquier, the Governor of the Colony of Virginia.

Wollaston's will gives very clear instructions as to how he wished his property to be divided up.[8]

> I give and devise all that my Estate at Sylham or elsewhere in the County of Suffolk and Norfolk which I purchased of Robert ffuller unto my second son William Wollaston and to his heirs and assigns for ever. I also give unto my said son William Wollaston five hundred pounds. I give and devise the estate late of Sir John Blomfield at Great Finborough in the County of Suffolk which I purchased of Ellis Ashpool and Wiston Styleman unto my third son ffrancis Wollaston and to his heirs and assigns for ever. I also give unto my said son ffrancis Wollaston two thousand pounds.

After Wollaston's death, his second son William, who would become MP for Ipswich and grand country gentleman, took possession of the estate at Great Finborough, Suffolk, and Francis, William's third son, whose main interest was science, made his home in London in the old house at Charterhouse Square and assumed ownership of the Monks Hall estate. They seem to have decided to swap legacies and that would have been consistent with their subsequent careers. An older son, Charlton, died soon after his father. There were many other family estates, in Essex, Leinster and Suffolk that were distributed to Wollaston's younger sons and still left a very generous income for his daughter Mary, who married Thomas Heberden FRS, scientist and physician.[9]

Before looking at the descent of ownership of Monks Hall via Francis Wollaston, it is worth a word about William Wollaston MP (1693–1764) and his son (1731–1797), also an MP for Ipswich. We have wonderful portraits of them, the family one by Hogarth above and two by Gainsborough of the son.

One might call them 'the owners who got away'.

The first William Wollaston MP married Elizabeth Fauquier, whose father was Governor of the Bank of England, and together they had eight children. In 1739, he had four of his children inoculated against smallpox, with the Ipswich Journal reporting that they were 'in a fair way of Recovery'.[10] His eldest surviving son, William (1731–1797) was himself MP for Ipswich from 1768 to 1784. An amateur musician, the younger MP gave Thomas Gainsborough two important commissions shortly before Gainsborough moved to Bath.

William Wollaston MP (1731–1797),
by Thomas Gainsborough, painted 1759.

Finborough Hall became the main home of William Wollaston MP but he owned several other properties in Suffolk, at Stradbroke and in Essex, so we will leave him there to enjoy the life of a country gentleman and return to his brother **Francis Wollaston (1694–1774),** who assumed ownership of Monks

Hall. Like his father he probably rarely visited, although his name appears on land tax records. It is thought that Francis Wollaston appears in Hogarth's family portrait standing behind the card table on the left, perhaps advising on her hand of cards to his seated wife Mary.[11]

Francis grew up in his father's London household in Charterhouse Square and read law at Sidney Sussex College, Cambridge, graduating in 1717. He never practised law but took holy orders, although he never served in an official position within the church. He had no need of a 'living'. He became a Fellow of the Royal Society in 1723. In the early 18th century it was not necessary to have achieved a great deal in science but to have attended regular scientific meetings and be generally known by other Fellows to be competent in some branch of science, sufficient to be recommended by other Fellows. From the records of the Royal Society it is clear he was a regular attender at meetings and played his part in the administration. He married the well-heeled Mary Fauquier (1702–1773) in 1728, sister of his brother William's wife Elizabeth.

Francis and Mary had five children. Their daughter Mary married a Heberden relative of her mother's. Francis the eldest son, an astronomer, inherited Monks Hall; the third child Charlton became a physician. William Henry Wollaston was fourth and their last son, George Wollaston FRS, was also interested in astronomy. George Wollaston was present at a celebrated event, the Transit of Venus watched by the King and Queen in 1769.

The second Francis Wollaston (1731–1815), Astronomer

The second Francis inherited Monks Hall estate when his father died in 1774. He too was educated for the law at Sidney Sussex College, Cambridge, graduating in 1754.[12] He entered Lincoln's Inn in 1750 to complete his law studies but, 'feeling some moral hesitancy in regard to an advocate's duties' as his biographer put it, he turned his mind to the church.[13] Lawyers in the early 18th century were regarded as both mercenary and devious. He was ordained deacon at the age of 23, and priest in the following year. About Christmas 1756 he undertook the morning preaching at St Anne's, Soho, where he became attached to a young woman parishioner whom he subsequently disappointed in favour of a London neighbour from Charterhouse Square, Althea Hyde, whom he married in 1758. They had no fewer than seventeen children together.

Francis Wollaston, age 69.

Drawn by H. Edridge, engraved by William Evans.

In the summer of 1758 Francis was instituted to the rectory of Dengie in Essex, then in 1761 moved to East Dereham in Norfolk, and later in 1769 to Chislehurst in Kent, where he remained for the rest of his life.[14] Church appointments in 18th century England were quite often sinecures that required little if any work. Parishioners were often profoundly dissatisfied with these absent priests, since most of the work fell on local poorly paid curates. In 1777 Francis was appointed precentor of St David's Cathedral in Wales and in 1779 he was also appointed rector of the united City of London parishes of St Vedast, Foster Lane, and St Michael-le-Querne. It is hard to believe Francis contributed much to these various roles. He retained all his preferments and the emoluments that went with them until his death on 31st October 1815 at the rectory, Chislehurst.

In 1801, 1802 and 1803, Revd Francis Wollaston appears in the published lists of 'Game Deputations' for Suffolk alongside the property 'Monkshall' Syleham. His tenant James Walne is also listed for the same address.[15] A certificate and annual stamps had to be purchased by the landowner and or tenant for each estate, and the details were registered with the Clerk of the Peace. One gamekeeper could be appointed per manor, and every deputation must be registered with the Clerk of the Peace. A stamp duty of £2 2s. per year was charged, in addition to the 10s. 6d. annual cost of the gamekeeper's licence. I think we can surmise that Francis Wollaston used his estate for shooting and possibly did so in the company of his tenant: 18th century clergymen often joined shoots and hunting parties. It was the later Victorian evangelists who heaped opprobrium on 'sporting vicars'.

Wollaston was the author of several books on the liturgy of the Church of England but his main fame attaches to his distinction as an astronomer. He had a private observatory with a triplet telescope by Peter Dollond, the optical instrument maker. Elected Fellow of the Royal Society in 1769, he later served on its council. He produced a catalogue of stars and nebulae in 1789, which was used by many including his friend William Herschel. His many scientific publications included 'Directions for making an Universal Meridian Dial, capable of being set to any Latitude' (London, 1793), 'Fasciculus Astronomicus; containing Observations of the Northern Circumpolar Region' (London, 1800), 'A Portraiture of the Heavens as they appear to the Naked Eye' in ten plates, (London, 1811). He also published ten astronomical papers in *Philosophical Transactions* between 1769 and 1793.

In 1795 he printed privately a few copies of an autobiography, curiously written in the third person, entitled 'The Secret History of a Private Man' which he distributed among his friends. This extraordinary little pamphlet is now available in print as a facsimile.[16] He certainly did not espouse conventional religious teaching, many have thought he was a Unitarian in outlook – that is, that he thought the doctrine of the Trinity was wrong and the Thirty-Nine Articles outdated – but in fact his beliefs were far more eccentric; he thought Christ was descended from the Archangel Michael, who was a kind of intermediary between God and man. He also thought there were other beings on planets in the stars.

Francis John Hyde Wollaston (1762–1863)

Francis Wollaston 2nd was buried at Chislehurst. Monks Hall was inherited next by the third Francis, **Francis John Hyde Wollaston** (1762–1863), a natural philosopher and Professor at the University of Cambridge. He too was educated at Sidney Sussex College, Cambridge, graduating as senior wrangler in 1783. He became a fellow of Trinity Hall in 1785, elected FRS in 1786 and ordained a priest in 1787. From 1792 to 1813 he was Jacksonian Professor at

Cambridge. He was obliged to resign his Trinity Hall fellowship in order to marry Frances Hayles in 1793, since it was still necessary to be unmarried to be a fellow in the 18th century. So he then became Rector of South Weald. In 1807, still yearning for a full-time academic life, he was elected Master of Sidney Sussex College, but the election was declared invalid on the grounds that he had never been a fellow of Sidney Sussex. On resigning his professorship in 1813, he assumed additional clerical 'responsibilities' as rector of Cold Norton and Archdeacon of Essex, but probably these positions did not require much personal activity.[17]

Wollaston delivered a Course of Chemical Lectures in 1794 but is best known for devising his thermometrical barometer (effectively a hypsometer) for measuring altitudes, and sent two papers on it to the Royal Society in 1817 and 1820.[18] Francis's younger brother **William Hyde Wollaston PRS (1766–1828)** was even more gifted. Astronomer, physician, chemist and botanist, he discovered a process for making platinum malleable. He was awarded the Copley medal in 1802, the most prestigious prize then awarded by the Royal Society, and served the Society in various offices until for six months he became President, an interim appointment because he did not wish to compete with Sir Humphrey Davy, who was in line for the role. He went on to discover palladium in platinum ores and rhodium, and published fifty-six papers on 'pathology, physiology, chemistry, optics, mineralogy, crystallography, astronomy, electricity, mechanics, and botany', and almost every paper marks a distinct advance in the particular science concerned. The majority were read before the Royal Society, and published in *Philosophical Transactions*. He invented the camera lucida and a goniometer for measuring the angles in crystals. William is included here for the sake of completeness of the family scientific generation. He was the most brilliant of an exceptionally gifted family.

Francis and William had another younger brother, **Henry Septimus Hyde Wollaston (1778–1867)**, who inherited the Monks Hall property in 1863 after his long-lived elder brother Francis died. Henry was also an inventor but not quite of the same dizzying order of brilliance as his brothers. He was more interested in business.

His anonymous biographer, writing on 'Ancestry.com' website so we read it with caution, notes that Henry Septimus was educated at Charterhouse.

At an early age he was sent with a label bearing his address pinned to him to begin life in a counting house in Amsterdam. He witnessed the entry of the French republican troops into that city in 1793 looking, he said, like a mere rabble, with torn and worn uniforms, and with loaves of bread stuck on their bayonets. He must have returned to England at the turn of the century, for he married his first wife in 1802 at Walthamstow. She is said to have been the daughter of his principal in Holland, though there is no evidence, apart from the name, to support this assertion.

There are no sources quoted for the information here.[19] Henry Septimus was said to be a volunteer at some time during the Napoleonic wars, although his name does not appear in the National Archive Navy List for the period. He claimed too to have mounted guard at Nelson's funeral in 1806 but that is also unlikely, as the Brigade of Guards who were present would have been long-serving men. Nelson's funeral was the grandest state occasion of the era and lasted over five days.[20] More than 15,000 people came to pay their respects. Henry Septimus may well have been in the crowd but one suspects Wollaston had a tendency to embroider the past. He probably was not a witness to the troops in Paris either. He was purely and simply a businessman and relatively modest banking official, although he was wealthy and had no need of a career at all.

After his first marriage he lived at Clapton, now part of Hackney, then almost in the country, and went daily into the City of London. He was reasonably successful in his profession and was able to avoid going bankrupt in the financial crisis of 1824–25 when six London bankers withheld payment. He also became deputy chairman of the Society of Merchants. After the death of his second wife he became, in 1828, the first Agent of the Exeter branch of the Bank of England. In 1831 he was transferred to the Bristol Branch of the Bank of England where he remained till he retired from the Bank in 1836, 'owing to some misunderstanding with the Directors' as his son William Monro Wollaston delicately put it. Whatever it was, the incident did not reach the local press.

In 1837 he went to live in Kent. In 1841 he settled at a house called Little Dawson, Welling, in the Parish of Bexley, Kent, where he remained till his death. In 1842 he was elected a director of the Equitable Assurance Association and a director of the British Plate Glass Co., and regularly went up to London at least one day a week. Henry Septimus estimated that at his death he would have given before his death, or left by will, to his family about £34,000 (about £3.6 million today).[21] Reading about Henry Septimus, one gets the distinct impression he could put a fine gloss on his biography; perhaps we should take some of the above material with a pinch of salt.

Wollaston wealth was made up of numerous estates and property, seemingly undiluted by having prodigious progeny because of their careful marriages. Henry married three times and like his brothers and father, had numerous children. In addition to Monks Hall, a property list in Kent County Record Office lists the property deeds of the Wollaston family between 1706 and 1948.[22] They held property in Kent, Surrey, Bedfordshire, Norfolk, Gloucestershire, Bristol, London and Canada in addition to those in Suffolk. In 1822, Henry Septimus submitted a patent application for a night bolt, an attempt perhaps to emulate his illustrious relatives.

H.J.S. Wollaston's name appears as owner on all tithe, property and land documents referring to Monks Hall until his death in 1867. In the light of his numerous properties he probably rarely visited but he may like his brother have used the estate for shooting in the season. After Henry's death in 1867, his son and heir, Revd Charles Buchanan Wollaston, Rector of Bognor, sold the Monks Hall estate to the sitting tenant James Read. If the Wollaston owners were not here in the 18th century, who was?

Notes
1. Theobald, J. (2001). '"Distant Lands": The Management of Absentee Estates in Woodland High Suffolk, 1660–1800'. *Rural History*, 12 (1), pp. 1-18.
2. Aldwell, S W H. 1936. 'A Short History of Syleham, its Manors and Church'. On page 2, Aldwell says about Monks Hall, "I have since found it was purchased by William Wollaston in 1722 from Robert Fuller". There is a copy of Aldwell's hand-typed book in SRO Ipswich and one in Monks Hall Archive. Will of William Wollaston 1724 TNA PROB 11/600/199.
3. Portrait of William Wollaston in National Portrait Gallery NPG D4886.
4. Porter, Roy, 2001. *The Creation of the Modern World: The Untold Story of the British Enlightenment* (New York: W. W. Norton & Company), p. 112.
5. Altmann, Alexander, 'William Wollaston (1659–1724): English Deist and Rabbinic Scholar', *Transactions* (Jewish Historical Society of England), Vol. 16, (1945–1951), pp 185–211.
6. Tweyman, Stanley, 1976. 'Truth, Happiness and Obligation: The Moral Philosophy of William Wollaston'. *Philosophy* Vol. 51, pp. 35–46.
7. Stephen, Leslie, 'William Wollaston (1660–1724)', Dictionary of National Biography 1885–1900. Vol. 62.
8. Will of William Wollaston 1674 TNA PROB 11/600/199.
9. Their son William Heberden described the eponymous Heberden's nodes of osteoarthritis.
10. 'Innoculation of Wollaston children against smallpox'. *Ipswich Journal* 14 April

11. Key to Hogarth's painting courtesy of Simon Lake, Curator of Fine Art, Leicester Arts & Museums Service.
12. The association of the Wollaston family with Sidney Sussex Collage and their scientific contributions has been reviewed in Archer, Mary and Haley, Christopher (eds) 2005. *The 1702 Chair of Chemistry at Cambridge: Transformation and Change* (Cambridge: Cambridge University Press), Chapter 4 (Haley C. and Wothers P.) 'Lavoisier's Chemistry comes to Cambridge', pp. 91–112.
13. Carlyle, Edward Irving 1901. 'Francis Wollaston'. Oxford Dictionary of National Biography, Oxford University Press.
14. Chislehurst Church can be seen at the bottom right of his portrait engraving.
15. Gamekeepers' Deputations and Game Certificates, Suffolk. Bury and Norwich Post, Wednesday 18 November 1801, repeated 1802 and 1803.
16. Wollaston, Francis, 1793. *The Secret History of a Private Man*. Facsimile edition published by Ecco Prints.
17. Clark, J. W. (Anita McConnell 2004). 'Wollaston, Francis John Hyde (1762-1823)'. Oxford Dictionary of National Biography. Oxford University Press.
18. A hypsometer is an instrument used to determine land elevation by observing the atmospheric pressure as measured by the change in the boiling point of a liquid, usually water. F. J. H. Wollaston's drawings of his thermometrical barometer, Royal Society Collection.
19. Biography Henry Septimus Hyde Wollaston by Moltenox online at https://www.ancestry.com/mediaui-viewer/tree/16008644/person/651235927/media/66c59805-0f27-454e-9d74-8ac215f1018f (accessed 9.8.2018).
20. Nelson's funeral described at http://www.rmg.co.uk/discover/explore/nelsons-funeral#GowolzsurFbGDTbo.99 (accessed 9.8.2018).
21. Historical Currency Converter. The National Archive. http://www.nationalarchives.gov.uk/currency (accessed 9.8.2018).
22. Deeds of the Wollaston Family 1706–1948, Kent Archives catalogued by D Gibson 1977. Ref U1509.

11

Monks Hall Tenants in the 18th Century

Farming on the Monks Hall Estate in the 18th century

While the Wollaston owners were surveying the astronomical and ethereal heavens, their minds on more lofty matters than soil, the tenant farmers of Monks Hall were unwittingly part of an agricultural transformation in England that produced an astonishing increase in produce.

Between about 1700 and 1850 agricultural output increased by approximately 350 per cent.[1] The phenomenal increase in food supplies enabled the population to increase by about 6.5 million with minimal need for imports. It has often been said that the industrial revolution depended on the agricultural one. In 1760 the output of each agricultural worker could feed one other person. By 1841 it could feed 2.7. East Anglia was the acknowledged birthplace of England's agricultural revolution, and there is a general consensus that a 'revolution' did indeed occur, albeit a slow, steady one. Historians argue over when exactly it occurred but during the 18th century huge improvements in machinery and techniques meant that farming was an increasingly prosperous industry. James Walne, the last of the 18th century tenants, would have produced more from his over 500 acres than any farmer before him.

In the Waveney Valley, however, the dairy herds still grazed the upper valley slopes and high plains, and hemp and linen were the most popular crops. Hemp grew both in meadows and 'bottom lands' in the valley, the same patch used repeatedly. Hemp stalks left over after 'retting' were tied into hemp-sheaves and used as fuel. Bullock fattening was common on the marshes.[2] About 40,000 firkins of butter were sent to London annually from Suffolk; the cheese reviled in London was popular abroad in Spain and Holland. Cows would have been the small polled type called 'Suffolk Dun', a small cow with lean dairy conformation, with a large belly to accommodate large amounts of poor roughage. It was a forerunner of the 'Suffolk Red Poll' introduced in the 19th century. Pigs were kept too, the short white breed of hogs usually. Warrens for rabbit breeding were confined to the sandy west of the county.

Suffolk produced the machinery that enabled the increased productivity: the Suffolk Spring plough, the horse rake for cleaning stubble, a drill plough produced by Henry Balding of Mendham and a scalp plough for destroying weeds. Landowners swapped information at the newly established agricultural society that met alternately at Melford and Bury in the late 18th century.

The state of development of local agriculture can be monitored by the timing of enclosing the open fields on an estate and turning wastes into productive arable or pasture. Surveys of Suffolk Agriculture in the 18th century found that there was little land that had not already been enclosed by the former manor estates, probably earlier than any other county. Although Arthur Young, the Suffolk observer of all things agricultural, said there were still 100,000 acres or so of commons and wastes unenclosed in the late 18th century.[3]

Horse rake.

There were only two enclosure acts in Suffolk between 1727 and 1760. The small Syleham Green, just 28 acres, was enclosed in 1854 under the later parliamentary enclosures acts but a 250 acre swathe of Brome, Oakley, Thrandeston, Yaxley and Eye was enclosed earlier in 1812.[4] Enclosures sometimes dispossessed the landless cottagers who used the wastes and commons to scratch a living. Often these poor folk received only small and short-lived compensation for loss of their grazing and gathering rights but in Syleham the poor had not had access to manorial land for centuries. Landless families would have been obliged to work on other people's land in summer when work was plentiful and save food for adverse weather when there was no work or seek assistance from the parish for bread or doles, 'outdoor relief' to tide them over.

Tracing the tenants

By the end of the 18th century Monks Hall had become the centre of a gregarious social circle, the tenants well documented in official records and newspapers. But the early 18th century tenants from 1725 to 1750 are rather more difficult to track down. The estate was still renting out tracts of land and houses to farming tenants and some of these are known, but the identity of the person who held the main demesne land and lived at the hall is not so straightforward.[5]

The usual sources for tracing house owners and occupiers of a significantly sized property are land tax records, poor law rate books, voting poll books, glebe terriers and newspapers. In the case of Monks Hall we are handicapped by the loss of all the poor law records and a very meagre survival of tax records for the parish of Syleham. We can identify some tenants through a process of exclusion, and make an intelligent guess about others.

It is always easiest when researching house history to start at the end and work backwards, and this was especially helpful for the 18th century history of Monks Hall. The Land Tax Redemption Records of 1798 are the most useful documents extant for showing the relative ownership of parish land and property at that time.[6] Land tax had been imposed on owners since the late 17th century but in 1798, land tax became a perpetual charge, which could be redeemed by the payment of a lump sum; landowners were thereby exonerated from future tax, although the redemption was optional. The lump sum equalled fifteen years tax and purchased 3 per cent 'consols', a government stock investment without a maturity date, which would yield an annuity exceeding the tax by a fifth. So the records now in the National Archive list the sums to be paid by owners to escape tax in future. From the government's point of view this was a very attractive tax as it appeared to be optional. About a third of landowners paid the redemption charge.

The land tax list for Syleham shows that the highest rate, £16 0s. 0d. for the largest block of land, was being paid by occupier James Walne, for the owner Revd F. Wollaston, clearly for the Monks Hall estate. Wollaston also owned three much smaller pieces of land in the occupation of Jonathan Theobald and two in the occupation of John Bond. The remainder of the land in Syleham was divided mainly between Miss Barry of Syleham Hall, the curate Revd Whitacre's glebe land on the slopes behind and beside the Old Vicarage, and the large block of land owned by a wealthy entrepreneur, the miller William Mann, who was the proprietor of the house now called Syleham Manor. Mann had acquired 'manor lands' from the old Syleham Comitis manor, formerly owned by the Barry family.

Mann's property also includes the former Syleham lands of the Cotton family, who lived in Brockdish, and former lands of the Spalding family, whose line died out in the early 18th century, plus several other smaller holdings. The only other owner-occupiers in the land tax list were Ezekiel Backler, who lived in Hoxne but farmed in Syleham, Stradbroke Town vestry (equivalent to the parish council), which owned a few charitable acres farmed for the poor of Stradbroke, and John Richards, who owned a middling number of acres farmed by himself. Altogether Miss Barry's tax came to £12, Wollaston's adds up to £34 12s. and Mr Mann's also comes to about £34 12s. The glebe land generated £6, Ezekiel Backler's £4 12s. and John Richards' £3 12s., giving a broad indication of relative wealth in the parish.

In 1798 then, Wollaston owned and James Walne farmed 576 acres or 36 per cent of the total parish acreage of 1600 or so acres. Monks Hall had become a substantial estate by the end of the 18th century, not a rival for the vast estates of north Norfolk such as Holkham or Houghton, nor indeed as grand as the 1200 acres owned by Sir Edward Kerrison at nearby Oakley Park, or the 900 or so acres of the 2nd Marquess of Cornwallis' Brome Hall, but a respectable size to provide a good living. In the same record book, Walne was also farming land owned by Wollaston in Stradbroke parish.

The Syleham tax redemption document also mentions several other families and their relative holdings and gives clues as to how to interpret earlier documents, such as the glebe terriers and the polling lists for voters registered in the early part of the century. If we return to the glebe terriers noted in the Barry family diaries described in the last chapter, we find that there is only one 'principal' inhabitant in 1725 whose land we cannot identify, that is a man called Richard Molly, or possibly Mully/Mulley, who also appears in the parish registers for the first time the same year.

> 14 August 1725. Carolus, filius Richardi et (text unclear) Mully baptizatus.

Then again in 1727,

> Aprile Vicesimo Tertio (23 April): Maria fila Johannis et (text unclear) Mully baptizata.

Sara, a second child of Richard, is born in 1728 and a son Martin in May 1730.

The Molly/Mully family disappear from Syleham after 1730.[7] Finding them without reasonable certainty about their name is challenging. There was a Richard Mully, a dyer living in Norwich in 1769, who was the beneficiary of the will of a gentleman, William Groom of Rattlesden, Suffolk, but I can find no further trace of this family among the middling families in Suffolk and Norfolk who could afford to rent the Monks Hall estate. Mully seems therefore an unlikely tenant.[8]

The later signatories of the glebe terriers do not include anyone who could have been living at Monks Hall until 1784, when James Walne makes his entry as a 'principal inhabitant' and remains there until the Read family appear in the mid 19th century. So we must now look down other avenues; voting lists are promising.

Clues from voting lists

The earliest surviving Poll Book for Suffolk was drawn up in 1727. An act of 1696 designed to prevent electoral fraud authorised the publication of copies of the results of polls for the election of Knights of the Shire and Members of Parliament. Throughout the 18th century, the right to vote was the privilege largely of landowners and those who rented property of a sufficient value. They usefully tell us who owned freehold property that entitled them to vote and where. They also list parish of residence where it is different from the parish where the qualifying freehold was owned.[9] The Syleham list for 1727 reads as follows:

Syleham Poll List 1727

Anthony Barry	Syleham freehold, lived at Syleham Hall manor
Ezekiel Backler	Syleham freehold, lived in Hoxne
Samuel Fullpot (Philpot)	Syleham freehold
Henry Richards	Syleham freehold, (owned a small farm in Syleham)
Charles Wyth(e)	Brockdish freehold (owned The Grove, Brockdish)
John Ownsworth	Syleham freehold
Samuel Browning	Needham freehold

The Wollastons do not appear in this list, although William Wollaston appears in the list in Stradbroke, a reminder that these lists are not totally reliable. The voting of each person is recorded. Apart from Anthony Barry, who supported the two sitting Tory baronets, the Syleham voters all supported Sir John Holt, a Whig gentleman who lived at Redgrave Hall. The Tories retained the two seats for Ipswich by a huge majority.

Richard Molly does not appear in the list, adding further weight to his not being tenant at Monks Hall. The only two people who could be our tenants are Charles Wyth (usually Wythe) and Samuel Browning. Charles Wythe is referred to as a 'gentleman' in a later poll list of 1734 but he is a tenant in Syleham, not a freeholder, an encouraging piece of evidence that makes him a contender as tenant of Monks Hall. Samuel Browning of Needham died in 1740, leaving a short will that makes clear he was living in Needham, Norfolk and has no major property to bequeath.[10] The author considers it likely therefore that Charles Wythe was the tenant of Monks Hall from about the late 1720s for some years until he moved to Hoxne Abbey in the mid-1740s. As yet there is no firm proof of Wythe's tenancy and the author stresses that until further evidence comes to light, this next section is hypothetical.

Charles Wythe (1677–1757)

Charles Wythe was a disagreeable, litigious character whose local reputation was not good.[11] The Wythe family were landed yeomen who were based at the Grove Estate in Brockdish. Branches of the family lived in Eye and Hoxne and were closely intermarried with other landed yeomen families such as the Catons at Thorpe Abbotts, the Crickmeres and the Spaldings.

Charles Wythe's shameless behaviour over the disappointing will of his first cousin Margaret illustrates his nature rather well.[12] If Margaret had made no will, the Spalding estate in Brockdish would have fallen on her death to Charles, which would conveniently have added 100 acres or so adjacent to his already substantial holdings at The Grove. Margaret had other ideas. Her entire estate was to be sold and generous bequests made to various relatives and a goodly sum of about £500 bequeathed to female friends, servants and the needy of local villages. The total sum of her bequests of £1,389 was worth £2.25 million in the 21st century. Nothing was left to Charles. He complained loudly to all and sundry about the will; he made various shifting and inconsistent claims, that Margaret had made no will and the will was a forgery, then that she was not in her right mind when the will was drawn up. Wythe repeated these claims in public, making himself a thorough nuisance to the executors, who decided to take him to the Court of Chancery to get a declaration in their favour.[13] Wythe was summoned to make a deposition before lawyers at Bungay in January 1744. He produced no evidence to back his claims and indeed denied he ever said such things. The Court adjudicator asked him to shut up and he said he would! So Margaret's female-friendly will stood and Charles got nothing.

If this had been the only litigation Charles Wythe was embroiled in we might perhaps attribute his behaviour to a one–off disappointment but he has no fewer than nine surviving legal actions in the National Archive. Beginning in 1729, he sued Sir Benjamin Wrench MD, a distinguished Norwich physician, Wrench's daughter Rebeccca and her husband John Jermy about property in Old Buckenham. The case went on for two years until he lost.[14]

Charles' next attempt to claim property began when he moved in the 1740s as a tenant to Hoxne Abbey, a desirable local estate owned at different times by the related Chauncey and Blackman families, descendants of John Thurston, or Thruston, who had built the house adjacent to the ruined abbey after the Dissolution, partly from the dilapidations.[15] These families were distant relatives of the Wythes. Thurston descendants occupied the house for six generations.[16] In the 18th and early 19th centuries, Hoxne Abbey was another estate owned by absentee landlords and rented out to tenants, a slightly grander estate than Monks Hall.

While he was a tenant there, Wythe conceived a notion, and persuaded his widowed sister Philippa Caton and another relative to join him in the action, that an early Thurston had intended to bequeath Hoxne Abbey estate to a forbear of the Wythes and that now the Abbey really should belong to him and the other complainants.[17] Wythe's claim failed and eventually Wythe settled back in Brockdish, where he died in 1757. If Wythe did tenant Monks Hall for a few years in the late 1720s and 1730s, as seems possible, he was probably an unreliable and difficult tenant, whom the Wollastons and their land agent may have been pleased to be see depart.

The next family at Monks Hall, about whom we have much clearer evidence, were the Corboulds and Walnes and they are much more attractive people.

The Corbould family and James Walne c 1750–1835

The author's impression of the branch of the Corbould family that tenanted Monks Hall for over eighty years is of gregarious social climbers who were keen to be counted with the grand families of the county. Their property possessions were modest but they rented in a style to which they aspired and one cannot help but be drawn to these friendly hospitable people and their determination to live life well.

The Corbould family, originally from Cotton, Suffolk, spawned many branches, including five generations of successful artists. Edward Henry Corbould was commissioned to paint Queen Victoria's children; his extensive portfolio is well represented on the web.[18] A genealogy and description of the various branches of Corboulds was published by the Suffolk Institute of Archaeology in 1935 and while it turns out to be not wholly accurate it contains numerous anecdotes and insights about the characters.[19]

Richard Corbould (1714–1814)

The first Corbould to move to Monks Hall was **Richard Corbould**, the youngest child of Richard and Martha Corbould of Harts Farm, Cotton, from whom most of the Suffolk Corboulds were descended. He married Susannah Bunn at Onehouse, Suffolk, in 1740 and it may have been after their marriage that they moved to Monks Hall. Certainly their children, two sons William and Pelham, always described themselves as coming from Syleham. William was born in 1740, Pelham in 1741.

The choice of the name Pelham for their second son came from a family legend that the Corboulds were descended from the 15th century Sir John Pelham, a glamorously heroic knight. The story goes that this knight would not marry the heiress chosen by his father, who disinherited him in consequence. Soon after 'the press gang got hold of him' but he escaped abroad and returned to England a few years later to Bristol, where he was known as 'the dark gentleman who rode a white horse'.[20] There is not a jot of evidence that this lineage is correct and indeed only this branch of the many Corboulds of Cotton claimed such descent. The story seems pure fantasy, especially as the navy press gang did not operate until the late 17th century. It was a sufficiently compelling story that various Corboulds have been named Pelham down the centuries up until the 20th century.

Richard and Susannah's older child William (1740–1791) married a widow, Sarah Welton, at Syleham on 22nd December 1775. They moved as tenants to a small farming estate in Eye called 'Clint', which still exists as an equestrian centre.[21]

The second son **Pelham Corbould** (b. 1741) remained at Monks Hall and married **Catherine Lorimer** (1754–1831), the daughter of Suffolk couple Samuel and Ann Lorimer, at Eye on 17 June 1765.[22] Catherine was as gregarious as her husband. The social whirl that centred on Monks Hall began when she was married to Pelham and continued with her second husband after Pelham's death. 'Pelham was famous for his lavish hospitality', remarked a relative but in Catherine he had clearly met his match.[23]

Whether Pelham's early death, in October 1771, was the consequences of too much good living we cannot know. He was only twenty-eight years old, leaving poor Catherine with three young children. Pelham's father Richard would live on to survive all his children and also several of his grandchildren and may have continued to live with Catherine and the children at Monks Hall after his son's death.

Pelham and Catherine had three children, Pelham Jnr (1766–1811), Elizabeth (born 1767) and William (1768–1811). William eventually went to London. Pelham Jnr and his wife settled as tenants at nearby Hoxne Abbey, mentioned above.[24] They established themselves as 'Maltsters and Wine, Spirit, Ale and Porter merchants' in Harleston, a business their son, also Pelham, continued after their demise.[25] Elizabeth married John Theobald of Starston in 1792, a farming landowner and tenant farming neighbour in Syleham.

James and Catherine Walne

After Pelham's death, Catherine married **James Walne** (1742–1835)[26] at his home parish of Starston on 31st December 1772. James came from very similar background to the Corboulds. His father was one of an extended family that owned property all over Norfolk and Suffolk. Thomas Walne at The Grove in Brockdish, a first cousin of James Walne, who died in 1825, (having taken over the Grove from the Wythe family) was possibly the wealthiest but there were prosperous Walnes up and down the Waveney valley and beyond. James Walne's father was another Thomas Walne, a farmer in Starston, almost certainly an uncle of Thomas Walne of Brockdish.[27]

James and Catherine's marriage witnesses were Charles Tuthill and Jonathan Theobald (John Theobald's father). Catherine's son by Pelham, Pelham Jnr, married Sarah Theobald, John's sister. We can see how very closely these families mingled as they hovered on the lower echelons of gentry.

Life in Syleham in the late 18th century

Families in rural villages worked hard at maintaining social contact. The well-to-do farmers, minor gentry and the parson were in a perpetual state of 'rotation' between their homes for dinners, taken about 4.00–5.00pm, suppers and afternoon gatherings. Rural society was a gregarious, gossipy, backgammon-playing, gambling, heavy-drinking and heavy-eating society. Food was relatively cheap for the propertied classes and the Corboulds and Walnes would eat meat most days of the week, beef on special days. Game and domestic ducks and geese they had caught or reared themselves were available. Fruit and vegetables were more frequently grown as the enthusiasm for gardening advanced in the 18th century.

The neighbours were crucial for social intercourse. There was a succession of curates at the Vicarage at Syleham Cross, the priest who did most of the work in both Wingfield and Syleham. William Gould, then Edward Vaughan, then Thomas Whitaker, all educated at Emmanuel College, Cambridge, were younger sons from 'good families'. Curates were often quite impecunious and reliant on tithes to sustain their families but were on a social par with the lesser gentry and part of their circle.

In his introduction to Parson Woodforde's diary Ronald Blythe memorably describes the Church of England of the late Georgian period as 'spiritually comatose'.[28] Dissenters had toned down their 17th century ranting, the Unitarians were in an elegant intellectual ascendancy in the thinking classes without any troubling fervour of faith, and Methodists had not yet quite roused their Wesleyan enthusiasm. The relationship between the established church and the ordinary parishioner was not one of acquiescence and subservience. The church was there to baptise, marry and bury you; the rest was optional as far as the congregation went. Very few people actually attended church. James Woodforde's three hundred or so flock in Weston Longville, eight miles west of Norwich, were only occasional worshippers. The only community occasions when the whole village attended church were few, to give thanks for the recovery of health of the monarch, or the funeral of a popular villager, or to pray for troops setting off for combat. Most Sundays the parson was pleased to see 'two rails', about thirty communicants.[29]

Farmers also harboured a growing resentment of the church tithes. As agricultural productivity increased, so did the local parson's 10 per cent share, without the church making any significant contribution to the investment needed for new equipment and materials. Parson Woodforde's annual tithe dinners for the farmers were famously generous but even he was subjected to 'unseemly talk' in the 1790s.

The Barry family at Syleham Hall continued to occupy the majority of Syleham parish acreage not owned by Monks Hall estate. Anthony Barry's son, Lambe Barry (1706–1768) was High Sheriff of Suffolk in 1748.[30] Named after his mother's family, Lambe and his wife Susan had two daughters, Ann, who died age 58 in 1808, and Isabella who lived on until 1825 aged 86. Neither Barry sister married but continued to inhabit Syleham Hall after their parents' death, the last of their line. Lambe Barry lived very well and was part of the upper echelons of county gentry. He had his portrait painted by Thomas Gainsborough, now displayed at Gainsborough's House in Sudbury. Barry has a wonderfully diffident but superciliously amused expression.

Lambe Barry (1704–1768), Thomas Gainsborough, painted in 1758.
Courtesy of Gainsborough's House, Sudbury, Suffolk.

Syleham Hall was a vast grand mansion demolished later to make way for a Victorian house and now replaced again by a more modest farmhouse. The Barry sisters sold much of their land to William Mann, the canny entrepreneur and mill owner who bought Syleham Manor house and turned it from a Tudor house into a splendid Georgian one.

Other likely companions of the Corboulds would be the prosperous Cotton family in Brockdish and Weybread, the Walne family at The Grove in Brockdish, perhaps the Maynards at Hoxne Hall (later called Oakley Park) and other local families owning property nearby or renting from the estate, such as the Theobalds, who were not especially well off but were long established in Syleham and Starston. The Corboulds probably did not mix much with the Cornwallis family at Brome Hall, who were the intellectual aristocracy of the county with extensive property holdings, but Catherine and James Walne were clearly social climbers and may have found a way to connect.

In the 18th century visiting friends and relatives would arrive unannounced, which meant one needed to be in a constant state of readiness to entertain, an expensive business when storage of meat was difficult. But the Corboulds and Walnes were famous for their hospitality and must have kept stocked up with a suitably generous offering of delicious victuals. There is no mention of servants in official documents but they almost certainly had live-in help in the shape of a cook and maids. Between 1740 and 1770 the Corboulds would probably have powdered their hair with starch or worn a wig on Sundays and special occasions, as illustrated by Lambe Barry's elegant hairstyle, using the services of the village barber and peruke maker. By 1770 the wig habit and hair powder were gradually dying under the influence of the pricey powder tax.

Well-off folk travelled around in phaetons, the sports cars of their age, if they could afford it.[31] Otherwise they hired post-chaises, rode considerable distances on horseback or went on foot. Much mail-coach travel was overnight, although being robbed at gunpoint by highwaymen was a rare but greatly feared risk on all major routes. Stage-coaches stopped at the White Lion in Eye and the Greyhound in Brockdish, the latter possibly a more convenient location because you could hire a driver and chaise from a cab rank owned and run by William Mann the miller, another of his entrepreneurial initiatives.[32] But the roads were bad and travelling was expensive, so for much of the time acquainted neighbouring families were interdependent, often marrying within a relatively small group of local families of the right social stratum. The novels of Jane Austen are set at this period, providing sharp insights into the edgy social milieu of families living in rural proximity but careful of maintaining and enhancing their status through marriage.

There were good opportunities for polite society to meet with like-minded folk. Assemblies in newly constructed Rooms at Ipswich, Norwich, Bury and Bungay provided more drinking and gambling. Bungay flourished throughout the Georgian period: the King's Head and Three Tuns opened fashionable assembly rooms providing music and entertainment, a theatre was built in the Castle Yard in 1773, and a spa and bath house was established just across Outney Common at Ditchingham.

Even nearer to Syleham, a small theatre opened in 1783 at Eye in the assembly room of the old coaching inn, the White Lion. William Cobbett lectured there on his tour through East Anglia and found the tiny room packed with local farmers 'from Diss, from Harleston and villages roundabout'.[33] It was also common for the literate classes to buy plays and music and put on their own performances among friends. In 1796 James Walne subscribed to *The Generous Attachment, A Comedy in five acts* by George Smythe.[34] Think of Catherine and James and their friends reading aloud to each other at a soiree after a good dinner at the hall.

There was horse-racing at Beccles and Newmarket, cock-fighting at The Scole Inn, and worse, bull-baiting at Ipswich, although both these two latter pastimes were rapidly becoming unacceptable to polite society. Local fairs, for the sale and purchase of livestock, where news of improvements in agriculture and local gossip were shared, were held in Hoxne in Spring, Eye at the beginning of December and twice in July and August at Stradbroke.

The Corbould/Walne menfolk would have hunted, fished and coursed hares, as was normal for gentlemen of their rank. James Walne figured in the list of Suffolk men applying each year for game licences for gamekeepers. In the first decade of the 19th century Francis Wollaston applied for a gamekeeper's licence every year and may well have hunted with James Walne. The Walnes probably kept one or more domestic dogs as pets. When a stray pointer wandered in, the Walnes looked after it and tried to find its owner.[35]

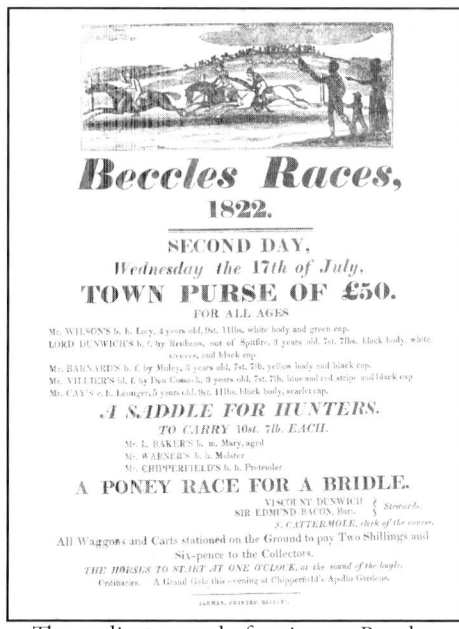

The earliest record of racing on Beccles Common was in July 1709.

The better sort of farming family like the Corboulds were loyal to their Hanoverian kings, especially to George III (reigned 1760–1820), whose passionate interest in agriculture earned him the nickname of 'Farmer George'. They would have followed the national news eagerly and in Syleham this arrived daily on the mail coach from London, which stopped at Brockdish. The first Suffolk local newspaper, the *Suffolk Mercury*, was published around 1717, 'an impartial collection of the most material occurrences, Foreign and

Domestick'. It contained little or no local news but, hot on its heels, the *Ipswich Journal* first went to press in August 1720. This was a publication that was to last for nearly 200 years. The first issues were few in number, and expensive; only about 250 gentlemen paid 'three half-pence' for their 'local' newspaper but items were mainly of national and international interest. If local items appeared at all, it was because they had appeared in a London newspaper first. Many of the early stories came courtesy of *Stanley's News Letter*, published in London and distributed by mail coach three times a week. Hence, by the time it was printed, news was often as much as a fortnight old. In the early days of the *Ipswich Journal* and *Suffolk Mercury*, news of Cadiz and The Hague was more plentiful than that for Ipswich or Bury St. Edmunds, though as the readership grew, adverts for sales stimulated interest in local affairs and the reporting of local crime naturally awakened interest.

There was no police force in Suffolk until 1840 but local landowners usually subscribed to local associations to pay the expenses for the apprehension and prosecution of suspected criminals and to bring private prosecutions in their area. James Walne was a member of the Hoxne Association and attended the annual meeting along with thirty or so others at The Swan in Harleston in April 1817. Dinner was included.[36]

The last years of the 18th century were troubled by riots and the fear of riots in London and many other urban and rural locations. There was mass rioting at the main market place in Great Yarmouth in October 1792, largely due to dissatisfaction with wages and the increasing price of provisions. 'The confusion that ensued was general throughout the market. Provisions of various sorts, and in considerable quantities were either destroyed or purloined'. The swift arrival of the military dispersed the crowd and no one died, although many rioters and onlookers were seriously battered with staves. Thomas Maynard chaired meetings of the Suffolk 'Loyal Association' at The White Lion, Eye, and The Swan, Hoxne, to express gentry support for the King although there is no evidence that the Corboulds/Walnes took an active interest in local or national politics.

The Corboulds probably bought smuggled goods. Free trade had scarcely been born and high protectionism was national policy, with the consequence that universal smuggling was accepted. Parson Woodforde bought smuggled tea and a barrel of gin as readily and as free of guilt as some people today buy smuggled tobacco in the pub.

Catherine Walne died in August 1826 at the age of 86, 'much lamented by her relatives and friends', 'a woman greatly esteemed by her numerous acquaintances for her hospitality and for her kindness and attention to the poor'.[37] The Walnes's hospitality had become legendary. A sentimental poem appears in the Corbould Genealogy, apparently written after Catherine's death, and originally published in the *Ipswich Journal*.[38]

> Syleham indeed, a heavy loss deplores!
> But not alone; for every parish round,
> Walne's name, if not his residence, adores,
> And owns a loss with sympathy profound.
>
> O I have join'd the hospitable board,
> And often view'd the venerable pair;
> Exulting that their gifts they could afford,
> And so much bounty from their substance spare.
>
> One soul directed both; let who would come,
> A friend or worldling, both alike appear'd,
> And never guest but found himself at home,
> In gladness welcom'd, and in sorrow cheer'd.
>
> It seemed a favour to partake their fare
> And such abundance greeted ev'ry guest,
> That was their heaven, promptly to prepare
> A room for feasting and a room for rest.
>
> Nor care nor poverty had a need to fawn,
> Or cringe for proud and ostentatious aid;
> A look, a word, from 'Aunt' or 'Uncle' Walne,
> The very fears of poverty allay'd.
>
> Dear, good old man! Thy years so honor'd blest
> I would the moisture from thy forehead wipe;
> And still beside thee, with an honest jest,
> Enjoy the social converse with a pipe.

Sustain his years ye kindred souls who own
The honour due to age and manly worth;
There is, I know, a coveted renown,
A boast of heaven and a scorn of earth.

Springing from sources that I've not explored,
There is, of human worth, a saintly dread;
But if 'Aunt Walne' were honor'd and adored,
T' were less than human not to weep her dead.

There is one line in the first stanza that suggests maybe the Walnes lived a little chaotically, or perhaps the house was in need of repair. What is the meaning of 'Walne's name, if not his residence, adores'? But if the house was by then rather run-down, the Walnes probably did not notice as they sat looking forward to their visitors.

After Catherine's death James Walne lived on at Monks Hall until 1835. The house and estate of course belonged to the Wollastons but he had his farming live and dead stock to sell. An advert appeared in the Suffolk Chronicle.[39] James, by then 93, was probably becoming frail and moved to spend his last months with Catherine's daughter Elizabeth and John Theobald in Starston, where James had grown up.[40] He died in December 1835 and was buried in Syleham on Boxing Day.[41]

James' will provided an annuity to his son James of £70 per annum and money for Catherine's children and their spouses, with the proviso that the John Theobald would not receive his part until he had paid off a debt owed to Sir Edward Kerrison for which Walne had stood guarantee.[42] The sum of £70 is now worth £3000 or so per year, not a particularly generous amount but at a time when agricultural wages were about 10s. per week, that is about £25 a year, son James was left comfortably set up.[43]

The Wollastons now needed another tenant and a highly suitable and ambitious farmer, Alfred Read, took on Monks Hall estate next.

Alterations to the house in the 18th century

The house shows little evidence of change dating from the 18th century except for the large casement windows with large panes at the front, which were inserted to give more light presumably, in the late 18th or early 19th century. Inserted is the wrong word; as the current 21st tenants point out, the openings were roughly hacked out but the frames are merely tacked on the outside, not inset into the walls. These were probably put in by the Walnes. Some of the range of back rooms near the kitchen may have been put in then too but there is no clear evidence. The house would have been lime-washed inside to spruce up the appearance every few years, odd maintenance jobs done perhaps but essentially Monks Hall remained as the Fullers had left it.

Notes

1. Overton, Mark, 1985. 'The Diffusion of Agricultural Innovations in Early Modern England: Turnips and Clover in Norfolk and Suffolk, 1580-1740'. *Transactions of the Institute of British Geographers* 10, pp. 205–21.
2. Starr, A. J. 1941. '18th Century Agriculture in Suffolk'. *Geography* 26, pp. 116–25.
3. Young, Arthur, 1797.
4. Tate, W E. 1952. 'A Handlist of Suffolk Enclosure Acts and Awards.' *Proceedings of the Suffolk Institute of Archaeology and Natural History* Vol. XXV, Part 33.
5. Deeds re Pescodd's tenement in Syleham with pasturage on the common belonging to the manor of Monks Hall in Syleham 1732, 1736 Released by Thomas Brown and Mary his wife, Edward Lawes and Elizabeth his wife, Sarah Balls, Deborah Balls (daughters and co-heirs of Thomas Balls) to Robert Bearcroft, 1732; lease assigned by Edward Lawes and Elizabeth his wife to Robert Beare, 1736. NRO. Haggard of West Bradenham and elsewhere, Deeds and Family Papers. HAG 65, 601x7.
6. Land Tax Redemption Office: Quotas and Assessments, 1798, Suffolk, Volume 2, p. 415. Records of the Boards of Stamps, Taxes, Excise, Stamps and Taxes, and Inland Revenue. The National Archives. Series IR23.
7. Last reference to Molly/Mully 1530. The Parish register of Syleham Suffolk Vol 1, 1535–1779, transcribed by Andrew Gray. Parish records, courtesy Mary Lewis.
8. Will of William Groom of Rattlesden, Gentleman. Archdeaconry Court of Sudbury. 3 October, 1769. Online at http://www.fullerfamilyhistory.org.uk/pdf/Will_Beneficiaries.pdf (accessed 10.8.2018).
9. UK Poll Books and Electoral Register 1538–1893. A Copy of the Poll for the Knights of the Shire for the County of Suffolk 1727. Syleham parish.
10. Will of Samuel Browning of Needham, Norfolk. NRO, ANF will register 1731-1737 fo. 154, 1740–1742 no. 20, MF227.
11. Charles Wythe's Dates from Ancestry.co.uk. Norfolk, England, Church of England Baptism, Marriages, and Burials, 1535–1812, Brockdish. Charles Wythe is discussed in Murphy. E. 2015. *The Moated Grange* (Book Guild, Hove), Chapter 7: 'The Last Spaldings 1705-1743', pp. 144–65.
12. Will of Margaret Pell and Inventory PM. 1743 NRO Norwich Diocesan Archives DN/INV 81C/5.
13. Greenwood v Whythe (spelt Wythe in body of deposition) William Greenwood, gent of new Buckenham, Norfolk and John Chappell fellmonger of Brockdish executors and devisees of Margaret Pell, widow deceased of Brockdish. NA

C11/2094/15. 1743 (This deposition of the plaintiffs was written by lawyer 'M. Rant Esq". Meux Rant was an experienced chancery lawyer.)
14. Title: Release in Trust Messuage and lands in Old Buckenham 1729 NRO MC 124/5 600 x 2. Wythe v Blackburn. Bill and answer. 1730 NA. Charles Wythe, gent of Brockdish, Norfolk. Defendants: Moses Blackburne, John Jermy, Sir Benjamin Wrench, kt and Rebecca Marcon. NA. C 11/2254/45. C 11/2298/59 Short title: Wythe v Mann. Bill only. Plaintiffs: Charles Wythe, gent of Brockdish, Norfolk. Defendants: Edward Mann.1731 NA C 11/2298/59. Wythe v Wrench. Answer only. Plaintiffs: Charles Wythe, gent. Defendants: Sir Benjamin Wrench bart, Norwich Rebecca Marcon, widow and John Jermy, esq.1731 NA C 11/1492/27.
15. John Thurston. Biographical note in Venn, John Biographical 1897 History of Gonville and Caius College: 1349-1897, (Cambridge: Cambridge University Press) Vol I. Alumni Gonville and Caius College p 308.
16. Deeds relating to property in Worlingworth, Tannington, Wilby and Hoxne. 'Clynte' about 5-6 acres. Hoxne Abbey in possession of John Thruston of Hoxne in 1634 Suffolk Record Office HA116/4/1/2, 1400-1637.
17. Short title: Wythe v Chauncy. Bill and answer. Plaintiffs: Charles Wythe, Philippa Caton, widow and Arthur Chauncy. Defendants: Elizabeth Chauncy, spinster and others.1746 NA C 11/2111/27. Short title: Wythe v Thurston. Bill and answer. Plaintiffs: Charles Wythe, gent, Philippa Caton, widow, Arthur Chancey, esq and Elizabeth Chancey, spinster. Defendants: John Thruston alias John Mott, doctor in physic of Weston, Suffolk and others.1746 TNA C 11/2109/49. Short title: Wythe v Blackman. Two bills and two answers. 1747 TNA C 11/2118/49. Short title: Wythe v Squire.Depositions.1748 NA C 11/2336/31. Charles Wythe gentleman and Philipa Caton widow …TNA C78/1943,1749.
18. Edward Henry Corbould 1815-1905. http://www.avictorian.com/Corbould_Edward_Henry_1815-1905.html (accessed 10.8.2018).
19. Poulter, George C. B. 1935. 'The Corbould Genealogy' (Ipswich: Suffolk Institute of Archeology), online at http://www.corbould.com/genealogy/tcg.html (accessed 21.10.17), Chapter VII Corbould of Bath and of Monks Hall Syleham and Hoxne Abbey, Suffolk, pp. 49-62.
20. Poulter. 'The Corbould Genealogy', p. 52.
21. SRO Ipswich, HD11/475/Eye/631 'The Clint Farm in Eye in occupation of Mr Wm Cobbold Tenant, [should read Corbould]'. 'Mr Lathburys' Estates in Eye, field names, acres, adjacent landowners and occupiers, road to Thorndon and Eye St, Occold Hall lands, glebe, kiln and yard, pightle." In 1781 some labourers unearthed a lead box by the river at Clint. The box contained about 600 Roman gold coins dating to the reigns of Valens and Valentinian I (reigned 364–375), Gratian (375–383), Theodosius I (378–395), Arcadius (395–408), and Honorius (393–423). This was the largest hoard of Roman gold coins ever discovered in Britain, similar in content to the 20th century find, the Hoxne Hoard.
22. Catherine Lorimer. Baptism 6 January 1754. Suffolk baptisms FHL Film 887380.
23. Poulter. 'The Corbould Genealogy' p. 50. Quote of a relative, R. T. Corbould.
24. Pelham Corbould of Hoxne Abbey, death reported 1811 in *The Monthly*

Magazine or British Register Vol XXXII, part 2 p. 512. Abstract of Will of Pelham Corbould, Farmer of Hoxne Suffolk, Proved in the county of Suffolk 28 November 1811. TNA. IR 26/397/397.
25. White, W. 1844. *White's Directory* (Sheffield: R. Leader), p. 754.
26. James Walne. National Burial Index for England and Wales. Syleham 26 December 1835.
27. Walne genealogy courtesy of Elizabeth Walne Budd.
28. Woodforde, James, ed. Blythe, Ronald. 1999. *The diary of a country parson 1758-1802* (Norwich: Canterbury Press), Introduction.
29. Ibid. p. vii.
30. Page A, p. 422; Venn, *Alumni Cantabrigienses*, Vol. 1, p. 98.
31. This is a memorable 'Roy Porter-ism' from his unbeatable book, Porter, Roy, 1982. *English Society in the 18th Century* (1st edn Allen Lane; rev. edn 1990, London: Penguin), p. 228.
32. William Mann's chaise stop. Articles of Agreement. (1) John Cotton of Wingfield (Suffolk), gent. (2) William Mann of Syleham (Suffolk), esq. For hire of a house in Brockdish. 7 April 1806. NRO. NRS 1737, 10F7.
33. Cobbett, W. 1830. *Rural Rides* (Public Domain edition for Kindle), p. 500. The Eye Theatre at the White Lion opened again in 2001 but did not survive.
34. Smythe, George, 1796. *The Generous Attachment: A Comedy in five acts* (Printed for the author in London: E. Hodson, Bell-Yard, Temple-Bar). Entered at Stationers Hall.
35. Pointer dog advertised by James Walne, *Ipswich Journal* 31 August 1776.
36. Annual meeting of the Hoxne Association. *Ipswich Journal* 5 April 1817.
37. Death of Catherine Walne. Death notices, *Bury and Norwich Post* 30 August 1826.
38. Poulter 'The Corbould Genealogy', p50. Poem appeared in *Ipswich Journal* 16 September 1826 p. 4.
39. The *Suffolk Chronicle; or Weekly General Advertiser & County Express*. Saturday 12 September 1835.
40. Report of James Walne's death at the home of Mr John Theobald of Starston. *Ipswich Journal* 5 January 1836.
41. James Walne 1742–1835. National Burial Index, Suffolk 26 December 1835, St Mary's (sic) Syleham.
42. Will of James Walne, Gentleman of Syleham, Suffolk 1836. Norwich Consistory Court Probate Records NCC will register Smith 109 microfilm MF 486.
43. National Archive Currency Converter. https://www.nationalarchives.gov.uk/currency/about1800s.htm. Lyle, Margaret. 2007. 'Regional agricultural wage variations in early nineteenth century England'. Agricultural History Review AgHR 55, I, pp. 95–106, online at www.bahs.org.uk/AGHR/ARTICLES/55_105Lyle.pdf (accessed 11.4.2018).

12

The Read Family
Victorian farmers

Alfred Read was an experienced farmer from an extended local farming family when he took on the tenancy of Monks Hall and its estate in 1838. Perhaps he was gripped by the great wave of optimism that swept the nation after the accession of the new young Queen Victoria in 1837. Alfred Read was ambitious for his estate and soon took on other roles that would give him a respectable position in local society. He became interested in agricultural politics and, unlike the Fullers of the 17th century, was happy to advertise his opinions and act as spokesman for local landowner and tenant interests.

Branches of the Read family had been farming in Suffolk and Norfolk area for generations and still do. Throughout the 19th century there were Reads with substantial farm holdings in Chediston, Hoxne, Linstead and throughout the Waveney Valley and further south in Huntingfield and Cookley. Alfred was the second son of James and Sarah Read of Hoxne, born about 1793. His older brother James farmed all his life in Linstead Magna. We know little of Alfred's early life but at the age of twenty-three he married Elizabeth Manby Cracknell, born in Dennington, at Stradbroke on 1st September 1818. He may have farmed first in Wilby, where his oldest son Thomas Cracknell Read was born in 1819. We know Alfred was later farming in Chediston, probably at Gate Farm, where their children Elizabeth (1821), Edgar (1823), John (1825), Sarah (1827) and James (1829) were all born. Tom, John and James all became prosperous local farmers, with substantial acres under their own tenancies, the youngest James being the one to follow their father at Monks Hall. Their second son Edgar stayed at home with his father and then lived

Monks Hall in the late 19th century, with its beams plastered over and a Victorian lean-to conservatory on the south-west elevation.

with his brother. No occupation was recorded for Edgar in the censuses and he died relatively young, aged forty-five; he may have suffered from long-term sickness or been disabled in some way.

Alfred's father died in 1832, perhaps providing his sons with an inheritance sufficient to invest in larger tenancies.[1] We know that by August 1838, Alfred was living at Monks Hall. On 1st October that year, Alfred hosted the meeting of landowners and tithe owners held to agree on the cash commutation of Syleham tithes.[2] Under the recent Tithe Commutation Act all tithes would be substituted by, or 'commuted' to, a cash sum, under a rather complicated formula that had to be formally agreed locally. The act introduced the long campaign to abolish tithes in their ancient form. This was the first of many references to public meetings being held at Monks Hall, usually chaired by Alfred as a man of consequence in the local community. The final tithe apportionments for Syleham were decided by the government commission in 1842 and once again the meeting to hear any objections was held at Monks Hall.[3]

A survey of the whole of England and Wales was undertaken in the decade or so after 1836, to establish the boundaries of each parish and assess the amount of tithe due for each parcel of land within it. This resulted in the survey of all tithe-able land in each parish, the production of a map covering the whole parish and a reference book (apportionment) identifying each plot of land and who owned/occupied it. The tithe maps and apportionments are an important source of information about the history and topography of a parish. The tithe map for Syleham still exists in the National Archive and a rather faded copy is held in the Suffolk Record Office in Ipswich.

Alfred Read was landowner of three plots and tenanted thirty-four further plots of land owned by Francis Wollaston in Syleham, comprising in total about 236 acres in 1842.[4] He also owned three plots in Hoxne occupied by tenant William Rush. The Monks Hall land is described as 'marshy' although the sloping hills above the valley were very fertile. White's Trade Directory for the period described the road running along the valley bottom as 'now well drained' but 'formerly being famous for the "Syleham Lamps", or "ignis fatui" ("foolish fire")'. The ghostly light sometimes seen at night or twilight over bogs, swamps and marshes, perhaps from methane gas, is traditionally called will-o'-the-wisp. It resembles a flickering lamp and is sometimes said to recede when approached. Local superstition said the light could lure travellers away from the road into the river, a scary thought that put locals on their guard.

Two years after they moved into Monks Hall, Alfred and Elizabeth's older daughter Elizabeth died aged eighteen 'after a long affliction'.[5] His younger daughter Sarah also died young, aged seventeen, in 1844; both may well have suffered from consumption, the scourge of Victorian families of all classes.

From 1838 Alfred assumed several responsible positions. He was appointed a trustee of Hoxne Trust Property, a local charity administering land for the benefit of the poor, and in 1842 was appointed as Chief Constable for the Hoxne Hundred, a job shared with Joseph Bloomfield of Laxfield.[6] He seems to have taken this job seriously, bringing a number of prosecutions to the courts, although not always successfully. There was no police force in Suffolk until 1840, when East Suffolk Constabulary was set up. Policing in Suffolk changed little between the 12th and early 19th centuries. The county remained dependent on the established system of Justices of the Peace, parish constables and town watchmen. Each hundred had a High Constable who was directly responsible to the Justices for the maintenance of public order within the hundred.

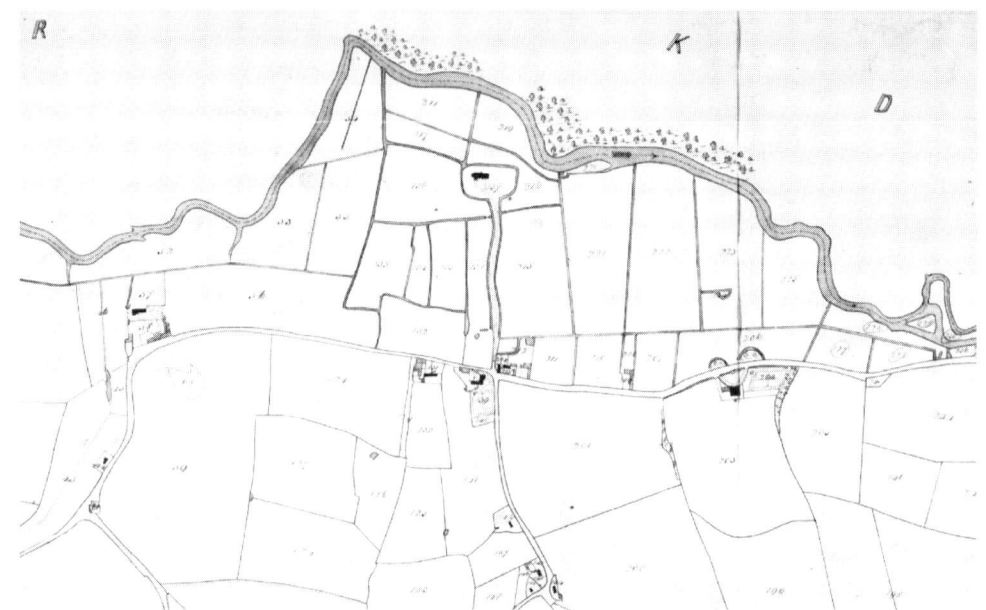

Part of the Syleham Parish Tithe Map 1839 showing some of the numbered plots farmed by Alfred Read.

Syleham Tithe map 1839 SRO. IR 29/33/402.

In 1840 the Justices of the Peace for East Suffolk, unhappy with the inadequate system of parish constables, made application to the Secretary of State to set up an organised police force under the Rural Policing Act. At the March Quarter Sessions, John Hatton was appointed Chief Constable for East Suffolk. But many local hundreds kept their own Chief Constables, as Hoxne did, and only gradually merged their local voluntary constables in the parish with the paid professional police constables. Quite how it all worked is not clear, nor to whom members of the public turned to report crime and look for assistance. Though local voluntary constables maintained a rhetoric of gentlemanly independence and sometimes outright opposition to the powers of the government-appointed constables, they were a crucial ingredient in the justice system. In important respects, local constables seem to have complemented and strengthened the new centralised force in maintaining law and order in a period of social, economic and political turbulence.[7]

Farming in Victorian Suffolk

First and foremost, however, Alfred Read was a farmer. And like many early Victorians he took his agriculture seriously, joining the Royal Agricultural

Society of England in 1841 and becoming a leading light of the East Suffolk Branch.[8] He subscribed to *The Farmers Magazine*, the farmers' bible of modern methods launched at the end of the 18th century.

Wealthy men set up model farms. Even Prince Albert had a go on a vast scale at Windsor, but few of these 'demonstration projects' made any money because of the imperial-sized excessive capital investments rich men put into them. It was the era of the Agricultural Show, which rapidly provided the main gathering place for all farmers, landlord and tenant, to learn about the latest improvements. Suffolk Agricultural Association and Annual Show began in 1831.

Mechanisation of farming gradually took hold. In the 18th and 19th centuries farm produce was grown mainly for market rather than for the subsistence of the growers, as it had been in earlier days. At the same time, industrial machinery was being created for agricultural purposes. Until the middle of the 19th century mechanisation made less headway than it might have done because of the surplus of agricultural labour in rural areas for which employment had to be found, the alternative being to support the parish unemployed via the provisions of the poor law, an expensive business for landed owners and occupiers. Simply put, the poor rate went up when employment went down. Many machines that could have saved labour were resented by farm workers who feared that they might be displaced, as indeed they eventually were. But by the middle of the century farm labour was becoming scarce, as canny workers moved to better paid jobs in the new Midlands factories. The high price of horses gave an additional reason for introducing labour-saving machines.

Early in the century a winnowing machine was introduced and by 1770 a machine was made that cleaned and sorted grain. Experiments were being made with threshing machines in the 1780s. A portable threshing machine was exhibited in about 1800. The early models were all operated by horse labour, and it was not until the 1850s that steam-driven machines that could thresh 60 quarters of wheat a day replaced horse threshers managing 7 quarters a day. By 1867 the advantages of the steam-driven over the horse thresher were so great that the judges at the Royal Show recommended that prizes for horse-drawn threshing machines should be discontinued.

By 1830 seed drills had already been designed which would sow seed in combination with manure. By 1860 most of the features of the modern drill had already been incorporated. The stimulus for double-furrow ploughs came through the shortage of labour. The 19th century was notable for the steam plough as the 20th century later became for the tractor plough. A system of ploughing with an endless steel rope moved by a windlass was patented in 1832 and by the middle of the century it was being used commercially. In 1867 it was estimated that 200,000 acres out of 12 million acres of arable were steam tilled. Alfred Read's tenure of Monks Hall was a relatively good time for farmers although hard times were on the way for his sons. He probably had the money to invest in new machinery.

The coming of the railways

Transport was vital to farmers. The advent of the railway meant stock could be transported to the London markets quickly without drovers and grain could be moved quickly to where it was sold. At a public meeting in November 1844, enthusiasts for alternative routes expounded their arguments over the route of the proposed new Diss and Colchester Railway from Norwich to London through the Hundreds of Hartsimere and Hoxne. Chaired by Lord Henniker, the majority of the meeting supported a deviation of the route through Eye and away from Diss. But Alfred Read and his neighbour Augustus Cooper the curate from Syleham, a considerable landowner and gentleman farmer himself, both felt that a direct route from Norwich to Ipswich via Diss would be preferable and tabled an amendment to that effect. Diss was a mile further away from Syleham than Eye but the road connection was much better. They lost the local vote in 1844 but history supported them.[9] The line was routed through Diss, which had an enormously positive effect on the prosperity and growth of that town. Eye got its own station on a later branch line, of much less importance, connecting the small town with Mellis, but that eventually closed to passengers in 1931 and goods in 1964.

Alfred and his family were not living especially wealthy lives in the early 1840s. The 1841 census for Monks Hall finds Alfred aged forty-five, Elizabeth his wife aged forty-three, and three children Edgar (fifteen), Sarah (fourteen) and James (twelve). Also resident with them were James Carter, an agricultural worker, and his wife Sarah, three other young labourers, Nat Hammond, Richard Denny and Thomas Evans, and two domestic servants, Esther Baxter and Sarah Bloomfield. There was a third daughter, Mary, who does not figure in the census and who later married William Buttram, a prosperous grocer and provision merchant in Ipswich.[10] She probably also lived at Monks Hall. It was a crowded household, although not atypical of the period. The two older boys, Thomas and John, were probably already working on farms elsewhere.

White's trade directory for Suffolk describes Syleham as having a total population of 399 and acreage of 1003. The Barry sisters had died; now Syleham Hall, 'a handsome mansion with grounds and plantations' was occupied by the rather grand 'perpetual curate' the Reverend Augustus Cooper, BA, who both owned the hall land and the living and the financial tithes that went with it. Cooper served as curate in Syleham for no less than fifty-four years.

Thomas Dyson, an impressive entrepreneur who owned half of Diss including the bank and the brewery, inherited Syleham Manor from his younger brother John, who had bought the lands formerly owned by William Mann. Dyson was formally Lord of the Manor of Syleham Comitis. There were no fewer than ten farmers listed in the directory, although only Alfred Read and Henry Stannard at Red House Farm are identified at a particular property.

Syleham still had its White Horse pub near the Green (closed in 1965), the miller was George Dye, and Charles Godbold was described as a wheelwright but also had a thriving building company, working for some years on the renovations of Brockdish Church. White's directory for 1845 records a 'ladies' boarding school' in Syleham run by Miss Caroline Thurtell, although she does not appear in the censuses of 1841 or 1851, so it must have been a short-lived venture.

Ten years later in the 1851 census, Alfred's son John, aged twenty-five, had returned home and was also farming, probably part of the family holdings which he would later inherit. Son James was also still at home in 1851, with two male farm servants and two indoor female domestics.

During the 1840s, the popular campaign to repeal the Corn Laws was making good progress and landowners and tenant farmers were not pleased. The Corn Laws were tariffs and restrictions on imported food and grain ('corn') enforced between 1815 and 1846. They were designed to keep grain prices high to favour domestic producers like the Reads. The Corn Laws imposed steep import duties, making it too expensive to import grain from abroad, even when food supplies were short, as it often was in the growing towns. The Corn Laws enhanced the profits and political power associated with land ownership. The laws raised food prices and the costs of living for the British public, both in rural areas and towns, and hampered the growth of other British economic sectors, such as manufacturing, by reducing the disposable income of the general public. Many ordinary people were near starving, their main income being largely spent on bread. This led to riots, to the demonstration that ended in the Peterloo massacre in Manchester, and to a national campaign led by Richard Cobden, a radical Liberal statesman and manufacturer, to rescind the acts.

The laws became the focus of opposition from urban groups who then had far less political power than rural Britain. Conservative landowners and well-to-do tenants like Alfred Read supported the laws but they were strongly opposed by Whig industrialists and workers. The first two years of the Irish famine of 1845–1852 forced a resolution because of the urgent need for new food supplies. Prime Minister Sir Robert Peel, a Conservative, achieved repeal with the support of the Whigs in Parliament, overcoming the opposition of most of his own party. Economic historians see the repeal of the Corn Laws as a decisive shift toward free trade in Britain and a triumph for working artisans and labourers.

Alfred Read was a leading light in the East Suffolk Agricultural Protection Society; its members opposed the repeal of the Corn Laws, which they foresaw would have a catastrophic impact on farming.[11] Lord Rendlesham, Member of Parliament for East Suffolk from 1843, voted against the repeal as expected but was not effective enough for Alfred, who announced publicly that he would be willing to offer himself as a protectionist candidate in opposition to Lord Rendlesham at the next election.[12] In the event he did not. Protectionist arguments included the importance of maintaining a stable rural society and the support of farm wages. However, with 170 years of hindsight it is now accepted that the repeal of the Corn Laws was a democratic advance that is now considered to have been beneficial to the general population and to have supported the growth of industry; it did not have quite the catastrophic impact on landowners that was envisaged.

It has been argued that the high duty on corn mattered little because when British agriculture suffered from bad harvests, this was also true for foreign harvests and so the price of imported corn without the duty would not have been lower. The real threat to British agriculture came about twenty-five years after repeal from the development of cheaper shipping, faster and thus cheaper transport by rail and steamboat, and the modernisation of agricultural machinery. The prairie farms of North America were able to export vast quantities of cheap grain, as were peasant farms in Russia, grown with simpler methods but cheaper labour. Every wheat-growing country decided to increase tariffs in reaction to this, except Britain and Belgium. The next thirty years were difficult for farmers and the slump in farm incomes would certainly have affected Alfred Read and his sons. Agriculture's contribution to the national income was about 17 per cent in 1871; by 1911 it was less than 7 per cent. The golden age of farming ended and has never recovered without subsidies.

The final land enclosures

The Victorian era witnessed the final stages of land enclosure. Syleham land was generally enclosed very early, mostly in the Elizabethan era, leaving only the greens in Syleham and Wingfield to be divided up between landowners. Claims were lodged to an 'Inclosure Commission' in 1850 by local landowners in Syleham who considered they had a claim and wanted to acquire pasture and grazing rights. In 1854 freeholder Henry Septimus Hyde Wollaston Esq. 'Lord of the Manor or reputed Manor of Monks Hall Syleham' was awarded a tiny plot, number 22 on the map, one acre 37 perches, but Alfred Read was granted an award as freeholder of 14 acres of Syleham Greens, mostly in the parish of Wingfield. They were in possession of his tenant Robert Juby in 7 pieces of land, numbers 351–357, just a little more to add to his already substantial holdings.[13]

By 1861, Alfred and Elizabeth were employing twelve men and three boys, and son James living with them was farming 120 acres of his own with six men and two boys.[14] There were still four servants living in the house with them and unemployed thirty-eight-year-old Edgar.

Changes of landlord and tenant

The landlord changed in 1863. Francis Wollaston died and Henry Septimus Hyde Wollaston took over. We do not know if this made any practical difference to the Read family. Alfred Read died in 1865, in his late 60s. There was no automatic right of his sons to inherit the tenancy although it is clear that his youngest son James, who was living at Monks Hall with his mother, did take on the tenancy from Wollaston. But perhaps Alfred wanted to divide his personal assets from the farm and hall between all his living sons. On Friday 21st September, the executors of Alfred's will, John Read and James Read, sold 'All the valuable live and dead farming stock' at Monks Hall, consisting of:

> 15 extremely valuable young fresh fine-shaped Cart mares, geldings and

colts,

6 very choice young milch cows,

Superior two years old Shorthorn bull and 3 weanels

80 capital shearling sheep

42 head of swine

3 excellent breasted road wagons, harvest ditto, 5 capital three-quarter load tumbrils, excellent 18 coulter corn drill and sledge, manure drill for beat and turnips, lever horse drag rake …[15]

and many other farming implements.

There followed a list of furniture including 'mahogany post and other bedsteads, 4 feather beds, mahogany, loo and other tables, 2 capital mahogany escritoires with glass fronts, mahogany hair seat Trafalgar chairs, mahogany frames sofa in hair cloth, dairy and brewing utensils and effects'.

Alfred's widow Elizabeth lived on until her ninetieth year; did she mind all these household goods being sold? What was the purpose of the sale? We do know their son James assumed the tenancy of the hall and farm. Elizabeth moved out into a small home of her own just near Gate House Farm in Syleham, where her son John and his wife Sophia lived.

A marble plaque high up on the south nave wall of St Margaret's Church commemorates Alfred and Elizabeth Manby Read, their two daughters, Elizabeth and Susan, and Mary Kate, four-year-old daughter of their son John Read at Gate House Farm.

James Read buys Monks Hall

When James took on the tenancy he was thirty-six years old, still a bachelor, and lived at Monks Hall with some farm servants. Henry Septimus Hyde Wollaston died in 1867, leaving his various properties to his son, the Reverend Charles Buchanan Wollaston (1816–87), Rector of Feltham, near Bognor Regis, who seems to have had no interest in running the estates. This provided James with an opportunity to buy the freehold of the Monks Hall estate. It is not clear how he raised the capital to buy Monks Hall. The mortgage indenture document between James Read and Wollaston is still held in the Monks Hall archive. Essentially the mortgage documents sold the estate to James over a five-year period between 1867 and 1874, for a total sum of £10,000, to be paid in equal instalments. This represented a colossal sum, about £4m today, and James may well have had to borrow heavily to purchase his farming empire, which included over 275 acres in Hoxne and Syleham. The money could have come from Wollaston himself or from a bank but later events suggest that at least part of the sum was borrowed from his elder brother or other prosperous relatives.

James was now a freehold owner and an increasingly confident one. The 'Golden Age' of English agriculture when farmers did well lasted from about 1850 to 1879. Wages for farm workers rose during the years of prosperity, yet they did not rise as fast as the price of food, with meat in particular prohibitively expensive. The general increase in labourers' wages did not increase standards of living. Farm workers in Suffolk were among the most poorly paid in the country, receiving about two thirds of the wages of industrial labourers in the Midlands and the north. Rural living conditions for labourers and tenant farmers with very small land holdings were shockingly poor. A report in 1871 by Julian Jeffreys on the employment of women and children in agriculture was commented on in the *Bury and Norwich Post*.

> The average dietary of the labouring population in rural areas in Southern England may be described as following: beef and mutton was rarely tasted so that they do not form part of their diet ... Bread and cheese forms the main part of the diet for adults, the poor mans cow being a blessing of the past as milk does not or rarely forms much part of the diet in village children, even in infancy ... I know a large parish in Suffolk mainly dependant on ditch water in certain seasons the administrations of vermifuge would expel from the bowels of perhaps half the children, worms many inches long.[16]

Even given journalists' gift for hyperbole, the hard life that labouring families endured is shocking. We simply do not know whether James was a sympathetic employer.

Fire destroyed one of the estate double cottages in July 1873.[17] The newspaper report remarked, 'The building was old, and there being a great deal of timber in its construction, it was soon found that it would be useless attempting to extinguish the fire.' We do not learn what happened to the occupants of the cottages.

James was still caring for his brother Edgar, who died in 1869. By 1871

James was providing lodgings for another young farmer, William Smyth, who had 100 acres in Chediston. And that is probably how James met his wife, William's sister Susan, who had grown up at The Grove Farm in Chediston, whose family had built a new farmhouse in the early 19th century. It may be that the final instalment for acquiring Monks Hall having been paid in 1874, James had the confidence to marry; he was now a man of substance, with property and land.

Susan was twenty-five, considerably younger than James, who was by then in his mid-forties. Susan may not have been much of a cook; an advertisement appeared in the *Diss Express* in January 1876: 'Good Plain COOK in a farmhouse where no cows are kept. Please Apply personally to Mrs James Read Monks Hall Syleham.'[18] The significance of 'no cows' is difficult to fathom – no milking? That is about all we know about this young woman.

Within two years Susan was pregnant with their first child. She went home to her mother's to have the baby in late December 1876 and never returned, dying in the postnatal period on 7 January 1877, leaving her infant son Percy James Read to be brought up by his father.[19] We can only imagine the tragedy this was for James. He never remarried and he seems to have thrown himself into expanding his farm, growing the business and becoming a pillar of society. He held the same politically Conservative views as his father, being registered in the late 1880s as a member of the Primrose League, an organisation dedicated to principles of conservatism articulated by Disraeli.

By 1881 James had 375 acres at Monks Hall, employing thirteen men and three boys. Young Percy was four years old, looked after by an elderly housekeeper, Mary Ann Galton, and a young maidservant, Eliza Cutting. James kept up what he regarded as his social responsibilities. The *Diss Express* of Friday 30 December 1881 reported on his ' Seasonable Benevolence': 'During the past week the labourers working at Monks' Hall, the widows of the village, and several other persons were presented (by James Read, Esq.) with gifts of meat, rabbits, Christmas fruit, tea, and sugar. The recipients wish to thank that gentleman for his kindness.'

James also served on the Board of Guardians of the Hoxne Poor Law Union, an organisation that had a good reputation on the governing national Poor Law Board for efficient administration and fair dealing.[20] Hoxne closed its own workhouse early and sent any needy paupers to the Eye workhouse that later became Hartismere Hospital; it was thought to be a decent place. By the late 19th century, workhouses were full of dependent elderly people without family help, mentally disabled children and adults and the chronically sick. The Guardians were unpaid volunteers, although many tradesmen Guardians hoped to get local contracts to supply the union. There would have been few benefits for James except perhaps the opportunity to recruit apprentices from among young people in the House. Like many men he probably did it because he felt it was his duty to the community.

But Monks Hall must have been a rather dour place for young Percy to grow up and that maybe one reason why when he became an adult he decided to move away. One sad event at Monks Hall, the suicide of a young servant girl Alice Dade, was explored in great detail in the local press. The Coroner's Inquest was held at Monks Hall on 9 November 1892.

SAD SUICIDE AT SYLEHAM[21]

On Wednesday morning Mr. Coroner Chasten held an inquiry at Monks Hall, Syleham, into the circumstances attending the death of Alice Dade, domestic servant, aged 28 years, whose body was recovered from the River Waveney on Monday last. The first witness was John Dade, agricultural labourer, living at Syleham, who said the deceased, who was his daughter, had acted as his housekeeper for several years. About a month ago, as a consequence of his marrying again, she had entered the service of Mr. James Read of Monks Hall, Syleham.

The witness had said nothing to the deceased about his proposed marriage and believed her first knowledge of it was from the publication of the banns. Witness said he had never known his daughter to be strange in her manner, or thought her to be other than right in her mind and responsible for her actions. He had never heard her threaten to commit suicide, and had last seen her alive in the back kitchen at Monks Hall at 4 p.m. last Saturday. The deceased then seemed in her usual health and spirits. In consequence of what afterwards came to his knowledge, the witness assisted in dragging the River Waveney on Sunday last. At about 10.30 in the morning he saw her body recovered from the water. She was fully dressed. Witness believed she threw herself into the river. It might have been because she was upset about his marriage. He believed she was well treated at Monks Hall.

Rosa Dade, sister-in-law of the deceased, deposed that deceased had told her that her father ought to have made known to her his intended marriage, as then she would have known what to do. She further assured witness that she need not be surprised if she drowned herself. Leonard Hood, agricultural labourer, said he last saw deceased, whom knew well, at seven o'clock on Saturday evening last in the kitchen at Monks Hall. She seemed in her usual health and spirits. Sunday morning, in consequence of being told she was missing, he looked for the footprints of her shoes, and found they led from Monks Hall gate, across the marshes, through water about a foot deep, to the river, a distance of 200 yards.

Mrs Gorton, housekeeper at Monks Hall, said that she had no complaint to make against deceased. The latter was dreadfully upset about her father. In summing up the coroner remarked that it would have been better if deceased's father had been more kind and considerate to the deceased, and had intimated personally to her his intended marriage. The jury returned a verdict of Suicide, while the jury returned their thanks to Mr. Read for placing a room at Monks Hall at their disposal for the inquiry.

Poor Alice Dade, why had her father not told her of his plans to marry? Why was she so despairing? Poor Percy was just fifteen when this tragedy occurred at his home.

The last Reads at Monks Hall

James Read died on 13 April 1894, aged 65, leaving his estate not to his young son Percy James Read but apparently to his older brother Thomas Cracknell Read in Chediston. His executors were his solicitor and his siblings Thomas Cracknell Read and Mary Buttram, who was by then widowed and living with brother Thomas. Was there a rift between James and his son? It seems more likely that the money to buy the Monks Hall estate had originally come from Thomas. When Thomas Read died in 1912 he left £8000, a tidy sum worth about half a million pounds today. Percy was an executor and probably a beneficiary.

The entire Monks Hall estate was advertised for let on 28 November 1894.[22] It included Monks Hall farm but also Gate House Farm and possibly Church Farm, Syleham, occupied until then by various Read relatives.

> Three Capital farms, containing together 430 acres, or separately; two farms of 100 acres each and one of 230 acres. The whole of the arable

land is good mixed soil and there is a good proportion of pasture … to each there is a good house and a full complement of buildings. The sporting rights are let with the farms and afford capital sport. Six cottages will also be let in part or together.

In January 1895 the Executors held a sale of all the effects at Monks Hall, ' a tent being provided' for the sale by the auctioneers, Moore, Garrard and Son.[23]

All the well-made household furniture, including mahogany dining, loo and card tables, dining room and fireside chairs, enclosed sideboard, couch, handsome well preserved antique carved oak cabinet and hall chair, pair of plated candelabras, two barometers, butler's tray, carpets, pictures, curtain poles and curtains, handsome half tester and other bedsteads, 4 feather beds, bedding, 4 chest drawers, 4 marble top and other wash tables, washing ware, duchesse dressing table, 3 others, 4 glasses, chairs, set of 4 plated dish covers, dinner, tea, breakfast and dessert services; Bradford's patent mangle and culinary requisites; modern safety bicycle with pneumatic tyres in good order; riding saddle and bridle, about 60 head of poultry.

Probate was granted the following February 1895, the sale having generated £1335 3s. (c. £470,000 in 21st century terms).

Percy seems never to have lived at Monks Hall after his father's death. He first moved up the hill to farm at Gate House Farm, Syleham, which had been farmed by his uncle John and which he shared with his second cousin Ernest Capon Read, a bank clerk, and a housekeeper, Ellen Josling. At the turn of the new century Monks Hall was occupied by George and Eliza Bullingham and their four children and a grandson. The Read family's connection with Monks Hall was almost over but members of the Read family, probably Percy Read, seem to have retained the ownership of the estate until it was finally sold in the 1930s. There are sadly no land registry records to confirm the ownership of Monks Hall between 1895 and 1930s, although we know who the tenants were.

Percy James married Helen Riches from Thrandeston in 1902 and they moved to The Laurels, Hoxne, and although he continued to call himself a 'farmer', he dedicated himself to field sports, featured regularly in local newspapers for his hunting, shooting and fishing successes. He died in 1932 aged fifty-five. Probate on his estate of little more than £1000 was granted to his wife but there were disputes about the land he owned until 1955, when three siblings called Threadkell were granted some land by the probate court. Monks Hall was however sold after Percy's death.

19th century changes to Monks Hall

The Reads built on the back of the house the various accretions that Victorian domestic life required: the extended kitchen, scullery, storage houses and perhaps also the Victorian lean-to greenhouse on the south front that was demolished in the early 20th century. But they did not change the house fundamentally. They may have inserted some of the dormer windows in the north face and certainly put in some of the bedroom fireplaces.

It is not clear when Monks Hall exterior walls were rendered but it may well have been in the 1870s when a fashion for lime or cement rendering may have seemed the right and modern thing to do. It was perhaps one way for James Read to express publicly his new pride in ownership of the old house. We cannot tell whether the render in the period picture is of lime base, which would not have damaged the house, or the less porous cement render, which did tend to trap water and cause damp problems to the underlying building. Fortunately the basic house slumbered underneath this new coat, waiting for 20th century owners to beautify it once again.

Notes
1. Death of James Read of Hoxne, father of James and Alfred Read. *The Suffolk Chronicle or Weekly General Advertiser & County Express*, Saturday 07 July 1832.
2. *The Suffolk Chronicle or Weekly General Advertiser and County Express*, Saturday 22 September 1838.
3. Tithe Commission Apportionment meeting. *Ipswich Journal*, Saturday 16 July 1842.
4. Tithe landowner records held by National Archive for Alfred Read, *Tithe Apportionments*, 1836-1929 [database online]. The Genealogist.co.uk 2017 Original data: "IR29 Tithe Commission and successors: Tithe Apportionments" The National Archives.
5. Elizabeth's death announced in *The Bury and Norwich Post* Wednesday 17 July 1839.
6. Swearing in as Chief Constable Hoxne Hundred reported in *The Bury and*

Norwich Post Wednesday 26 October 1842. June 1838 Alfred Read was appointed as a Trustee of Hoxne Trust Property (note addressed to J. L. Moore Esq.) SRO Ipswich FC82/L/1/5.
7. Philips, D. 2004. 'A "Weak" State? The English State, the Magistracy and the Reform of Policing in the 1830s'. The English Historical Review 119, Issue 483, pp. 873–91.
8. Alfred Read recorded as a member of the Society in 1845, elected 1841. *Journal of the Royal Agricultural Society of England* 6 (London: John Murray).
9. 'Diss and Colchester Railway'. *The Suffolk Chronicle*, Saturday 16 November 1844.
10. Buttram was the main corn supplier to the Union workhouse at Ipswich and was much criticized in the Ipswich press for the poor quality of his provisions.
11. Public Petitions 18–20 February 1846, p. 78. Parliamentary Papers.
12. Representation of East Suffolk. A correspondent of Bell's Messenger states that, whenever an opportunity occurs Alfred Cooper Read Esq of Monks Hall, a staunch protectionist, will offer himself as a candidate in opposition to Lord Rendlesham. *Bury and Norwich Post*, Wednesday 05 November 1851.
13. Syleham Green Inclosure Awards 1854 SRO. FC 84/N011010100002/1. 1851 Enclosure map National Archive PRO MAF 1/641.
14. 1861 census Syleham.
15. Monks Hall sale advertisement *The Ipswich Journal*, 15 September 1865.
16. *Bury and Norwich Post*, 14 March 1871, quoted in 'The Song of the Emigrant Ship' published online by the Foxearth and District Local History Society, http://www.foxearth.org.uk/Emigration2.html#third (accessed 6.3.2013).
17. Report of fire, *Norwich Mercury*, Saturday 19 July 1873.
18. Advert for Cook, *Diss Express* Friday 28 January 1876.
19. Report of James Read of Monks Hall Syleham marriage to Susan Smyth of The Grove Chediston (daughter Wm Smyth) at Chediston, Bury and Norwich Post, Tuesday 28 September 1875.
20. Norfolk Poor Law Unions. Hoxne and Hartismere. http://www.origins.org.uk/genuki/NFK/norfolk/poor/unions/hoxne (accessed 12.4.2018).
21. *Norfolk News*, Saturday 12 November 1892 .
22. To Be Let Monks Hall Estate, Syleham. *East Anglian Daily Times*, Wednesday 28 November 1894.
23. Advertisement for the sale of effects at Monks Hall *East Anglian Daily Times*, Friday 11 January 1895.

13

Bullingham the Bigamist and Other Tenant Farmers, 1895–1935

By the time the Reads left Monks Hall, the house had become a large rather sad-looking house of little distinction, a Sleeping Beauty hiding under the external render, described simply as a 'farmhouse' in trade directories. There were no significant changes to the building after James Read's death and as a consequence of the serious depression in agriculture at the end of the 19th and beginning of the 20th centuries, the tenant farmers who followed him struggled to make a good living. These were men of middling talent doing their best at a time when few landowners were making profits.

The next four tenants to occupy Monks Hall, **George Bullingham** (1839–1915) and his successors, **James Backhouse** (1860–1925), **Henry Redgrave** (1841–1922) and his son **Henry John Redgrave** (to 1935) were traditional yeoman tenant farmers paying rent to their freehold landlord, the last of their kind to live at Monks Hall and the last of that breed of relatively prosperous men who cultivated the land and employed local tradesmen and labourers to help in the task. They would have got their own hands dirty and shown by example how they wanted the work done but they would have employed many men to assist them, both long-term hired men and transient seasonal workers. These men did not aspire to join a higher social class as the Reads did; they were Suffolk farmers pure and simple. As characters they are diverse and some are highly diverting!

George Bullingham (1839–1915) took on the tenancy of Monks Hall estate some time between 1895 and 1898. We know that he was definitely living at

Monks Hall in March 1898 when his son Arthur, an employee butcher, was charged with an accomplice at Wickham Market petty sessions with stealing 19 lbs of beef, the property of his employer, who had suspected he was stealing for some time.[1] It was a first offence, his previous employer had given him a good character reference, and his father 'George Bullingham of Monks Hall Syleham' was asked to supervise him more closely. Arthur pleaded guilty, but was nevertheless jailed with a month's hard labour.

It was not the first or last time that members of the Bullingham family brushed with the law and George and his family were regularly featured in local newspapers throughout the late 19th and early 20th centuries, to the great good fortune of this local historian.

George and his twin brother Robert were born on 15 December 1839 in Mellis, Suffolk; their father, John, was twenty-nine, and their mother, Maria, was twenty-seven. John was a cattle dealer in Earlsford Road, Mellis, but also a butcher. And it was as a butcher that George first set up business in Yaxley in his early twenties, with his wife Maria Miller, who was just seventeen when they married in 1859. And that was when things started to go wrong. Maria ran off with another local youth in Yaxley, Lewis Bond, whose father had recently died. George found new work at Stradbroke but Maria did not go with him. Her new relationship with Bond did not last and Maria disappeared, leaving George wife-less, with no idea where she was. So, as often happened in the 19th century George didn't set about finding her; what was the point when they couldn't afford a divorce? He moved again for work, to Thorndon, where he began dealing in cattle. He met a girl called Eliza Sharman and got married again, in 1864. The problem was that by then Maria had reappeared, having eventually gone home to live with her parents in Thornham Parva. When she heard about George's new marriage she complained about it, leading to his arrest and a magistrates' court case. The case, which appeared in several local newspapers, caused considerable mirth in the court and the assize chairman's response was admirably robust.

> DOUBLE BIGAMY.[2]
>
> George Bullingham (on bail), was charged with bigamy at Stradbroke, on the 1st December, 1864. Mr. Cherry appeared for the prosecution, and Mr. Metcalfe for the defence. Abraham Brookes, parish clerk, Yaxley, produced a certificate of marriage between prisoner and Maria Miller, aged 15 [*in fact she was 17*], on September 12, 1859. He was present at the marriage. Prisoner was that man. Thomas Thurston,

registrar of marriages for the Hoxne district, produced the register of marriage at the register office, on the 1st December, 1864, of prisoner, in the name of "Bollingham," to Eliza Sharman. [*It still appears in the register as Bollingham. EM.*] Cross-examined: Thurston said he should not like to swear prisoner was the man, but he believed he was. Witness married them, the superintendent being present.

John Miller said:

"I live at Thornham, and Emma [*misreport, name should read Maria*] Bullingham, wife of the prisoner, is my daughter. I have seen her within the last six months."

Cross-examined: "I don't know where she is now. She was in Little Thornham when I saw her. She lived with me sometimes. I don't know where she lived when not with me. I don't know that she lived with a man named Lewis Bond, at Yaxley. I know nothing about it."

Mr. Metcalfe : "Why, did not the clergyman turn Bond out of his house ?

"—I don't know."

"Did you know of your daughter living with another man P—?"

"With her husband."

"But with another man ?—

"I don't know."

"Did you not tell the magistrates she lived with Lewis Bond ?"

"It is unbeknown to me if I did." [Laughter in court.]

"Don't you know she is married again ?"

His Lordship : "double bigamy, then. Don't you know she is married again, and is now living in London ?"

"—I don't know and I have a clear conscience."

"Don't you know she is married ?"

"—All I know is she married the prisoner. I only knew from prisoner and my daughter that they had separated. I don't know an agreement was drawn up."

Witness Emma Bullingham: "I am sister of prisoner. I was present at Stradbroke when he was married to Eliza Sharman. I don't know where his first wife is. They separated when living at Stowmarket. They separated three or four years after their marriage."

Cross-examined: "I heard that his first wife associated with other men; but I don't know that that was the reason they parted. I saw her when she was living with Bond at Yaxley. It caused great scandal at Yaxley, and the clergyman turned Bond out of the house."

Re-examined : "I don't know that she was living with Bond other than as a servant; but it was the common talk that she lived with him as his wife." Inspector Edwards: "I took prisoner into custody. I told him the charge, and he said, I did not think of the consequences at the time, or I should not have done it, but her (Eliza's) friends are very respectable, and did not like my living with her without my marrying her."

Cross-examined: "The first wife set this prosecution going, and her father is prosecuting. The last time I saw her was at the commitment. I now know she has married a second time, and I hold a warrant for her apprehension."

Mr. Metcalfe said it was singular fact that the prisoner married the second time on the 1st of December, 1864, and his first wife also married another husband on the 26th of the same month, and having married herself a second time she gets a warrant against prisoner for doing the same. [Laughter in court.]

Eliza Sharman: "I married the prisoner. He acquainted me with his first marriage, and told me he was separated from his first wife. I had no money. He has treated me well. I don't prosecute (she said with emphasis)."

Mr. Metcalfe said of course he could not contest the second marriage.

His Lordship said no, he could not. Generally in such cases the first wife was aggrieved, but in this case A had but little ground of complaint, and the wife did not complain at all. The prisoner might sit down, and he would consider the case.

His Lordship, in passing sentence at the termination of the Assize, said he "thought that under the circumstances justice would be done by sentencing the prisoner to a day's imprisonment."

George got off lightly and the marriage to Eliza remains on the register to this day. His children were registered as legitimate and everyone, save Maria perhaps, was perfectly happy with the outcome. George and Eliza proceeded to produce a large family; by the census of 1871 they had four children, by 1881, ten.

Maria did not remain with her second husband … and indeed I cannot find the alleged second marriage in the records but by 1871 she was living back at home in Thornham Parva with her parents, working as a 'taylores' under her maiden name.

Bigamy was of course as illegal in the 19th century as now. However, in an era when there was no divorce except for the privileged wealthy few, and it was far easier than now to remain undetected by the wider community when moving district and setting up a new home, many couples entered bigamous unions.[3] Most communities accepted these unions if they followed certain norms. The bigamist had to have a good reason to have left his or her spouse, had to have been honest with the second spouse, and had to be able to support multiple families. Within these parameters, neighbours and friends accepted illegal marriages, following in a long tradition of self-marriage and self-divorce. In fact, by the end of the century, judges followed community standards in their sentencing and often handed out nominal punishment to both male and female bigamists. In the 1880s and 1890s, law enforcement officials were wary of bringing bigamy charges because pressure from the public had so compromised prosecutions. It seems in George's case that he and Eliza did their best to make their marriage conform to society's expectations and the world was sympathetic.

Bullingham's Other Troubles

Shortly after this bigamy case, George decided to try his hand at managing a pub but he was refused an innkeeper's licence, presumably on the grounds of his character although no reason is given in the Hartismere petty sessions report.[4] If bigamy had been George Bullingham's only brush with the law we might have thought that he could still have been a good tenant farmer but several incidents in the last decade of the century suggest that George was an impulsive, heavy-drinking and larger-than-life character with little regard for his animals, not perhaps an ideal tenant.

In December 1875, Bullingham was prosecuted for driving twenty-two bullocks onto the highway at Dennington, when they were suffering from lameness as a result of foot and mouth disease, during an outbreak that had affected 157 cattle, sheep and pigs in the district that week.[5] He claimed he had bought them in good faith and believed they were recovering. After first pleading not guilty he changed his plea to guilty 'in order to be done with the case quickly'. He was fined £5 and costs of 10s. 6d. The vet who examined the animals found them lame, suffering and in poor shape, not a great testament to George's care of his stock.

George's cavalier approach to legal constraints put on farmers when an epidemic was in progress were evident six years later when he was prosecuted for allowing his son to drive a steer and a bullock on a main road at Laxfield without the necessary licence.[6] In fact it turned out he had obtained a licence under the Contagious Diseases Act from James Read, who was locally responsible but George had omitted to give the piece of paper to his son. The magistrate dismissed the case but berated his carelessness.

At some point before the 1881 census George and Eliza and six of their children moved into Church Farm, Syleham, the next door farm to the east of Monks Hall, where George was farming sixty-six acres, employing four men and a boy and dealing in cattle. In 1884, he and a bricklayer from Hoxne, Walter Huggins, were charged with assaulting George Pretty, another bricklayer from Scole, during an argument in Hoxne.[7] It has the hallmarks of a drunken brawl. Both defendants were found guilty and fined £5 each plus costs.

Only a month later, in May 1884 a catastrophic fire devastated the Church Farm buildings, destroying outhouses, where the fire first started before spreading rapidly to the farmhouse, only one small outhouse remaining.[8] The Brockdish fire engine was sent for but was totally inadequate to put out the fire. The family managed to save a good deal of household furniture but George lost most of his farming implements and a good deal of hay and straw. 'Since his occupancy Mr Bullingham has spent a good deal on improving the place and although it was partially insured he will incur heavy losses'. It was the kind of catastrophe that would distress any man. George probably relied heavily on his cattle dealing during these years. For a while he moved to Hoxne, presumably renting somewhere while his home was rebuilt. He did eventually build a new house for Church Farm, a solid brick home that still stands.

George was a character though, a big man weighing 17–18 stones. In 1895, probably the outcome of another pub visit, to the Railway Tavern in Harleston, he made a wager with a fellow drinker, who claimed that George was in no shape to run two miles in half an hour.[9] George boasted that of course he could and a crowd duly assembled to watch him do it. It was good cover for the local press on Christmas Day. He arrived attired in 'an appropriate outfit' and the run was well advertised. George did indeed run two miles in several minutes short of a half hour, rather to everyone's surprise and no doubt, delight.

George could not have been the ideal tenant. By the time he moved into Monks Hall, some time before 1898, Read must have known George well or at least by reputation. He was the nearest available person geographically able to take on the tenancy and perhaps that was the reason he was appointed. He did not give up Church Farm when he added the Monks Hall estate to his responsibilities and eventually retired there. The Bullinghams were at Monks Hall for about five or six years, years not without incident.

There were good times: George won first prize for a hackney mare called Polly at Eye Colt Show in July 1898.[10] But there were also bad times; 1898 was the year son Arthur was convicted of stealing. Then in 1899, there was another serious fire, started it seems by George's grandson, named in the paper as 'Reginald Cranford' but actually named Cranfield.[11] When two serious fires devastate the property of one person, one might suspect arson-induced insurance claims – these were common at this time – but genuine accidental fires were also common, especially in haystacks. George was insured although his neighbour Mr Colman, whose straw elevator and stacks were destroyed, was not.

George Bullingham retires

In 1905 George Bullingham placed an advertisement for a sale on 4 October of 'all the live and dead stock' at Monks Hall Syleham as 'Mr Bullingham is retiring from farming'.[12] Whether he changed his mind, or the sale went ahead and the proceeds were insufficient is difficult to fathom but a year later he was still farming at Monks Hall. In February 1906 another advertisement appeared in the Diss Express.[13]

> WANTED before next Michaelmas, House and Stabling, with about 400–500 acres Shooting.— Apply Monk's Hall, Syleham.

This rather implies that the lease was coming to an end and that George was looking for a new farm in the locality … or was this advert placed just to convince the owner he intended to leave? George sold '280 Black-faced Lambs and Ewes' in June 1906[14] and then George and Eliza gave their usual Harvest Home supper in Syleham Schoolroom in September 1906:

> The evening was spent in toast, song, and dancing. Mr. G. Bullingham presided, Mr. A. H. Bush, of Needham Mill, being in the vice-chair. Songs were sung by Messrs. Bullingham, Thrower, Miles, and Bush, while Mrs. Cranfield [George's daughter] also contributed two capital songs. The toast of the evening was The Host and his family.[15]

Another advert appeared for a sale of live and dead stock in early October the same year, again 'because Mr Bullingham was retiring from farming' and it seems on this occasion he did give up the tenancy of Monks Hall and retreated to Church Farm.[16]

A later incident at Church Farm in 1913 suggests that George's propensity to get into trouble continued unabated. Harry Revill, a labourer from Syleham, was summoned for assaulting George Bullingham, 'dealer', and his daughter Agnes Bullingham.[17] On 8 February, about 10.45 p.m., according to George, Revill came to his house with a gun in his hand, 'which he delivered up to his wife (Mrs Bullingham) when requested'. Revill followed him about the room. Bullingham went into the back scullery and shut the door, but then 'Revill burst the door open and then struck him on the cheek, rendering him unconscious'. However, George 'got away and went into the parlour, where his wife had placed the gun'. Revill also burst this door open. 'In self-defence George took the gun and struck defendant'. Revill's story was very different: he had gone to the house, knocked at the door and was invited in, where he sat talking with Mrs Bullingham and her two daughters. George was not there at first but about ten minutes afterwards he came in [straight from the pub perhaps?] and struck Revill with the gun without saying a word. Agnes Bullingham had yet another story; she said Revill had struck her in the eye, blacking it, and her sister found her unconscious and bleeding at the ear.

Perhaps not surprisingly, the magistrate did not believe George's story and dismissed the first case, George having to pay the costs of 12s. In the second case, that of Agnes, Revill was found guilty and fined 2s. 6d., and costs, 8s. 6d. Clearly the magistrate thought the blame for this unseemly brawl was evenly divided.

George Bullingham died on 19 March 1915, aged seventy-seven.[18] He was buried at Hoxne. George's devoted, long-suffering Eliza lived on until 1926 when she died of a stroke aged eighty-one.[19]

James and Harriet Backhouse, Monks Hall tenants c. 1908–1909

James Backhouse was a short-lived tenant at Monks Hall but he is important because for the first time in this long story, we can put a face to a name! Both James Backhouse and his wife Harriet have photos posted by descendants on the ancestry.co.uk website.

James came from a farming family: his father Philemon Backhouse and his mother Sarah, nee Durrant, farmed at Bull's Hall, Knodishall, Suffolk, although James was born in Theberton in 1860.[20] On reaching adulthood, James soon established himself as a tenant farmer in Hazlewood, Plomesgate, Suffolk and was living 'in the farmhouse by the side of the turnpike' for the next thirteen years or so. In October 1881 James married a local girl, Harriet Merrells, from another farming family at 'the Sizewell Gap, Leiston' and they stayed at Hazlewood with their growing family of three daughters, Amy, Ethel and Mabel, until October 1893, comfortably off, with a live-in servant girl.

James was involved in an unsavoury court case in 1883 when a labourer, Edgar Morley, was summoned by William Scarlett, the Hazlewood estate gamekeeper, for having, 'knowingly and wilfully placed upon the ground in certain fields upon the farm occupied by James Backhouse, certain meal steeped or dipped in poison called arsenic which had been mixed, thereby to render such meal poisonous, and calculated to destroy life.'[21]

Harriet Merrells.

Courtesy Tim Evans.

The prosecution was brought on behalf of Colonel Thellusson, the person who held the shooting rights over the land. The magistrates however did not consider that it had been proved that Morley placed the poisoned grain on the farm, so the summons was dismissed. The magistrates then charged James Backhouse, with 'having placed, or caused to be placed, upon the farm in his occupation, certain meal steeped in poison, with intent to destroy life.' The magistrates said that it was clear that poison had been laid upon the ground, but there was no evidence to connect the gamekeeper Scarlett with laying the poison. There was 'a second information' against Backhouse for having placed, or caused to be placed, poisoned grain upon the land with intent to destroy game. Whether it was

James Backhouse with an unidentified woman (a daughter?).

Courtesy Tim Evans.

Scarlett, Morley or Thellusson who accused Backhouse we do not know but after some consideration, the magistrates dismissed their own case. This odd turn of events ended by the chairman informing James that there was 'no reflection whatever upon his character'. Each party was ordered to pay their own costs. Thellusson knew that it must have been James or Morley who had done the deed but could pin the blame on neither. We shall never know who was responsible, nor why it was done. James may have resented the aristocratic Thellusson's shooting rights over the land he was tenanting but we cannot know for sure.

James himself was not an especially forgiving character. In 1887 three farm labourers from Aldringham all pleaded guilty and were fined 10s. each [about £30 today] for having stolen apples to the value of one shilling from James Backhouse's garden at Hazlewood.[22] One shilling was worth about £2.99; was it worth prosecuting? That's one August scrumping outing the three must have regretted.

James was a staunch member of the Leiston Conservative Club, but his real enthusiasm was sheep, like his father before him, and by 1890 he was active in the Suffolk Sheep Society, an interest he pursued vigorously throughout his career. He bred Southdown sheep, one of the oldest breeds of English sheep, and had a substantial registered flock in the 1890s.[23]

The family remained at Hazlewood until October 1893 when James acquired a much larger and better tenancy on Sir Thomas Gooch's vast Benacre estate at North Hall, Wrentham St Nicholas. We know the exact date of the move because the farmer who was to have moved into Hazlewood committed suicide the same day.[24] There were a dozen or more farms on the Benacre estate, which Sir Thomas ran in traditional patriarchal style, doling out modest prizes at the annual tenants' dinner for well kept farms. In 1904 James was the beneficiary of a prize of £4, which does not sound a great deal but had a purchasing power of about £200 today.[25]

James and Harriet stayed at North Hall, Wrentham, until 1908. He was there for the census in 1901 with his wife and two of their daughters and was still living there in 1906 when he brought a crown court prosecution against a dealer in Shadingfield for the £8 10s. that he was owed for turkeys.[26] But within two years he and Harriet had moved into Monks Hall as the next tenants. When exactly this occurred is not known but in September 1908 he placed an advert for 'a second horseman' at Syleham, quite a senior position in the agricultural employment heirarchy, offering a cottage and opportunities of employment for a son as a ploughman too.[27]

Why did James want to move to Monks Hall? It was a serious step up in size of tenancy and a much larger house. Perhaps at the age of forty-eight he felt this was the right time for a final move to stretch his farming ambitions. Certainly he continued to breed and sell his precious Southdown sheep and it is his advertisements for these sales that list him as living at Monks Hall. Like most of the tenants at Monks Hall he entered into local farming community life. In 1909 he and his neighbour William Groom, the tenant at Wingfield Castle Farm, organised a 'drawing match', horses and ploughs being supplied by the two of them.[28] But later the same year a new tenant, Henry Redgrave, appears in the records and the Backhouses had moved away from Monks Hall.

The 1911 census finds the Backhouses at a house in Weybread; he is recorded still as a farmer but it is not clear if he was working nearby. Was the larger Syleham estate too much for James, was he unwell? Or was there some other reason for surrendering the tenancy only a year or so after he had taken it? Clearly there is something of a mystery here and it may not be possible to establish the reason for his retirement. In the period between 1900 and the outbreak of war in 1914 farm incomes stagnated. In much of Britain there was an agricultural recession. It may be that James Backhouse realised early on in his tenancy that the estate had become unprofitable and wanted to withdraw as soon as he could. James lived on at Weybread, then in Chediston, until he died on 23rd March 1925, leaving £238 10s. 11d. to his widow Harriet, who died many years later.

Farming in Suffolk at the end of the 19th century

The 'golden age of high farming' in Suffolk lasted from the late 1840s for about forty years up to the late 1870s, when cheap imports of cereals from North America and Russia began to displace English wheat in bread-making.[29] In much of Suffolk, where good soil enabled farmers to carry the cost of the fall in wheat prices, agricultural wages remained stable and farmers could turn to other crops and to dairying. Some of the worst land, like the sandy coastal areas of Suffolk and some marshy, fen areas, went out of cultivation but in north Suffolk farmers and landlords adapted to the new imperative to find profitable activities, especially dairying and chicken and egg production. In 1872 the UK had 24 million acres under crops, or 51 per cent of the cultivated area. By 1913 this had shrunk by 10 per cent, leaving Britain heavily reliant on imports. At the outbreak of the Great War 80 per cent of wheat and 40 per cent of meat were imported. James Backhouse's beloved sheep would probably have been unprofitable in 1908–9.

Henry Redgrave (1843–1922), who followed James Backhouse, farmed at Monks Hall between 1909 and 1922. One of the difficulties in being clear about the dates of these tenancies is that no contracts survive; the deeds do not reveal the names of tenants and we are dependant on trade directories, censuses and newspaper reports from the British National Newspaper Archives at the British Library.

Both Henry and his son were called Harry in some reports so they were probably called that by family and friends. Harry Snr was already in his late sixties when he took on the Monks Hall tenancy; he was another highly experienced tenant farmer who lived all his life around Suffolk. Harry's wife died in 1907 and two of his three children had died in the years just before that. His one surviving son, Henry John Redgrave, remained unmarried and at the age of thirty-eight accompanied his father to help run Monks Hall farm. It was difficult to find farm tenants in these first years of the 20th century, but perhaps Harry needed to do something, even if not very profitable, to keep himself occupied in widowhood. Many vigorous men just kept working as long as they could. There were no state pensions for men under seventy until 1925. In the earlier years before the turn of the century, successful tenant farmers were able to save a little and often enough to invest in smallholdings and properties of their own but in the early 20th century there were few profits to be made, farming was a tough job with few long-term rewards.

Henry Redgrave Snr was born in Frostenden, Suffolk in 1843, to an agricultural labouring family living on Clay Common.[30] By 1861 his father had died and Henry at nineteen was himself working as a farm labourer, living with his widowed mother Judith, older sister Emily and her son Joseph. Over the next ten years he must have proved to be a competent farmer, for in the census in 1871 he had been promoted to farm bailiff on Edward Hurren's estate at Kelsale. He had married Anna Thurston from Hedenham at Loddon parish church in 1864 and by 1871 there were three children, Rosa (6), James (4) and Henry James (2).

Two years later in 1873 the family were on the move, to a new bailiff position on a farm near Laxfield, Button's Farm in Brundish. Moving day was almost catastrophic.[31] The local Halesworth Advertiser reported that

> On Tuesday last Henry Redgrave, late farm bailiff at Mr. Edward

Hurren's, of Kelsale, was removing to another situation at Laxfield, and while passing through the village with three horses and a waggon containing a load of furniture, stopped for some purpose, when the forehorse turned suddenly round and the waggon was completely upset, causing a terrible smash. The fore wheels and shafts were separated from the body of the waggon and dragged some considerable distance. Redgrave's wife and three small children were on top of the furniture and fell among the latter; but fortunately none of them were hurt with the exception of a few bruises. Another waggon was kindly lent by Mr. Asker, and with the assistance of several people on the spot, the furniture was quickly loaded up; but it had of course been seriously damaged, as well as getting very wet. Another man was with Redgrave in charge of the horses and waggon at the time, but no blame apparently can be attached to either of them.

The two eldest of Henry and Anna's children, James aged 10 and Rosa, only 5, died in 1877 and 1880. The loss of two children who had survived early infancy was becoming more unusual in the late 19th century and it must have been a sad blow for the Redgraves. They still had Harry and he remained single all his life, living with his parents until they died.

By 1891 Henry, Anna and Harry Jnr had moved again, to become farming tenants at Clubbs Farm, Denham Road, Hoxne, a property that survives today. At fifty-one years old, Henry could afford men to help him and also employed a servant girl Eliza. But Henry and Anna were using borrowed furniture and using books and other household goods lent or given to them by Henry Mutimer, a farmer who lived in nearby Denham and probably an old friend.[32] One wonders if the furniture lost in the accident twenty years earlier had ever been replaced. In 1893 Mutimer decided he wanted his furniture back but the Redgraves demurred. There followed an extraordinary court case: Mutimer brought an 'action in detinue' to recover possession of furniture, books and other effects to the value of £43, a substantial sum worth about £3,800 today.[33] Redgrave counterclaimed, saying the stuff had been deposited with him for safe keeping and he should be charging Mutimer rent for looking after the goods of £7 16s., and warehousing charges for two years. It was a long hearing, the magistrate was puzzled as to what exactly had happened and both parties were tight lipped. The outcome was that £3 was allowed Henry Redgrave for storing the goods and when that was paid over from Mutimer to Redgrave, all the furniture had to be returned to Mutimer. As so often with these curious cases, it is impossible to determine who exactly did what and why but Mutimer obviously thought Redgrave was taking advantage of his generosity; Redgrave disagreed. So for the second time the Redgraves needed a new set of furniture!

Henry's wife Anna died in 1907, Henry and his son were living alone together. Perhaps it was to escape painful memories at Clubbs Farm that early in 1909 the Redgraves took on the vacant tenancy at Monks Hall, after James and Harriet Backhouse moved out. The 1911 census at Monks Hall also includes a twenty-year-old single housekeeper called Hettie Mutimer. Mutimer is an unusual name but not uncommon in Norfolk and Suffolk so there may be no connection between Hettie and the Henry Mutimer of the furniture tussle but one cannot help but wonder if there was more to that case than meets the eye.

The First World War

The Redgraves were farming at Monks Hall all through the Great War. Farming was a bleak prospect for many landlords and tenant farmers in the first years of the 20th century but the outlook changed dramatically with the outbreak of war in 1914. The tension between the need to expand production of food and yet to raise a volunteer army of young men for the front was most keenly felt in the countryside. East Anglian landowners encouraged their workers to join up to what was believed at the outset to likely be a short-term loss to the land.

The government also believed at the beginning of the war that overseas imports of food would be uninterrupted. Lord Lucas, the President of the Board of Agriculture, told the House of Lords on 4 August 1914 that 'there was no occasion whatever for public alarm over food supplies'.[34] This turned out to be true at first; in 1914 and 1915 the yield of cereals was increased and prices were buoyant, but the increased productivity was gained by omitting the traditional root crop break in the old rotation system, impoverishing crop yields. Then in 1916 imports from North America were hit by poor harvests and the closure of the Dardanelles halted imports from the Black Sea area. By 1916–7 the German U-boat campaign was effectively interrupting supplies.

The need for government intervention in food production policy was clear and state support was provided first in incentives to plough up grassland and plant cereals and then to guarantee the prices of wheat and oats. The Corn Production Act of 1917 was successful in maintaining bread supplies, or was considered to be then, and an Agricultural Act also established a minimum wage for farm workers and local agricultural boards to set fair wages. The Suffolk County Agricultural Wages Board was meant to determine wages locally but was slow in making up its mind, and eventually a national minimum wage of 25s. a week was set by central government. This represented a substantial increase for farm workers but was affordable for farmers as a result of the new guaranteed prices the government was funding. The Corn Production and Agricultural Acts created the culture of subsidised farming which we still have today with all its challenges, resentments and successes.

During the war the Redgraves would have done all right financially although recruiting labourers was tricky. Farmers themselves were exempt from enlistment. Retired men, young boys and women were the only people available as the village young men volunteered or later were conscripted. The impact of women on agriculture was surprisingly small. There was an increase nationally of only 9,000 women who took up farm work; there were too many better paid jobs in munitions factories and other work, even around north Suffolk. So instead, boys over twelve years old were taken out of school by means of an official School Exemption Certificate.[35] A whole generation of young men received minimal education as a result. The local flax crop had a brief resurrection during the war because it was needed for uniforms.

The war's main impact of course was the loss of ten young men from the village who never returned, recorded on the war memorial in the church. It is difficult to trace some of these lost men's connections in the village; some may have been employed at the drabbet mill in Syleham. One of those who died was George Cranfield, a grandson of George Bullingham.

Sale of Monks Hall estate 1920

The subsidised farming system established in the war continued afterwards, although canny landowners must have wondered for how long these halcyon days would last. Many farms in England were sold to tenants after the war. The increase in Schedule tax on income from land was at a historically high level, which encouraged landowners to convert a highly taxed income into zero-tax capital gain. Nearly a quarter of agricultural land in England was sold by the end of 1922.

So it is not surprising that the landlord Read decided to sell his extensive Syleham and Hoxne estates, who by 1922 included three major farms – Gate

House Farm, Park Farm and Monks Hall, a total of 443 acres. An advert appeared in the *Framlingham News* in April 1920.[36]

> By Auction for sale by Moore Garrard and Sons.
>
> SYLEHAM. THE GATE HOUSE FARM, MONKS HALL, and PARKES FARM, containing about 443 acres.

Gate House Farm and Park Farm were sold, but Monks Hall was not. A further advert appeared in July the same year.[37]

> RESIDENTIAL ESTATE of about 252 a. 1r. 36p. of good corn growing Arable Lands, Low Meadows and old Pastures, known as MONKS' HALL, with fine old Residence, ample ranges of Home and Off Premises, and Three Cottages, together with 6 acres of Plantations, as in the occupation of Messrs. Redgrave. Particulars, with Conditions of Sale, may be obtained of Messrs. Foyer, White, Borrett and Black, Solicitors, 26, Essex Street, Strand, London, W.C.2; or of the Auctioneers, Hoxne and Eye.

Neighbours were selling up farms too. Syleham Manor farm owned by Jethro Elsey was advertised in September that year. The Syleham Hall estate of 301 acres with hall, six cottages and other property was sold with three of the estate's tenanted farms.[38] Landlords wanted to get out as fast as possible.

But who, if anyone, bought Monks Hall estate is not clear. There was no report in local newspapers but that is not unusual. There is no record in the Land Registry of a change of owner at this time. The Redgraves stayed on as tenants. It is possible that there was no change of freehold until fifteen years later, simply because there was no available buyer. Henry Redgrave Snr died two years later in 1922 but his son continued on the farm alone.

Henry John Redgrave 1869–1941

Harry Jnr lived at Monks Hall until he retired in 1935, when he was 'declining farming, on account of the holding having been sold.'[39] The sale included

> a bay gelding, 6 years old 49gns; a chestnut gelding 42 gns, two others 30 gns each, six forward North Country steers £14 7s 6d per head; another six at £12 10s, sows and pigs from £8 to £12 10s; sows from £5 10s – to £8 and stores up to 28s 6d each. Among the dead stock, there were 'Scotch

carts' to £20, road waggons to £18 10s, ploughs £3 and £3 15s; 'D.F.' plough £45-; frame horse hoe £6 10s -; corn and seed drill £15 1s 0d; iron hurdles to 16s a piece ; 21-h.p. oil engine and iron saw bench £10 2s 6d, round iron pig troughs made from £11 to £1 each, iron watercart on wheels, £6: stack tilt £4.

It is difficult to know whether Harry was a good farmer. In 1932 he was prosecuted for 'failing to isolate pigs' during an outbreak of swine fever.[40] More specifically he had moved one boar from Harleston market to Monks Hall and then put it in a field with other pigs. He claimed he had kept the boar separately for 8 days but the pen was so small, 3 yards square, he decided to let the pig out and the local policeman appointed to follow up all pigs sold with a swine licence had arrived after the boar had been released. It emerged in court that Harry did not know the regulations, which had been in place for ten years and in any case were written clearly on the back of every licence. The magistrate was not sympathetic but nevertheless Harry was fined only £2 and ordered to pay just 10d. costs.

After Harry retired he continued to farm at his own smallholding of 22 acres at Low Street, Oakley, and in the last years of his life lived at The Nursery, Langton Green, Eye. He died aged seventy-three in December 1941 and is buried at Hoxne.

The end of the tenant era

The long period of tenancies was coming to an end. The era of the amateur gentleman farmer was beginning in this interwar period. The next owners wanted to live and work at a house that was now being appreciated as a stunningly beautiful medieval house in desperate need of renovation. The sale to the Leader family who were to be so vital to the survival and restoration of Monks Hall was by no means a straightforward conveyance. The next owner, if only for a matter of months, was an ambitious, risk-taking developer with a penchant for medieval timber-framed buildings and a habit of making over optimistic financial commitments. The story of **Richard Horry Winn** and his dealings with Monks Hall reads like fiction … and is coming next.

Notes

1. Petty Sessions Reports. *Ipswich Journal*, Friday 11 March 1898.
2. 'Double Bigamy'. *The Suffolk Chronicle; or Weekly General Advertiser & County Express*, Saturday 28 March 1868.
3. Frost, Ginger, 1997. 'Bigamy and Cohabitation in Victorian England'. *Journal of Family History* 22, pp. 286–306.
4. Hartismere Petty Sessions: Innkeepers' Licences August 23rd. *The Suffolk Chronicle or Weekly General Advertiser and County Express*, Saturday 28 August 1869.
5. *Framlingham Weekly News*, Saturday 18 December 1875.
6. *Framlingham Weekly News*, Saturday 05 February 1881.
7. Stradbroke Petty Sessions. *Framlingham Weekly News*, Saturday 26 April 1884.
8. 'Fire at Syleham'. *Thetford & Watton Times and People's Weekly Journal*, Saturday 31 May 1884.
9. 'Race against time, Harleston'. *Norwich Mercury*, Wednesday 25 December 1895.
10. 'Eye Colt Show prizes', *The Ipswich Journal*, Friday 8 July 1898.
11. Reginald Cranfield was the son of George's daughter Eliza (nee Bullingham) and John Cranfield. *Norfolk News*, Saturday 4 March 1899, and *Evening Star*, Thursday 2 March 1899. Reginald Walter Cranfield became a successful farmer himself, settling in Derbyshire; he died in 1951. There are two Cranfields named on the Syleham War Memorial, Reg and George, but Reg cannot be readily identified with the Cranfields who lived in Syleham. George's grandson Reg Cranfield survived to have a family himself. (Information from Sue Dixon, gt gt granddaughter of George Bullingham.)
12. Advert for sale in *Framlingham Weekly News* Saturday 27 August 1904.
13. Advert for sale in *Diss Express* Friday 2 February 1906.
14. Advert for lambs, *Diss Express* Friday 22 June 1906.
15. 'Syleham Harvest Home'. *Diss Express*, Friday 21 September 1906
16. *Framlingham Weekly News*, Saturday 22 September. "Thursday 4 October 1906 at Monks Hall 9 head horse stock, 20 head Neat Stock, Swine, poultry and dead farm stock by direction of George Bullingham who retires from Farming". George Bullingham appears in Trade Directories for Suffolk at Church Farm Syleham until his death.
17. Stradbroke Petty Sessions. *Diss Express*, Friday 14 March 1913.
18. George Bullingham's funeral. *Diss Express*, Friday 2 April 1915.
19. Eliza (Sharman) Bullingham. Death certificate image on Ancestry co. uk. https://www.ancestry.co.uk/mediaui-viewer/tree/13118647/person/12589559507/media/26ee4090-e58b-468a-833e-123dbb8cb573 (accessed 10.8.2018).
20. Census Knodishall Suffolk 1841.
21. Petty Sessions. *Framlingham Weekly News*, Saturday 19 May 1883.
22. Petty Sessions, *Framlingham Weekly News*, Saturday 20 August 1887.
23. Press reports from 1893 in eastern region newspapers up until *East Anglian Daily Times*, Saturday 13 June 1908, and *East Anglian Daily Times*, Saturday 10 July 1909.
24. Report of suicide. *Norwich Mercury*, Saturday 14 October 1893.
25. Sir Thomas Gooch of Benacre Estates gives prizes to tenants. (£4 to James

Backhouse of North Hall Farm). *Eastern Daily Press*, Wednesday 04 May 1904.
26. Crown Court Reports. *Norfolk Chronicle*, Saturday 13 January 1906.
27. Advert for second horseman. *East Anglian Daily Times*, Friday 18 September 1908.
28. 'A Drawing Match'. *East Anglian Daily Times*, Tuesday 01 June 1909.
29. Perren, R. 1995. *Agriculture in Depression 1870–1940* (Cambridge: Cambridge University Press). Holt, H. M. E., and Kain, R. J. P. 1982. 'Land Use and Farming in Suffolk about 1840', *Proceedings of the Suffolk Institute for Archaeology & History* 35, part 2. Online at http://www.suffolkinstitute.org.uk/online-proceedings-contents (accessed 12.4.2018).
30. The Redgrave family appears as 'Redgraft' in the census of 1851.
31. 'Accident and Narrow Escape'. *The Halesworth Times and East Suffolk Advertiser*, Tuesday 18 March 1873.
32. Court Report, *Norfolk Chronicle*, Saturday 14 January 1893.
33. An action in 'detinue' is to recover the wrongful taking of personal property. It is initiated by an individual who claims to have a greater right to immediate possession than the current possessor of the goods.
34. Hansard 4 August 1914, quoted in Whetham, Edith. 1978. *The Agrarian History of England and Wales. Vol Vlll: 1914-39* (Cambridge: Cambridge University Press), p. 70.
35. Mansfield, Nicholas 1988, 'Land and Labour', in Gliddon, G. (ed.), *Norfolk and Suffolk in the Great War* (Norwich: Gliddon Books), pp. 74–83.
36. Advert for estate sale. *Framlingham Weekly News*, Saturday 17 April 1920.
37. Advert for estate sale. *Framlingham Weekly News*, Saturday 03 July 1920.
38. Sale of Syleham Hall estates, *Yarmouth Independent*, Saturday 17 July 1920. *Framlingham Weekly News*, Saturday 18 September 1920. *Yarmouth Independent*, Saturday 17 July 1920.
39. Sale of Stock. *Diss Express*, Friday 11 October 1935.
40. 'Failing to Isolate Pigs'. *Diss Express*, Friday 04 November 1932.

14

Richard Horry Winn, 1900–1942, owner of Monks Hall 1935–1936

A romantic dreamer, a dedicated house restorer, a scoundrel, an over-ambitious fool with the knack of persuading others he was a well-meaning unfortunate, or a tragic man hounded by his own incompetence? The 1935 purchaser of Monks Hall may have been all of those things. In his short life Richard Horry Winn changed his given names on paper but was called neither of those names by his friends, for whom he was always Mike. He moved many times, making it difficult to track his history, and he and his wife Freda went bankrupt four times. He clearly loved ancient and beautiful houses but had no money to restore them, constantly on the edge of penury, moving swiftly around the country, one suspects escaping creditors. It is unlikely he ever lived at Monks Hall and he was the owner for a relatively short period from 1935 to 1936 but he is part of the house's story, especially as he carried out substantial restoration work on the house and the appearance today owes much to Winn's work.

There are no surviving property conveyance documents or deeds for the sale of Monks Hall in 1935, no newspaper advertisement for a sale either. We know only from newspaper reports that the estate was sold privately by local auctioneers and land agents Moore Garrard, who had an office in Hoxne. The contract of sale to Richard Horry Winn was exchanged on 8 February and completed on 30 April 1935. Harry Redgrave's retirement announcement of a sale of his farming live and dead stock because of a 'change of owner' is one piece of evidence, but definitive evidence comes from the court record of a case of alleged breach of contract brought a year later by Winn against the auctioneer, Arthur Taylor Bland, who worked for Moore Garrard at Hoxne in 1936.[1]

Winn's complex claim, for £40 against Arthur Taylor Bland, auctioneer, at Moore Garrard, 'for alleged breach of contract in connection with the demolition of certain buildings at Monk's Hall, Syleham' was heard at Eye Crown Court in October 1936.[2] Winn gave his address as Manston Hall, Whepstead, Suffolk, a fine timber-framed house with similarities to Monks Hall. His case was that on 8 February 1935, he had entered into a contract 'to purchase certain property known as Monks Hall, Syleham'. Winn wished to do various repairs and alterations on the property before completion, which he was allowed to do under an unusual clause in the contract, and he proceeded to instruct a builder, Mr Limmer of Dickleburgh, to provide an estimate.

Winn also wished to get rid of certain exterior buildings at the property, old cottages, and he thought Arthur Bland 'was a likely person who could help him in this'. Bland agreed to get the demolished buildings taken away, saying the buildings were not worth more than the cost of pulling them down. Winn wanted to get the property renovations finished by 31st March, presumably to facilitate a resale, one suspects because his profit depended on a quick sale to pay off what he had borrowed to purchase the property and carry out some restoration. His urgent need to get a resale was probably the reason he had insisted on the unusual clause in the contract in the first place. But time went on and nothing had been done to the buildings by 30 March, so Winn 'thought he had better make other arrangements'. He therefore asked Limmer to remove the buildings, and Limmer agreed to reduce his estimate for the work on Monks Hall in consideration of being allowed the building.

On 1 April, Winn wrote to Bland, cancelling the authority given to him to demolish the cottages but Bland replied stating that the work of demolition 'was proceeding' and would be finished in a few days; he could not therefore accept the cancellation. Bland further claimed Winn had given him an extension of time over the telephone. Winn on the other hand said that on 13 March he rang up Bland, which to the best of his recollection was the 'only telephone conversation he had with the defendant' and told him to stop the demolition, as Limmer would be doing it. About 27 or 28 March, Winn went to Monk's Hall and found there were no men working there. In consequence of that, he went to see Mr Limmer about taking the buildings. But the work of demolition was started by Bland's men during the first few days of April and Bland had taken away most of the valuable parts of the cottage buildings, including some thousands of tiles, oak boards and roof rafters —in fact everything except the skeleton of the walls.

The arguments about who said and did what and when, and who was at fault, were tossed about in the court for four hours. The county court judge finally decided that Bland should not have continued to authorise demolition work on the cottages after Winn had told him to stop on 1 April, and awarded damages of £40 against Bland. This is the only one of Winn's court cases that he won and if the Eye court judge had known the rest of Winn's story he might not have been so quick to find against Bland. But at least we know when Winn bought the property.

Who was Richard Horry Winn?

Winn died tragically in an air crash in Westmorland in 1942. Quite recently Yorkshire aircraft historians researching the crash site tried but failed to trace his birth in the UK.[3] In fact it has been possible to trace his real name and origins from the unusual name of his wife and his two daughters, who are all now dead. We do know that his wife called him 'Mike'.[4] He was proud of his middle name and corrected an entry in the London Gazette when it was misspelt as 'Harry'.[5]

He was born William Berger Horry Winn into a middle-class family in Fulham, London, in 1900. His father was a 'petroleum merchant', evidently a successful one as the family moved to Hill Top House, Wheathampstead in Hertfordshire, while 'Richard' or 'Mike' was growing up. He later said that he went to school nearby in Harpenden in Hertfordshire. We know little of Winn before his marriage in Dorking, Surrey, in summer 1925 to the unusually named Frieda (later Freda) Mary Phizacklea, born in Harriston near Tamworth, Warwickshire, in 1903. Freda's background was also solidly middle-class. She was away at boarding school at the age of eight in the 1911 census. The name Phizacklea is probably a phonic corruption of the town name of Fazakerley, near Liverpool. The couple was mentioned in the Surrey electoral registers as living at 'Wayside', Reigate, in 1925.

Soon after their marriage, on 28 November 1925, Winn signed up to become a pilot in the early days of the RAF, when he received a short service commission to the rank of 'Pilot Officer on probation'. He was confirmed in the rank of Pilot Officer on 28 May 1926, posted to 9 Squadron at Manston,

Kent, on 9 November 1926, and was promoted to Flying Officer in 1927.[6] By now the couple had a baby daughter, Anne, born in 1926.

In August 1927, he resigned his commission and transferred to the RAF Reserve because 'he was suffering from neurasthenia' in consequence of a near catastrophic experience in March 1927, when he and three others flying an aeroplane over the North Sea beyond the Thames Estuary crashed into the sea and they all hung on to the side of the wreckage for seven hours till they were rescued.[7] The term 'neurasthenia', no longer used, covered a wide range of mental disorders but probably these days we would say he was suffering from PTSD (Post-Traumatic Stress Disorder), which can be chronic and disabling. It certainly explains why Winn, probably unable to work for some time, was so impecunious afterwards, while not entirely explaining his erratic attempts to become a property developer.

By 1931 the couple had another baby daughter, Philippa Jane, and insufficient funds to stay out of debt. His first bankruptcy announcement in the *London Gazette* was recorded in January 1931, stating that he had been living in Shipston-on-Stour, Worcestershire, but at the time of the hearing he was living in Steeple Claydon, Buckinghamshire. Perhaps his bankruptcy accounts for him relinquishing his commission on 10 August 1931 on completion of his period of service in the Reserve.

Bankrupt or not, later in 1931 he appeared in court at Diss, giving his address as Ufford Hall, Fressingfield, a rather grand address for someone with no cash. Ufford Hall is another strikingly beautiful timber-framed medieval house. Winn was charged with obtaining money, £3, under false pretences, from Victor Golding, a baker in Diss.[8] Arrested at Halesworth on 2 November, he was remanded in custody for nine days. 'His mother-in-law offered bail but the Police were not inclined to accept her security' so he 'was held in custody until satisfactory bail was forthcoming'. Winn had asked Golding to exchange a cheque for £3 for cash, which he had done, expecting Winn to return with the cash later the same day when he collected some bread. But Winn arrived without the cash and the cheque bounced. Winn and Freda had closed their joint account in Norwich in June earlier that year.

Police records revealed that Winn had given out other dud cheques, one for £10 to a Mr Walne, a motor engineer of Framlingham, 'returned no account', although the money was paid later in notes. There was another bad cheque presented in Harleston, but no charge was laid in this case.

Winn pleaded guilty and elected to be dealt with summarily. He set out his story of the crash and subsequent breakdown and understandably the magistrate was moved to be sympathetic. Winn said he had been in receipt of approximately £100 year Reserve pay, but this had ceased when he left the Reserve, and from time to time he had been assisted by friends. He was 'in a hard way in September' and 'improperly drew cheques'. Now he was anxious to make a clean breast of the whole matter. He had also given a bad cheque to the Hotel Cavendish (Great Yarmouth?) for £5 and several other misdemeanours were admitted. The magistrate decided against punishment and bound him over to keep the peace for a year.

Between 1931 and the court case surrounding the purchase of Monks Hall in 1935 there are no further mentions of Winn in the local records or news. But afterwards, in September 1938, he pops up in the bankruptcy court again, then living at West Tisted Manor near Winchester, brought to court by a builder and decorator. This manor house was another very ancient moated medieval house that was sadly destroyed in the mid-1950s. It was another ambitious but unsuccessful move and by October 1938 his address was listed as 'unknown'.[9] He and Freda and, by now, four children – Ann, Philippa Jane, Stephen (born 1934) and Nicholas (born 1936) – may have gone to live in the United States, but immigration and passenger lists draw a blank. However there is a record of claims for US social security support for Philippa Jane and Ann Winn, by their mother using her maiden name.[10]

The US record does not reveal where they were living and they cannot have stayed very long as at the outbreak of war the family returned to Britain and Winn volunteered for the Air Transport Auxiliary (ATA). When he applied, the family was living at Knapp Cottage, Corscombe, Dorset, yet another historic building, then on joining the ATA he gave his address as Carleton Hall, Penrith, a beautiful early 18th century house that now serves as HQ for the Cumbrian police. How accurate his claim was is difficult to know. Carleton Hall was partly restored in 1937 but it would have been way beyond the Winn family's means even to be a rental tenant there. Winn may have been involved in the restoration there.

The ATA was a civilian organisation set up in May 1940, headquartered at White Waltham Airfield; it ferried new, repaired and damaged military aircraft between factories, assembly plants, transatlantic delivery points, maintenance units, scrap yards and active service squadrons and airfields. It also flew service personnel on urgent duty from one place to another and performed some air ambulance work. Notably, many of its pilots were women, and from 1943 they received equal pay to their male co-workers, a first for the British government.

Winn returned home to the UK to serve as a pilot at a time when many people were heading in the opposite direction across the Atlantic. It would appear that he flew as a pilot with the ATA until his death in 1942. But while 'Mike' was flying planes, his wife Freda, who was then living in Widworthy Barton, near Honiton, Devon, 'of no occupation', was declared bankrupt on 21st January 1941.[11] It is tempting to wonder if it was Freda's spending that was at the root of their penniless wandering. This was wartime; it was not unusual for a wife and her young children to decamp to the country while their husbands were serving in the war, but it is not clear how she got into such debt.

Mike Winn's plane disappeared on 28 January 1942.[12] In all probability he had collected the aircraft, a Miles Master T8614, from RAF Kinloss on the Moray Firth the day before and had flown to Prestwick where he remained overnight. The plane had just been allotted to No.12 Group HQ (Fighter Command) at RAF Watnall, Nottinghamshire, but this was not a flying unit and it had no airfield, so the intention seems to have been to operate the aircraft out of nearby Hucknall airfield as part of No.12 Group Communications Flight. The following morning, on 28 January 1942, Winn set out from Prestwick heading for England. It is thought he landed at Dumfries to refuel and then set out south again on a course between Dumfries and Catterick. He seems to have flown into bad weather over the Pennines. It was colder than average that month and in the week before this incident there had been both snow and rain. The Met Office's archived weather report suggests that snow was lying at Stainmore and on the hills, and that rain and/or snow may have been exacerbated by low cloud; visibility would therefore have been very poor as he flew the common ATA route across the Pennines, using the Stainmore railway line and the A66 road as navigation aids. The aircraft flew into high ground in the Stainmore area near to Beldoo Hill and disintegrated. Winn was killed in the crash. Because of the time of year, and because the crash site was well out of sight of the road and railway line, nothing was seen of the missing aircraft until 4 April 1942. His body was then recovered and the crash site was cleared. Fragments of the plane have been found recently.

Winn's body was taken to RAF Catterick prior to burial at Maidenhead Cemetery in Berkshire. The RAF Benevolent Fund came to the help of Freda and her four children, providing money for school fees and helping with clothes for the children. The Official Receiver dealing with Freda's bankruptcy acted as helpfully as he could. It transpired that Winn owed £2,349 and Freda owed £80, but consideration was taken of the fact that Richard lost his life in the service of his country. The Official Receiver could have taken the full £2000 from the ATA insurance policy for the creditors, leaving Freda and the four children penniless, but she was allowed to keep £1000 of the insurance for the maintenance and education of the children.[13]

Freda remarried in Bodmin, Cornwall, in 1946, a US Navy Lieutenant from Boston, Massachusetts, called David Lincoln Bateson. He was just twenty-three, she was forty-three. She gave her address as Coombe Mill, St Breward, Bodmin. A year later, they set sail from Southampton for New York, travelling first class on the *SS Washington*. The three younger children went with them but Ann, now 21, did not accompany them, although she later settled in the US.[14]

Poor 'Mike' Winn never did get to restore one of the historic properties he loved so much. He was obviously a complex man, more honoured in death than in his rather convoluted lifetime. He was obliged to sell Monks Hall in 1936 and he did so to the glamorous John and Weeny Leader.

Alterations to Monks Hall 1935–36

Winn made significant alterations to Monks Hall, presumably to help him sell it. We know that he intended to do some building work, first tearing down some old cottages that were on the site, but he seems to have gone much further. Old timber-framed houses were at last beginning to be appreciated and in the mid-1930s there was a boom in the mock-Tudor cottage style for new smaller semis and suburban detached houses. At some point in the first half of the 20th century, Monks Hall lost its surface render that we can see so clearly in the late 19th century illustration, and the beams were exposed to reveal the fine timber frame we see today. It seems unlikely this was carried out by the earlier tenants – they had little incentive to do so – but Winn may have recognised that a well-heeled buyer would be more attracted to the property if it had the desirable exposed beams. He probably dismantled the Victorian lean-to greenhouse too, no doubt in poor repair by then.

The author has concluded that Winn also put in the new 'Tudor'-looking windows with diamond panes to improve the light inside the house. It is easy to see the changes on the north front from the late 19th century rendered building shown on page 164. The photos taken of the house soon after the Leaders moved in show the diamond panes already in place, and by Weeny Leader's account to Andrew Gray, they did not engage an architect or begin their own renovations until the mid-1940s.[15] It is likely that all the smaller windows with diamond leaded glass were inserted by Winn, including the windows to the side of the porch and on the west side of the crosswing. Similar leaded glass was added to the large first-floor porch window. The model for these was probably the fourlight mullion window on the upper story eastern façade in the western crosswing.

Sketch by Andrew Gray of one of the new windows, inserted into an old mullion on the south façade, c 1935.

Notes

1. 'Monks Hall Syleham sale of farming stock by Moore Garrard and Sons, Hoxne'. *Diss Express*, Friday 11 October 1935. 'Damages awarded against Hoxne auctioneer'. *Diss Express*, Friday 30 October 1936.
2. The value today of £40 in 1936 varies between £6,000 and £9,000 but was a significant sum.
3. Yorkshire Aircraft Co. history. Miles Master T8614. http://www.yorkshire-aircraft.co.uk/aircraft/planes/dales/t8614.html (accessed 12.4.2018).
4. England, Andrews Newspaper Index Cards, 1790–1976. Richard Horry Winn 22 April 1942.
5. *London Gazette,* 29 May 1928 p3737, original error made on announcement of appointment as Flying Officer, August 1927.
6. Confirmed as Pilot Officer after probation by Air Ministry. *Western Morning News*, Wednesday 23 June 1926.
7. 'Airmen rescued from Thames. Plane nearly submerged, six hours in face of death.' *Leeds Mercury*, Thursday 24 March 1927, also in *The Scotsman*, Thursday 24 March 1927.
8. 'Fressingfield man charged.' *Diss Express*, Friday 6 November 1931.
9. *London Gazette* bankrupt list. Richard Horry Winn, 14 October 1938.
10. Ancestry.com. US Social Security Applications and Claims Index, 1936–2007 [database online]. Provo, UT, USA: Ancestry.com Operations, Inc., 2015. Original data: Social Security Applications and Claims, 1936–2007.
11. *London Gazette* bankrupt list. Freda M. Winn, wife of R. H. Winn, January 1941, p. 453.
12. The account of R H Winn's final flight by Jim Corbett, personal communication, derived from official records.
13. Personal Communication Jim Corbett, 2017 from research on ATA personnel, unpublished.
14. UK Outward Passenger Lists 1890–1960. Ancestry.co.uk. Southampton January 1947.
15. Gray, A. 1995. 'Monks Hall Syleham, a Vernacular Survey'. Unpublished MHA. Gray quotes Weeny Leader.

15

The Leader Family at Monks Hall 1937–2016

Johnny and 'Weeny' Leader brought a glamour to Monks Hall that Syleham had not witnessed since the days of Catherine and James Walne at the turn of the 18th to the 19th century. They were young, uncommonly good-looking, with the loud confidence born of two families of impeccable heritage. Their noisy charm, gift for entertaining and endearing devotion to English country living shaped Syleham social life and the lives of their many friends for seventy years. They belonged to a way of life that is now dying if not dead, an existence played out in this beautiful house surrounded by a social circle of well-heeled local gentry and landowners, retired officers and churchmen from similar backgrounds, and a regular traffic of visitors from home and abroad. Without any pressing need to make a living, which was just as well given their inability to make their farm pay, they sailed through life adding sunshine to the locality and most importantly for this story, restoring Monks Hall as they thought it ought to look and doing a very good job of it too. But there were consequences of their charmed existence that left their two sons an unenviable legacy.

Who were Johnny and Weeny (or often Weenie)? To give them their full names, Lt Colonel John Temple Bouverie Leader (1913–2008) and Amoret Fitz Randolph Leader (1914–1996) were just twenty-four and twenty-three years old when they moved into Monks Hall. They had seen the advert for Monks Hall in *The Times* in 1936 and it appeared to offer a more manageable size of property than their current home, Tidcombe Hall in Devon, and gave them enough land to finance their life there, they thought.[1] They moved in between the end of March 1937 and 14 May 1937, when their first visitor arrived.[2]

John Leader's background

John Temple Bouverie Leader came from a distinct class of Anglo-Irish protestant aristocracy that served in the British military. Their home from the 18th century was the Keale House estate in County Cork, a relatively modest demesne although the existing house, built in 1834, is valued for the quality of its architecture.[3]

The family history is extensive, researched in minute detail by Johnny's brother Michael Leader (1915–1998), an obsessional genealogist, vice-president of the Irish Genealogical Society, who left copious, detailed family trees painstakingly recorded in a minuscule hand. Many are preserved in the Monks Hall Archive. These trees are soporifically tedious to scrutinise, so this author is going to stick to the forebears who had a direct bearing on Johnny's life.

Johnny Leader came from a long line of military men, all called John Leader, who served across the globe wherever the British Empire dictated, educated their sons in England and spoke English without an Irish accent. Their loyalties were always to the British crown. They traced their heritage to one John Temple of Keale who fought at the Battle of the Boyne with King William in 1690 and 'took such an important part in the conflict that King William renamed him Leader, and Leaders they have remained'.[4] Well that's all complete nonsense, as Michael Leader showed. The name Leader can be traced back to rather more humble origins. Nevertheless the name Temple was incorporated into family myth, explaining Johnny's second name.

John Temple Bouverie Leader

Members of the Leader family had arrived in Millstreet, Cork, in the late 17th century during the Cromwellian settlements. They purchased a large estate at Mount Leader, which became the main family home until the early 19th century.[5] By 1876 the family owned almost twelve thousand hectares in County Cork in fourteen separate holdings. Among their possessions were the extensive and valuable collieries at Dromagh and Dysert, providing employment to many local people for over a century. They had other homes but Keale had become the main family home by the end of the 19th century.

Johnny's grandfather, Surgeon-Major Colonel John Leader (1843–92), served mainly in India. As a consequence Johnny's father, also afterwards called Colonel John Leader, was born in Quetta, now in Pakistan, in 1877. Educated first at Wellington College, Berkshire, a school created after the death of the eponymous Duke to educate the children of the military, and then Sandhurst, John Leader Snr was gifted linguistically, eventually mastering five or more languages, including some Chinese, Arabic and Japanese. He served in the Anglo-Boer War, then with the expeditionary party sent to China to quell the Boxer Rebellion. At the outbreak of the Russo-Japanese war, Leader went to the Far East again, this time in the position of interpreter of Japanese. In 1907 he went from Siberia to India, and in 1908 fought in Arabia where he distinguished himself in the field. When he retired from active military service in 1909 he relocated to British Columbia with his new aristocratic English wife, Eveline Pleydell-Bouverie. Eveline was the daughter of Colonel John Pleydell-Bouverie, former commander of the 17th Royal Lancers and his wife Grace (*nee* Mallaby), and the granddaughter of the 4th Earl of Radnor. Born in India, her background was very similar to her husband but even 'posher'.

In Canada, the colonel started an export/import business that soon flourished and he and Eveline started a family. Johnny was born in Vancouver in 1913 and his brother Michael in 1915, so both Johnny and Michael had Canadian citizenship. When the Great War erupted in Europe, the Leaders returned to England. John was sent to Ulster to recruit troops before taking command in October 1914 of the 16th Royal Irish Rifles. He served two years on the front and was lucky to survive a period of intense warfare, but he was wounded at the Battle of the Somme and sent home to serve in an Officer Training Corps.

When the University of Oregon wrote to the British War Office in autumn 1916 asking for a man to drill its troops, the office sent back a list of men that were available. The university selected Colonel Leader, so he arrived in Eugene, Oregon, with his family at the end of 1917. He helped to train a university battalion for the war effort, and was instrumental in forming the Reserve Officers Training Corps (ROTC) program at the university in 1918.

Leader was the second-highest ranking British officer to reside in the United States during World War I, giving speeches throughout Oregon and preparing coastal communities for potential attacks from the Pacific, although the expected assaults never happened. He became well known in Oregon, not only for his military training and alerting the public to the threat of war but also because he was a seriously good polo player. His 'thorough friendliness, impulsive enthusiasm, restless energy, his genuine good humor – these and other admirable traits have won for him a high place in the hearts of students, faculty and friends of Oregon. If the Great War has done no other good thing, at least we can be grateful that it brought Colonel John to the University.'[6]

Eveline gave birth in 1922 to their third son, Deryck Pleydell Leader, while they were still in Oregon; quite soon, however, the family moved back to Vancouver, where Leader's business grew larger and he served for a period as the President of the American Pacific Export Company. In the 1920s he became involved in the Chautauqua Movement in Canada, being one of its main promoters there, and gave a lecture tour in 1921 across Australia and New Zealand. The Chautauqua Movement was an adult education movement in the USA; highly popular in the late 19th and early 20th centuries, it had roots in Protestant Methodism, although later it became less religious in focus.

At the outbreak of the Second World War, John and Eveline Leader again returned to London and he became attached to the Intelligence Division where he was among other things occasionally in direct contact with General Charles de Gaulle. Characteristically he said he would have preferred to get a command 'in the field'.

Col. John Leader (1876–1967).

Eveline Maud Pleydell-Bouverie (1883–1972).

He returned to Vancouver after the war and died on 8 March 1967. Eveline died in 1972. John Leader was an intelligent and gifted man, competent in management and an inspirational leader as a young man. Young Johnny Leader had an awful lot to live up to.

John Temple Bouverie Leader (Johnny)

Johnny's early years were spent between Canada, Oregon and England, where he was sent to school at Blundells, a well-known public school in Tiverton, Devon, favoured by West Country families. He was not especially intellectually gifted but a phenomenally good sportsman, especially at tennis. His parents by then spent part of their summer in Nice or Monte Carlo and it was on the Riviera that he started to play serious amateur competitive tennis, winning tournaments and, more importantly, enjoying himself enormously. His father was also a good tennis player and they often played together. Johnny's tennis was professional standard, holding his own with the famous French 'Four Musketeers', Jean Borotra, René Lacoste, Henri Cochet and Jacques Brugnon. He played in Monte Carlo with King Gustav V of Sweden, who represented his country at tennis under the name 'Mr G'. Johnny was invited to India to teach the grandson of the Maharajah of Kutch, or Cutch, to play tennis. In 1932 he played mixed doubles at Wimbledon with Sheila Hewitt and made a good showing, losing in the second round but only just.[7]

Johnny was spotted, it is said, by Benito Mussolini, who invited him to Italy to play tennis and whom he taught to play table tennis. Well, that is the story and it may well be true. Mussolini famously spent holidays on the Adriatic Riviera, not in France, and I can find no record of Mussolini visiting France or Monaco in the most likely years between 1929 and 1933. Johnny, however, was impressed with the Fascists and admired Mussolini, as did many English people of his age and class in the 1930s, when the perceived alternative, Communism, was regarded as a realistic threat to Europe. He kept a folder of Fascist cuttings illustrating the successes of the Italian and German Fascist dictators in the 1930s that survives today in Monks Hall. Like many others, as soon as war was declared against Germany, his loyalties were unshakably British and he rapidly rejected his earlier enthusiasm. His horror of socialism, though, persisted for a lifetime. When Attlee's Labour government was elected after the Second World War he sent to the *Diss Express* an American press cutting containing dire warnings about the consequences of socialism.[8]

Weeny's background

If the Anglo-Irish military was the key to understanding Johnny's outlook on life, then Baltimore Old Money aristocracy was at the core of Amoret Fitz Randolph Leader. She was born in Morristown, New Jersey, in 1914 to Robert Fitz Randolph and his wife, Vera, the baby being named after her maternal grandmother Amoret Cameron Price. Vera's money came in part from her father's successful business as a lumber broker and his later role as vice-president of a huge Baltimore-based national insurance company, the US Fidelity and Guaranty Co., but both parents had inherited wealth too.[9]

Amoret (Weeny) Fitz Randolph

The marriage did not work. Three years after Amoret was born, Vera's husband Robert left, going home to live with his mother in New Jersey, so Vera fell back on her Baltimore relatives in Maryland. Vera remarried well and successfully, to a Baltimore judge, William L Henderson, who eventually became Chief Judge of the supreme court of the U.S. state of Maryland, in the Court of Appeals. A half brother Jud was born in 1924.

The family figured regularly in the society pages of *The Baltimore Sun*. Amoret's coming out parties as a debutante in the 1933 season included a dizzying round of beach parties, lunches and grand suppers given by debutante mothers around the Gibson Island private, gated, exclusive enclave where they lived.[10] You still cannot buy a home of any size in Gibson Island for less than a couple of million dollars.

Johnny meets Weeny, Summer 1933

Amoret, who from childhood was always called Weeny by family and friends, was not thought to need much of an education, like many young women of her generation and class. Finding the right man was the objective, preferably one with breeding, style and money. But travel broadened the mind and brought opportunities to mix with the right kind, so her grandmother, Amoret C. Price, a travel enthusiast, took young Weeny to London in 1928. Then, as the launch to her debutante season in April 1933, they embarked for Europe again, spending some weeks in Majorca, then London, and finally ending up in the south of France.[11] There is some disagreement about whether the beach party where Johnny and Weeny met was in Majorca or France but France seems to fit the immigration and passenger lists for the relevant transatlantic liners, although it really could be either. It would have been a party for an English-speaking set, wherever it was.

So we will say it was in France at a beach party either in July or early August 1933 that eighteen-year-old Weeny met the dashing, athletic twenty-year-old Johnny Leader, outgoing, charming, a fabulously promising tennis player and utterly irresistible. It seems that Johnny was just as smitten. They were very young, too young perhaps, and we do not know what their parents thought about this sudden affair but they very quickly decided to marry and clearly had the support of both families by the time of the wedding. Weeny went home to do her debutante season as planned from September to December 1933, but the date for her wedding was fixed for February 1934.[12]

The wedding was a grand society affair at St Thomas Church, Garrison Forest, 'the most distinguished matrimonial alliance that has taken place in Baltimore society for many years' gushed the society hack. 'Mr Leader is related to half the peerage of Great Britain, being a great grandson of the 4th Earl of Radnor' and Amoret came from 'two of the best Old America families'. There were two columns of hyperbole about their distinguished lineage and an announcement that from March 1934 their home would be Tidcombe Hall, Devon, England, 'a beautiful old place in the south of England which has been in the family for generations'[13] – not quite true, but it sounded marvellous. The wedding dress[14] was designed to conform to the requirements for being presented at court. In early March, Weeny was congratulated on being the first of the 1933/4 Baltimore debutantes to secure a marriage.[15] Other debs must have felt just a little upstaged.

Tidcombe Hall, Tiverton

The reason for the young couple's decision to live in England is not entirely clear. Johnny's parents were still in Vancouver but Devon was the home of Johnny's mother's family, the Pleydell-Bouveries, who lived at Blackmore House, Sidmouth, about thirty miles away from Tiverton, and Johnny knew Tiverton well from his schooldays. Tidcombe Hall was in fact a wedding present from Johnny's father. One report says that the house was 'bought by John Leader when the family mansion in Limerick was burnt down in the Irish Riots of 1922.'[16] John Leader's grandmother's home, Roxborough House in Limerick, was indeed burnt down in June 1919, but there were continuing serious civil war riots in Cork in August 1922. Michael Collins, the Irish Republican leader, was murdered there that month. In fact by then Keale House was in the possession of other family members.[17] But Cork was a dangerous place for Anglo-Irish landowners and it would have made sense at that time to purchase a property back in England near to Eveline's parents.

Tidcombe House was a classically proportioned early 19th century house, spacious and grand, although with less attractive accretions of outhouses and a ballroom wing.[18]

The problem with Tidcombe was its huge size and lack of land. The young couple needed a larger income of their own to maintain such a place. They had

Tidcombe Hall, Tiverton, 1930s.

the idea of keeping chickens in the ballroom but found it was no easy matter running a profitable farming enterprise without any training. The investment in equipment was sizeable though, so they optimistically took their 150 Hudson battery cages for producing eggs with them to Suffolk and used them during the war. They finally sold them in 1948.[19]

The move to Monks Hall

Two years after moving in, the Leaders decided to look for a smaller place with more land to provide an income and found Monks Hall through an advertisement in *The Times*. Richard Horry Winn must have been keen to

Weeny and Johnny Leader at Monks Hall, late 1930s.

sell, probably in his usual desperate debt-ridden state, for less than someone else might have asked. It was a fairly random choice for the Leaders. They knew nothing about farming or Suffolk, but buoyed up with the optimism of youth and irrepressible personalities, they embarked on their great adventure. They paid £1800 for Monks Hall and 200 acres and took possession on 28 April 1937.[20] It was a bargain, £300 less than the asking price, worth about £700,000 at 2018 prices.

Minnie Roberts

The couple brought two staff with them from Devon, evidence of the rapid attachment these two could generate in those who worked for them. Albert Victor Bishop (Bish) (1902–1975), who lived in the lodge at Monks Hall until he died, and Minnie

Roberts (1911–1981)[21], an indispensable housekeeper who married local Hoxne man, George Chapman. Minnie's son and his wife describe her as a very caring person, quiet but knew her own mind and had a good sense of humour.[22]

The Second World War Years

Johnny and Weeny's first son, also John, but forever J to distinguish him from his father and grandfather, was born in February 1939 as the hovering threat of yet another war loomed over England.

Baby J's christening party, Monks Hall 1939. L-R Great Uncle Bertie Leader (brother of John Leader), Johnny holding J, Michael Leader, John Leader (behind) and Deryck Leader. This photo provides indisputable proof that the 'Tudor style' diamond pane windows were in place by early 1939.

Weeny volunteered for the Air Raid Precaution (ARP) service. John Leader was one of five Suffolk men who in May 1939 acted as recruiting support to Captain Mennear to re-form the territorial 5th battalion of the Suffolk Regiment at Eye.[23] Fortunately, at the outbreak of war he was transferred quickly from the Suffolks to the Royal Artillery and served partly at Walton-on-the-Naze on the Essex Coast. 'Fortunately' because the 5th Battalion of the

Suffolks were sent to defend Singapore, arriving just three weeks before the peninsula was overrun by the Japanese. Most became POWs, consigned to the notorious Japanese camps, many dying on the Thai Burma railway.

Walton-on-the-Naze was heavily fortified because the east coast was thought to be a likely site for an invasion. It was well defended with troops and artillery.[24] The Naze was covered with army huts, trenches, pillboxes and gun emplacements. The Naze tower had a huge radar aerial on the top, and barbed wire ringed the site. Along the cliff top were perched pillboxes, each with an anti-aircraft machine-gun on the top. Soldiers manning them would scan the horizon for a possible invasion fleet or low-flying aircraft intent on strafing the site. All along the beach below there was a continuous line of scaffolding erected as a barrier against landing craft or tanks. The site housed one of Britain's first guided missile test installations. It was not a difficult posting compared with many. In 1942, when the Americans arrived, Johnny became regional liaison officer between the British Army and the US 8th Army Air Force, which between 1942 and 1945 had 50,000 troops on thirty-four airfields and bases around East Anglia.[25] No fewer than 26,000 American servicemen died on active service in the 8th.[26]

Towards the end of the war, Johnny was sent to India and served there until 1947, achieving the rank of Lieutenant Colonel, which stuck to him to the end of his days. When the author met him in the late 1970s he was introduced by his courtesy title of 'Colonel Leader'. Weeny

Johnny Leader during the war; photo taken outside Monks Hall.

bore a second son, Robert William (Bill) in 1942. She took on much of the work of supervising the farm, but relied mainly on 'Bish'. Johnny was away in India for about three years, from late 1944 to 1947, years when his two baby boys were growing from babies into boyhood.

Farms survived in wartime because of huge state subsidies to extend arable farming, reduce beef cattle and introduce state control of stock sales. Business was under the direct and strict control of the local East Suffolk War Agriculture

Committee, the 'War Ag', which even the local MP for Eye, Edgar Granville, complained was profligate.[27] The 'war ags' were spending £12 million a year by 1944, of which over £2 million was spent on the expenses of running the committee machine, and the rest was flowing into farmers' pockets, happily for them. The committee encouraged local farmers to produce more milk and to turn bullock-grazing land into arable fields, although few farmers did so in the Waveney Valley. There was encouragement too to keep chickens; the Leaders dutifully complied and presumably the battery cages came in useful.

During his later schooldays Johnny's younger brother Deryck stayed with them during holidays. Deryck was just seventeen at the outbreak of war but served in India in the early 1940s. Invalided out in 1943 following an episode of typhoid fever, Deryck came to stay at Monks Hall for the remainder of the war.[28] He may well have been a considerable help to Weeny during Johnny's absences. Deryck returned permanently to his parents in Vancouver in late 1944.

After the Second World War

After the war the family settled down to country life and local society. Johnny became a magistrate, sitting on the Stradbroke bench. He served on East Suffolk County Council from 1967 to 1974, then when East and West Suffolk Councils merged, on the new Suffolk County Council until 1985. He was Chairman of Syleham Parish Council for countless years, Vicar's Warden to St Margaret's Church Syleham and Chairman of Governors at Diss Grammar School. Margaret Gray, who served as parish clerk in the late 1960s and 1970s, remembers Colonel Leader as an extroverted, lively but extraordinarily generous man. 'He talked over people, didn't always listen but you couldn't ignore him'.[29] He was always shouting some repartee but 'an unforgettable and very loveable character'. Until Syleham parish hall was restored, parish council meetings were held in the parlour at Monks Hall, 'which was always a little chaotic'.

The Great Flood of 1968

Monks Hall sits right by the River Waveney in the flood plain. Surprisingly, it rarely floods. But the earliest built west crosswing is seventeen inches lower than the rest of the house, lowered further by alterations to the floor by the

Leaders in the 1940s. In 1968, the Great Flood of Sunday 15 September, caused by a pronounced trough of low pressure bringing exceptionally heavy rain and thunderstorms to the whole of southeast England, brought the Waveney straight into the kitchen hall, fortunately doing little permanent damage but leaving mud and detritus behind. A 'height of the flood' plaque on the outside wall still shows where the flood reached.

Life at Monks Hall

From the moment the Leaders arrived in Syleham, friends and relatives from Britain, Canada, and USA came to stay, all documented in the visitors' book started at Tidcombe and continued in the same book until 2015. Weeny's grandmother, Amoret Price, was one of the first visitors to both houses. Parents, brothers, friends from London, Devon, all were given a warm welcome. There were shooting parties, meetings of the Waveney Harriers hunt, fishing parties, tennis parties round the grass court in the orchard, lunches and dinners. The game-shooting ledger is preserved, with the names of the guns, economically using the same ledger left behind by a former tenant, started in 1904.

Monks Hall was the venue for village fetes, church fund-raising events and children's parties, where Colonel and Mrs Leader were ever present, the life and soul of every party.[30] The hall was their milieu where they had a palpable 'presence'. They rarely ventured away from their own social circle and when they did, friends observed they were like fish out of water. They lost their *joie de vivre* and confident demeanour, strangely 'a little diminished' in unfamiliar territory, uncomfortable in a London club or restaurant, for example. But at Monks Hall and among their friends they were stars, Weeny shrieking with laughter; Johnny's 'Hey, Attaboy, Attagirl!' interspersed with his eternally optimistic opinions.

Johnny and Weeny were undoubtedly devoted to each other but not necessarily in a conventional way. When asked to describe his home life, their son Bill would later say 'We do not have conversations in this house, we all just shout at each other'. They had little understanding of their two growing sons, who were a puzzle to them and something of a disappointment; sadly they made that all too clear to both of them, showering them with exhortations, injunctions and advice that neither were able to take with equanimity. Bill escaped quite quickly abroad, J stayed on, trying to please. He took a long time to develop a life of his own; but more of J later.

From the extensive accounts preserved in the Monks Hall Archive, meticulously maintained through the Leaders' years at Monks Hall, it is clear that the farm never made a profit. It probably did not worry them very much. Weeny still had a million US dollars in the bank when she died.

> AMORET FITZ RANDOLPH LEADER
> OF MONKS HALL SYLEHAM
> AND GIBSON ISLAND MARYLAND U.S.A.
> 1914 - 1996
> Lt. Col. JOHN TEMPLE BOUVERIE
> LEADER R.A.
> OF MONKS HALL SYLEHAM
> AND VANCOUVER B.C. CANADA
> 1913 - 2008

The memorial to the Leaders at the west end of the south wall of the nave, St Margaret's Church Syleham, is headed by the Leader coat of arms. The motto with the arms reads Probum Non Poenitet, which can loosely be translated as 'Good deeds are not regretted' or 'An honest man does not repent'.

Weeny died in 1996, nursed devotedly to the end by Johnny. He died in February 2008, at the age of ninety-three, supported in those final years by J. In later years Monks Hall, which had never been centrally heated, became more uncomfortable and unkempt, a little *distrait*, like an ageing courtesan, still obviously beautiful but in need of some serious restoration. The stylish farmyard gates rotted away, some makeshift repairs were done but rather badly. The render turned a ghastly mauve pink. It was meant to be the rose madder shade of traditional Suffolk pink but an unwise choice from a shade card left the house looking a little like 'Essex girl' when it should have been Suffolk *grande dame*. It was sad to see, given the enthusiastic work that the couple had put into transforming the hall in the mid-1940s and 1950s, work that simply needed to be revealed and re-burnished to bring out the quality of the building again.

The Leaders' restoration of Monks Hall in the 1940s and 1950s

Monks Hall c 1950.

The Leaders started planning the renovations during the war and engaged an architect, M. W. Poray-Swinarski, to draw up a design for further improving light to the house and adding some internal architectural features. Most of the work was completed in the late 1940s after the war, some in the 1950s.[31]

The architect, Matthew Woodrow Poray-Swinarski (1918–2005) was Polish-born but educated in England. He served as an artillery officer in the Polish Brigade in the British Army before becoming a Prisoner of War.[32] His obituary reported he had escaped from POW camp back to Britain. He was certainly in England at the end of the war and then migrated to Canada, practising architecture in Ottawa and later Toronto. It must have been in 1947 or 1948 that the Leaders engaged Matt Swinarski before he and his wife Sophie left for Canada. Swinarski clearly had a feeling for the Suffolk vernacular and no dramatic changes were made.

On the north side of the house two modern windows were inserted, one an amusing but not strictly historically correct 'oriel window' and another plainer metal window that may originally have been designed as a doorway but has been cut short. A dormer window was put in to provide light to the roof space.

The basic internal arrangement of rooms was preserved. The parlour was covered in fine oak panelling purchased from a local 16th century house, Haywards at Chickering.[33] The floor-to-beam plank and muntin partition was moved slightly west although the original position can still clearly be seen. This late 1940s renovation included a new fireplace, thought to be a 20th century copy, though it looks wonderfully old. A photo of the room, with an oil painting above the fireplace, was taken after the original work in the late 1940s.

Sketch of the 20th century Oriel Window on the north facade, by Andrew Gray.

The parlour in the late 1940s.

Dominating the room now however is an elaborately carved fire surround purchased from Ufford Place, near Woodbridge, for the princely sum of ten shillings. The provenance of the fire surround is not entirely clear. Ufford Place was a substantial 18th century classical mansion, remodelled and extended at the end of the 19th century. The estate was broken up in two sales in 1921 and 1930 and the house itself was demolished in 1956. It was certainly after that that the fire surround was installed at Monks Hall. The surround, which is earlier than the 18th century date of Ufford Place, may originally have come from somewhere else. It arrived in three pieces; the Leaders used the central section but the flanking pieces were given to Graham Baron Ash of Wingfield Castle, a neighbour and close friend of the Leaders, who later disposed of them through Christies.[34] The fire surround is early William and Mary in style, c. 1690. Johnny Leader said one of the two 'roses' in the twirls on the panel was damaged and remade after installation.[35]

The Parlour, Monks Hall in the 1960s with the Ufford Place overmantel.

The pine drawing room, late 1940s.

The easternmost reception room is completely pine panelled, the panelling probably put in in the late 17th or early 18th century. There is a fine cast-iron fireplace dated to the 19th century and a door now in disuse that once gave access to the garden.

Travelling back west inside the passageway down a slope to the crosswing, a small passageway north opens onto a bathroom installed in 1994. A domestic kitchen area was refashioned at the back of the crosswing from a 19th century extension.

The Leaders made some alterations to the range of buildings at the west

Dining Hall in the crosswing c. 1950 showing new supporting upright beam.

end but found they needed to do some structural support to the axial beams in the dining hall of the crosswing, inserting a strong support post in 1950 to prevent further bowing, replacing an earlier beam which had become worn and worm eaten. An original three layered brick floor in the hall was removed and a wooden floor put down at a lower level, it is said to give a better height to the room. The Leaders told Andrew Gray for his vernacular survey that the small bricks had been laid on puddled clay but no clear record was kept at the time.[36] Most of the west crosswing's features internally are original except for the leaded light window cut into the old 19th century west doorway.

Upstairs, alterations above the porch created a library. New bedrooms and a bathroom were fashioned rather haphazardly without changing the various inconvenient, staggered levels in the upstairs passageway. The 19th century cast-iron fireplaces and some early tiles were left intact. Also left was the ancient newel staircase that opens up into the loft, with its 19th century hearth, presumably valued by the 19th century servants who used it.

The new gates, c 1950.

Part of the garden, c1950s/1960s.

The Leaders filled their newly beautiful house with family heirlooms, some paintings and treasures they collected themselves, and created a home that looked the part of the ancestral manor. They gave the house new gates to smarten up the 19th century wall and created new gardens, an orchard and of course the all-important grass tennis court. As a silver wedding present, Graham Baron Ashe gave the Leaders a magnificent set of garden gates; the card that went with them said 'for Junk Hall'.

John ('J') Leader (1939–2016)

The story of Monks Hall comes up to date in the 21st century with the Leaders' elder son J. He loved this house, his village, his Suffolk roots and his life immeasurably enriched the community he lived in.

J Leader took his own life, with a shotgun, in the afternoon of Thursday 7 April 2016. The shockwaves that travelled through the tiny Syleham community and the villages around brought well over 200 people to gather spontaneously in the tiny church of St Margaret's, to question why, to express shock and grief, disbelieving that someone so beloved in the locality could have left it in such a desperate and shocking manner. His close friends knew that he was going through a 'bad patch', that his severe depression felt bleak and hopeless to him. He had begun medical treatment and friends had been rallying round to support him but even they were unprepared for this final act.

Very few people knew J well but he did have some very close friends in whom he confided about his sense of failure. The author does not recall she ever really had a serious conversation with him but like many others was the observer of his unfailing if eccentric hospitality and irreplaceable position in the village and church, where keeping the church going has less to do with faith in God than with keeping faith with the historic heart of a Suffolk village. His final act was atypical of the life he led. Often paralysed by indecision in his later years, this final irrevocable step was profoundly out of character. While writing this book, I have repeatedly been asked, 'Oh wasn't that the place the guy shot himself?' and have found this increasingly irritating; the man was far more complex and interesting than the manner of his going. I have been enormously helped to understand J by the friends and relatives who knew him well, and I have drawn on their memories extensively.

Both J and his younger brother Bill, to whom he remained close all his life, though living on different continents, grew up in the frenetic Leader household at Monks Hall with parental expectations that they would shine. They really only got to know their father after he returned from India in 1947, so were brought up as very young children mainly by their mother. This late family reunion may have had an impact on later family relationships.

Both J and Bill were sent to school at their grandfather's *alma mater*, Wellington in Berkshire, but they hated it and felt completely unsuited to the army life being planned for most pupils there. Bill in particular was miserable and badly behaved. He ran away on a couple of occasions. It is said that he tried to sign on as crew on a ship at Liverpool docks but did not have the requisite union card. He was sent back to school. He decided to go to America at the earliest opportunity and found a job as a journalist. He told friends his main reason for going was that he wanted to get away from his father, who treated him as a child. So he went to Texas and eventually ran a local newspaper. He never returned, settling in the States for good. He visited J at Monks Hall regularly in later years and kept in close touch with weekly phone calls.

J setting off for the Officers' Training Camp, late 1950s.

After school, loyally but reluctantly following his father's wishes, J set out to become the '14th generation of Leaders' to join the army and was sent to Officer Training Camp. J did not want to join the army and the army rapidly decided it did not want J. Next he was dispatched to agricultural college but that was not really J's cup of tea either. He was never really interested in the mechanics of farming, although he loved land and landscape. He was unmoved by commercial considerations. He returned home as often as he could until finally he stayed permanently. J loved Suffolk and thought of himself as a Suffolk man through and through, indeed he was a bit sheepish about the fact he had been born in a nursing home in Norwich, Norfolk.

His father often despaired of J doing 'something with himself' and referred to him as 'that darn fool of a son of mine'. J's personality and his father's could not have been more different. Where his father sailed through a troubling situation with a bombastic and canny charm, paying some attention to what the world expected, J's personality was neither confident nor outgoing and what he could not grasp he left to one side. He had a capacity to stuff problems away in some inaccessible cupboard of his mind until they spilled out, overwhelming him. But he had many other valuable qualities, perhaps not always appreciated by those who judge others on their worldly success. He was described in the eulogy at his memorial service,

> The stepping stones of ambition simply passed him by, he aimed at no exalted position, he strove for no proud place as head of anything. In a competitive world he had no desire to be better, quicker, loftier, more successful than anyone, to stand out from a crowd, to make himself noticed or to overtake someone else – competition was not for him either. Instead a human and humble spirit flourished within him, which permitted no jealousy, no resentment, no envy of others. Devoid of malice, of impeccably good manners, he possessed a mystique that drew people to him with affection, endeared him to them and entranced them. They don't make'em like that anymore, we said … and in truth they never had.[37]

Johnny and Weeny bought a farmhouse on Wingfield Green for J to live in, to give him some independence, but he returned to Monks Hall during the day, to continue his involvement with the estate. He never married but made some lifelong close friendships with women. After his mother died, J returned to Monks Hall to support his by then ageing father, for whom he cared devotedly.

One thing he absorbed from his parents, the commitment to Monks Hall being at the heart of village life. He had a love of the Syleham village community and St Margaret's Church, becoming churchwarden following his father, and gave generously to the church to support the fabric and other local charitable causes, even when he believed he had no money. He attended every event in person.

J did however find an intermittent escape from Syleham. He was visiting Winnipeg in the late 1960s when his brother Bill, who was then a local journalist, drove him and a friend west on to the prairies. Looking out over the vast, rolling wheat fields in the evening light, J immediately decided he wanted to farm there and found 3000 acres near Treherne, a tiny town in Manitoba.

It was to take four years for him to overcome his parents' objections and to get his money out of Britain. The landscape was similar to Suffolk and the soil was of better quality, though the climate was harsher than in Britain. But for J the prospect of more land was irresistible.

After first sowing winter wheat, spring barley and beans in Suffolk, he would fly out to plant spring wheat and sunflowers in Manitoba between mid-April and mid-July. He would then return for the English harvest before going back to spend September to mid-November getting in his prairie crop.[38] In Canada he lived alone in very simple style ten miles outside the small township of Treherne. After some ten years he decided to lease his two Manitoba properties but continued to visit every year. He bought a further tranche of land, largely to ensure that the farm was surrounded on three sides by a river. The proximity of a river was important to him in Suffolk, Manitoba and later Zambia. He maintained his connections to his uncle Deryck's family in British Columbia and Deryck's children Alan, Geoffrey and Anne and their children.

Africa provided another 'colonial' venture. While on holiday in Zambia with a group of friends, he invested in a safari lodge, Waterberry Lodge, upstream from Victoria Falls near Livingstone, in an idyllic location on the banks of the Zambezi, and also bought more land. J's passion for land was irrepressible. Through the commitment of one of the partners, the Lodge became successful and remains so. The partners embarked on a school building and education project for local village children which has continued to expand and develop. Two of his last visitors to Monks Hall were the Zimbabwean Ambassador to the UK and the High Commissioner of Zambia, effusively adding their appreciation in the visitors' book. His African ventures were enthusiasms that gave him enormous pleasure.

J was determined to continue the tradition of his parents' hospitality although sometimes his haphazard planning and carefree approach did not quite match his parents' style. There was the familiar wonky drinks table, made almost inaccessible by the armchairs which barred the way and were never moved, the mismatching glasses, the arbitrary bottles of red on the silver tray. J's annual Christmas Eve party, where invitations were issued to regulars by phone but also by proxy depending on who J bumped into, was legendary for its crowds, a mixture of friends and acquaintances from the local Suffolk community. Every year at least 150 people turned up. As one friend says, 'if you arrived early you couldn't get out and if you arrived late, you couldn't get in'. For someone who paid so little attention to his own wellbeing and comforts, J's generous entertaining was legendary, although it did rather depend on friends organising him. J was such a welcoming host that visitors to Monks Hall departed starry-eyed, their national flag flying on the flagpole in greeting.

None of these activities ameliorated his ingrained sense of inadequacy. He never knew what to do with his estate and even when he got his EU (CAP) grant he spent it on other things rather than reinvest it in the farm. The farm struggled to make a profit. He was unable and unwilling to manage staff; he was taken advantage of and frankly exploited by some. After his farm manager died he sensibly contracted out day-to-day farming responsibilities to a contract farming company and appointed a land agent, who began to get the farm in good order. His close friends devised a plan for him to manage his finances. In fact he had ample resources that could have sustained him comfortably but as he sank into severe depression he failed to believe it. J thought he was bankrupt; he was not, indeed he was by most people's standards exceptionally wealthy, but in his final weeks a severe depressive illness coloured all his thinking.

J, circa 2000.

J was probably very unhappy for many years before the final episode of depression but he was not someone who readily unburdened himself. His friends say he had a previous episode of depression perhaps about thirty years before his suicide and he had recovered but perhaps not fully. He had begun treatment for depression at the time of his death. The tragedy is that given time for the treatment to work he probably would have recovered to fight another day.

J led a privileged life by most people's standards. He inherited a beautiful house, sufficient resources to maintain it and all the trappings of a comfortable landowner. He had conventional conservative views and enjoyed campaigning for politically active Conservative Party friends but he was not really a political animal, even though he was President of the Hoxne and Denham Conservative Association at the time of his death. In later years he harboured a private admiration for Nigel Farage, although he would never have joined UKIP. Paradoxically, when he felt the Conservative government was neglecting the

Commonwealth he announced he would vote Liberal Democrat although he might have had difficulty in articulating their policies.

His problems were essentially those created by the personality he was born with and parents who found it difficult to accept. He simply never could be that traditional squire figure. Eulogies naturally tend to stress the good but no-one disagreed when J was described at his memorial service at St Margaret's as 'the most loyal and steadfast friend one could have had and one of the most loveable characters who ever walked this earth'. It was clear that the small church would be overflowing for the service, so a marquee was erected by the church and a public address system relayed the service. A second marquee was ordered when the numbers expected soared. The church filled to bursting, then the two marquees for the 'overflow' got uncomfortably crowded; then the graveyard filled up with villagers and friends. It was raining that summer day and the field allocated for a car park near the church was a quagmire, but still they came down that long muddy path to the church. If only J had absorbed this affection before his death.

But what of Monks Hall? At J's death, the estate was beginning to be put in order and over the years he had made some urgent repairs to the building, rebuilding a chimney stack and, after much procrastination, investing in a new roof and renovation of the crowstep gable end and crosswing, generating funds by a judicious auction sale. Inside, the house needed modernising, untouched from the 1950s, and was desperately in need of redecoration and loving care.

As I write, the Trustees of J's estate are ensuring that his wishes are observed. The contents of Monks Hall, pictures, furniture and family mementoes were sold at a sale at Cheffins Auction Rooms in September 2016.[39] The heritage of the Leader family of Keale handed down over generations was dispersed. Essentially two hundred years of stuff was disposed of; such is the sad nature of post-mortem house sales but that was his wish, to generate cash for his beneficiaries.

As I write, the estate farm is in process of being regenerated and life is coming back to Monks Hall. The new residents show every sign of giving Monks Hall the love and devotion it deserves. Others will complete the history of this wonderful house.

Notes

1. The author has been unable to identify the advertisement in *The Times* archive but there were several small country houses with land in Suffolk advertised in 1936 that could be the Monks Hall estate. The Leaders themselves said they had seen the advert there. (Eulogy John Leader by Charles Michell, 2008).
2. Visitors Book, begun at Tidcombe Hall April 1934, continues as Visitors Book Monks Hall until 14 October 2015. Monks Hall Archive.
3. Keale House, Keale South, Co Cork. Buildings of Ireland National Inventory of Architectural Heritage Number 20903920…20903920 2 209
4. This myth of the origin of the name Leader was repeated by J. T. B. Leader to local friends.
5. Blake, Tarquin. 'Mount Leader', Abandoned Ireland http://www.abandonedireland.com/MountLeader_1.html (accessed 12.4.2018).
6. History of Colonel John Leader was assembled from a number of sources, but the most useful has been Zachary Bigalke, University of Oregon Department of History, and Geoffrey Leader's family tree on Ancestry.co.uk. Images from: Colonel John Leader, University Archives photographs, UA Ref 3, box 14b, Special Collections & University Archives, University of Oregon Libraries, Eugene, Oregon, 1922. John Leader, *Oregon Through Alien Eyes* (Portland: Meier and Frank). F881.L43 1922b. Also see an anonymous article in *The Register-Guard*, Eugene, Oregon, 18 September 1939.
7. Early years history from Charles Michell, Eulogy from JTBL's funeral 2008. Players in the 1932 Wimbledon Championships – Mixed Doubles listed at https://en.wikipedia.org/wiki/1932_Wimbledon_Championships_–_Mixed_Doubles (accessed 12.4.2018).
8. A Hint from the USA. Article about the horrors of communism, socialism and fascism, and the desirability of capitalism, explaining why no-one from USA would want to settle in Britain under the current socialist government, sent to *Diss Express* by J. Leader. *Diss Express*, Friday 17 February 1950.
9. Obituary of Herbert L Price, Amoret's grandfather, *Baltimore Sun*, 18 February 1918. He died of pneumonia in the Asian flu epidemic.
10. *Baltimore Sun* Social Calendar from September to November 1933, e.g. Beach Party for Miss Amoret Fitz-Randolph at Gibson Island 19 November 1933 *Baltimore Sun*, p. 78. Described as debutante in *Baltimore Sun*, 24 December 1933 p. 58.
11. The various transatlantic and other sea voyages of Amoret C. Price, Amoret Fitz Randolph and John Leader and his family are documented in passenger lists and immigration information from Ancestry.com. The circumstances of their meeting are from friends and relatives.
12. *Baltimore Sun*, 18 February 1934 p. 61. Lunch party and cocktail reception for couple. Announcement of marriage at St Thomas Episcopal Church, Garrison Forest.
13. 'Miss Amoret Fitz Randolph To Be Married On Wednesday'. *Baltimore Sun*, Sunday 18 February 1934 p. 61.
14. The wedding dress was designed to specifications from Buckingham Palace

for a gown suitable to be worn at a British court presentation, according to *The Baltimore Sun*, Sunday 18 February 1934 p. 61. A cutting of the wedding, possibly from *The Baltimore News,* appears as an undated scrap from Monks Hall Archive.
15. *The Baltimore Sun*, 8 March 1934.
16. Newspaper cutting about Tidcombe Hall, without source or date, found in Monks Hall Archive.
17. Personal Communication from Geoffrey Leader.
18. Tidcombe Hall later became a Marie Curie Nursing Home but for the past 25 years has reverted to a private house.
19. Advert for selling 150 Hudson laying batteries, Monks Hall, *Diss Express* Friday 9 July 1848.
20. Letter to Leaders from Constable and Moor Solicitors confirming date of possession. Monks Hall Archive.
21. Minnie Roberts was traced from an entry in the Visitors Book in 1986, when a Patricia Chapman came to Monks Hall and said her family had lived there. It was then possible to trace her to George Chapman and Minnie Roberts through the Ancestry.co.uk website.
22. Personal Communication, John and Margaret Chapman.
23. *Diss Express*, 12 May 1939.
24. Walton-on-the-Naze in WW2. http://www.walton-on-the-naze.com/wwii-trail.
25. Eulogy for J. T. B. Leader, Charles Michell 2008.
26. 8th USAAF losses in WW2. http://ww2f.com/threads/the-8th-air-forces-sacrifice-in-the-air.37649/ (accessed 12.4.2018).
27. Edgar Granville MP speaking in Debate on War Agricultural Executive Committees. House of Commons Debates Hansard 19 May 1944 vol 400 cc543-8.
28. Information from personal communication Geoffrey Leader, Deryck P. Leader's son.
29. Margaret Gray, personal communication 2017.
30. Newspaper references to events appeared annually from 1945 to early 1980s, in the *Diss Express*, e.g. 29 June 1945: 'Syleham Home Coming Fund fete and flower show Sat 28 July'; 1 July 1949: First of many summer fetes which continued annually in aid of PCC, Church and village causes. 1953 Coronation Celebrations raised £66 from a house to house collection to fund a party at Monks Hall. Later, Syleham Festivals 1981 (12–13 September) and 1986 (20–21 September) held events at the hall.
31. Mention of Swinarski in Gray, A. 1995. 'Monks Hall Syleham, a Survey and interpretation'. M. W. Poray-Swinarski, a Toronto-based architect, is listed in Bergeron, Claude, 1986. *Canadian architectural periodicals index, 1940–1980* (Quebec: University of Laval Press).
32. Obituary M. W. Poray Swinarski. *Toronto Globe and Mail*. 14 December 2005.
33. Haywards is now known as Chickering Corner farmhouse, listed IoE 281002.
34. The provenance of the fire surround was told by Amoret Leader to Andrew Gray, described in his study of the buildings, 1995. The price of ten shillings was mentioned by J. T. B. Leader in a home video taken by Geoffrey Leader at Monks

Hall 4 July 2003.
35. Reported on video by Geoffrey Leader 4 July 2003.
36. The sequence of renovations as described here was recorded by Andrew Gray directly from Weeny Leader.
37. Charles Michell. Eulogy for John 'J' Leader St Margaret's Church. Syleham 2016
38. Obituary John 'J' Leader. *The Daily Telegraph* 29 April 2016.
39. Cheffins Fine Art Sales Cambridge, September 2016. http://www.cheffins.co.uk/en/news/international-interest-at-the-fine-art-sale (accessed 12.4.2018).

16

A Manor through Time

The bustle in a house
The morning after death
Is solemnest of industries
Enacted upon Earth--

The sweeping up the heart,
And putting love away
We shall not want to use again
Until eternity.

Emily Dickinson 1830-1886

After the sadness of J Leader's death and the necessary pause to absorb and take stock, we leave Monks Hall at the beginning of a new era, in the good hands of people who will cherish and preserve it for at least one more generation. The house has acquired a new coat of optimistic pink render, the garden is cared for; there is a welcoming flag once more for enchanted visitors. The continuing survival of this ancient house looks assured but is Monks Hall an anomaly, a one-off survivor against the odds, or is it a common survivor typical of manors of the Waveney Valley and the wider East Anglian counties?

Monks Hall estate has many of the characteristics of the local north Suffolk landscape of boulder clay plateau but agriculture began in Syleham in the valley floor long before the plateau was cleared of woodland. The hall building nestled at the valley bottom is in a rather unusual position, very close to the river but just above the habitual flood reach. It was built on the most productive land in the parish in medieval times, in a location that separates the Hall from the marshy site of the medieval church, very probably a spot chosen for the practical reason of avoiding flooding. The Waveney riverbank site also precluded the need for a status enhancing moat, when in the 13th or 14th century so many moats were being constructed at other East Anglian manor halls of this period.

Monks Hall, together with its farmland, has survived for six hundred years as a private residential family estate, testament to the continuity of the local agricultural community but is also a lucky survivor. In Suffolk hundreds of smaller ancient timber framed buildings continue as family houses. These usually have plastered and colour-washed exteriors under peg-tiled or thatched roofs. Exposed beams are common enough, although it is not always easy to tell if the studs and rails were meant to be exposed originally. Larger ancient houses, which were never very numerous in the first place, have often simply disappeared and ancient great houses are rare. Among the few exceptions are the 14th century castle of the de la Poles, earls and dukes of Suffolk, on the edge of Wingfield Green, and the moated early Tudor brick mansion of Charles Brandon, Duke of Suffolk, on Westhorpe Green, demolished in the 18th century. Tilney Hall is another exception but that is now also merely a diminished fragment of its former glory. It is thought now that fire may have been a significant cause of destruction of many more timber framed homes than was previously thought, and the old manorial houses would not have been rebuilt in the same style once the administrative functions of the manor had gone.[1]

Post Reformation optimism and the wealth generated by the 18th century agricultural revolution led to the gentrification and aggrandisement of many ancient houses and imposed further risks to survival of early manor halls. Larger halls and manor houses were rebuilt and over-developed by ambitious proprietors in the 18th and 19th centuries becoming vast mansions that required armies of staff to run them efficiently. When the economics of owning a country house imploded after the Great War, these houses were abandoned.[2] At least 50 larger houses considered uneconomic as family houses or unwanted for institutional use, were demolished in Suffolk between 1900 and 1970. In the immediate vicinity of Monks Hall, Hoxne Hall, also known as Oakley Park, originally a Tudor house but expanded into elegant magnificence in the 18th century, was knocked down in 1923. Brome Hall, the ancient ancestral home of the Cornwallis family was destroyed later, in 1963. Syleham Hall, just up the road, the magnificent 18th century home of the Barry family, built on medieval foundations, has been reduced to a much smaller farmhouse to make it manageable. If manor houses of a middling size did survive they were often turned into country house hotels, schools, care homes or, as towns have encroached on countryside, offices for professional practices and businesses.

We can identify good reasons why Monks Hall survived in centuries past right up to the present day. Between the 14th and 16th centuries the hall and manor were protected by belonging to Thetford Priory. Religious institutions had sufficient clout to resist the ambitious predations of the great family of de la Poles who built and owned Wingfield Castle just a mile away. In the late 14th and early 15th centuries the de la Poles were notorious for grabbing manors and land around them when the opportunity arose and there wasn't much the less powerful could do. The de la Poles acquired the other two Syleham manors, Syleham Comitis and Essham Manor, in the 14th century, together with the manors of Fressingfield and Stradbroke, including Eye. Neighbouring Hoxne Manor was under the protection of the Bishop of Norwich and therefore not a threat and survived to be redeveloped later. Similarly, the manors of Mendham were owned by Mendham Priory and were sold intact at the Dissolution. Monks Hall Manor was important to Thetford priory, mainly because of its watermill and that must have been an important factor in its survival.

In the mid 16th century, Emery Tilney created the Monks Hall we see today and he no doubt was content with his creation during his tenure. It would have felt like a modern and prestigious dwelling. The following century the Fullers were modest Puritan yeomen farmers who probably did not want to change and improve. Their simple unadorned belongings listed in the post mortem inventories suggest they were folk without a need for prettifying or decoration. While East Anglia did not suffer as much physically in the Civil War as other counties further west, economic stagnation and recession affected everyone and it is likely that after the Civil War there was little spare cash for extravagant rebuilding.

Many ancient houses in Suffolk were given plain facades of classical Georgian architecture in the 18th century. It was too expensive to rebuild the house or indeed cover it completely in the new flat brick style, but a new elegant front or a wing could be added when the budget allowed. Whole streets of Bungay, Beccles and Bury St Edmunds have understated Georgian facades, with sash windows divided up by glazing bars and elegant door-cases. Behind are medieval beams and chimneys. Monks Hall's near neighbour, Syleham Manor House, has a classic Georgian façade and new front wing with the old timber framed house still tacked on the back. But Syleham Manor was occupied by an energetic local owner, *entrepreneur* William Mann, followed by John Dyson, a Diss brewer, who married a wealthy widow. Both these gentlemen had an interest in looking the part of the successful businessman. In contrast, the Monks Hall owners, the Wollastons, were far away in London and the southeast, interested in science not agriculture and for them the Monks Hall estate and their other property holdings were simply a capital investment providing a guaranteed source of income; they had little incentive to change the Hall.

By the time the estate was bought by James Read in 1867, the early Victorian 'golden age of English agriculture', that lasted between about 1850 and 1870, was almost at its end and farm incomes declined between then and the Great War, which is perhaps why the Read family made few alterations or embellishments. Yet more tenants followed and it was really only the extraordinary vision of the eccentric property developer in the mid 1930s, and the lucky happenstance of the arrival of the comfortably set up Leader family bringing some much needed American cash and dedication to style, that ensured the restoration and survival of the house.

Monks Hall has turned out to be older than originally thought, constructed out of a medieval hall and some farm buildings. Recently, academic scholarship has concluded that thousands of rural buildings in Britain are likely to be substantially older than previously believed. For example, research in 2014 at Letheringham Lodge, Suffolk, an exquisite small moated manor owned originally by the Wingfield family, revealed that the building was 15th century although it was for many years thought to be Tudor.[3] A larger survey in the Midlands has revealed that many similar buildings date from the 13th to early 16th centuries rather than the late 15th to early 17th centuries as assumed until now.[4] Thousands of rural buildings in Britain are likely to be substantially older than previously believed. Using the technique known as tree-ring dating or dendrochronology, archaeologists are able to work out the exact age of a piece of timber by examining its tree-ring pattern. Each sequence of rings acts as a chronological fingerprint for a particular series of years. One day perhaps Monks Hall will be dated accurately with these new techniques.

Monks Hall is and was always someone's residence. Even when the Hall had important manorial administrative and judicial functions, there were people living there, calling the Hall their home. The German philosopher Martin Heidegger (1889-1976) remarked that "dwelling is not primarily inhabiting but taking care of and creating that space within which something comes into its own and flourishes". That is how houses like this survive for six hundred years, each occupier in turn finding their own way to realise the home of their dreams. A last word from Victorian novelist and politician Benjamin Disraeli, who turned his rather plain Georgian manor of Hughenden into an extravagantly romantic baronial gothic fantasy:

> I have always felt that the best security for civilization is the dwelling, and that upon properly appointed and becoming dwellings depends more than anything else the improvement of mankind. Such dwellings are the nursery of all domestic virtues, and without a becoming home the exercise of those virtues is impossible.
>
> Benjamin Disraeli, 1804-1881.

Monks Hall is above all 'a becoming home' that we can all enjoy as we drive slowly by the chestnut tree.

Notes
1. Currie, C. R. J. 1988. Time and Chance: Modelling the Attrition of Old Houses Journal of Vernacular Architecture Vol 19, 1-9.
2. Lost Heritage. England's Lost Country Houses. Online at http://www.lostheritage.org.uk/lh_complete_list.html (accessed 6.8.2018).
3. A Heritage Asset Assessment of Letheringham Lodge, Edward Martin April 2014. http://www.letheringhamlodge.com/edward-martin (accessed 6.8.2018).
4. Alcock, N. and Miles, D. 2013. *The Medieval Peasant House in Midland England*, Oxbow Books, Oxford. Introduction, pp. 7-10.

Bibliography

MHA Monks Hall Archives. Records held at Monks Hall.
NCC Norwich Consistory Court records, Norfolk Record Office
NRO Norfolk Record Office, Norwich.
SRO Suffolk Record Office
TNA The National Archives, Kew

Aldwell, S. W. H. Vicar of Wingfield and Syleham. 1936. 'A Short History of Syleham, its Manors and Church c 1936', unpublished. SSF124 - SRO, Ipswich PRC 644.

Altmann, Alexander 'William Wollaston (1659–1724): English Deist and Rabbinic Scholar', *Transactions* (Jewish Historical Society of England), Vol. 16, (1945–1951), pp 185–211.

Archer, Mary and Haley, Christopher (eds) 2005. *The 1702 Chair of Chemistry at Cambridge: Transformation and Change* (Cambridge: Cambridge University Press).

Bailey, Mark 2007. *Medieval Suffolk: An Economic and Social History 1200–1500* (Woodbridge: Boydell and Brewer).

Banham, D. and Faith, R. 2014. *Anglo-Saxon Farms and Farming* (Oxford: Oxford University Press).

Barrow, Julia 2009. 'Ideology of the Tenth century English Benedictine "Reform"'. In Skinner, *Challenging the Boundaries of Medieval History: The Legacy of Timothy Reuter*.

Bergeron, Claude 1986. *Canadian architectural periodicals index, 1940–1980* (Quebec: University of Laval Press).

Botelho, L. A. (ed) 1999. 'Churchwardens Accounts of Cratfield 1640-1660'. *Suffolk Record Society*, Vol XLII. (Woodbridge: Boydell Press).

Brewer, John Sherren 1862. 'Letters and Papers, Foreign and Domestic, of the Reign of Henry VIII' preserved in the Public Record Office, the British Museum and Elsewhere in England.

Butcher, A. F. 1987. 'English Urban Society and the Revolt of 1381', in Hilton and Alton. *The English Rising*, pp. 84–111

Carlyle, Edward Irving 1901. 'Francis Wollaston'. Oxford Dictionary of National Biography, Oxford University Press.

Chaucer, Geoffrey c.1386. 'The Monks Tale', *Canterbury Tales*.

Clark, J. W. (Anita McConnell 2004). 'Wollaston, Francis John Hyde (1762-1823)'. Oxford Dictionary of National Biography. Oxford University Press.

Clark, James G. (ed.) and Preest, David (trans.) 2009. *The Chronica Maiora of Thomas Walsingham (1376-1422)* (Woodbridge: Boydell).

Clergy of the Church of England Database 1540–1835, The (CCEd), online at http://theclergydatabase.org.uk.

Copinger, W. 1905–1911. *The Manors of Suffolk: Notes on their history and devolution* (Manchester: Taylor, Garnett, Evans and Co.).

Corder, Joan 1965. 'A Dictionary of Suffolk Arms'. *Suffolk Record Society*, Vol VII.

Craig, J. 1999. 'Reformers, Conflict, and Revisionism: The Reformation in Sixteenth century Hadleigh'. *The Historical Journal*, 42 (1), pp. 1–23.

Craig, John 2005. *Reformation, Politics and Polemics: The Growth of Protestantism in East Anglian Market Towns, 1500–1610* (Aldershot: Ashgate).

Cromwell Association, The, 2017. 'Online Directory of Parliamentarian Army Officers', ed. Stephen K Roberts, online at British History Online http://www.british-history.ac.uk/no-series/cromwell-army-officers (accessed 5.9.2017).

Dalton P. and Luscombe, D. (Eds), 2016. *Rulership and Rebellion in the Anglo-Norman World c.1066–1215* (Farnham: Ashgate).

Defoe, Daniel 1722-24. Tour through the Eastern Counties of England (London). Online at http://www.buildinghistory.org/primary/defoe/suffolk.shtml (accessed 10.4.2018).

Dowsing, W. 'The Journal of William Dowsing 1643-44', online at http://www.williamdowsing.org/journalnoindex.htm (accessed 10.4.2018).

Dugdale, Sir William 1693. *Monasticon Anglicanum, or, The history of the ancient abbies, and other monasteries, hospitals, cathedral and collegiate churches in England and Wales. With divers French, Irish, and Scotch monasteries formerly relating to England.* (London: Sam Keble, Hen Rhodes), Vol. V: *Thetford Priory, Norfolk*, p 148. Online at https://archive.org/details/monasticonanglic00dugd (accessed 4.7.2017)

Dutton, Richard 2008. 'Tilney, Edmund (1535/6–1610), courtier'. Oxford Dictionary of National Biography.

Dyer, Christopher 1988. 'The Rising of 1381 in Suffolk: Its Origins and Participants'. *Proceedings of the Suffolk Institute of Archaeology and History*

36, pp. 274–87. Online at http://suffolkinstitute.pdfsrv.co.uk (accessed 9.4.2018).

Dymond D. and Northeast, P. 1995. *A History of Suffolk* (Chichester: Phillimore).

Dymond, D. 1995-1996. *The Register of Thetford Priory*. Part 1: *1482–1517*. Part 2: *1517–1540* (Oxford: Norfolk Record Society and Oxford University Press)

Dymond, D. and Martin, E. (eds.) 1999. *An Historical Atlas of Suffolk*, 3rd edn. (Ipswich: Suffolk County Council & Suffolk Institute of Archaeology and History).

Elmer, P. 2016. 'East Anglia and the Hopkins Trials, 1645-1647: a County Guide', online at http://practitioners.exeter.ac.uk/wp-content/uploads/2014/11/Eastanglianwitchtrialappendix2.pdf (accessed 11.4.2018).

Evans, N E. 1985. *The East Anglian Linen Industry* (Aldershot: Gower)

Federico, Sylvia 2001. 'The Imaginary Society: Women in 1381'. *Journal of British Studies*, 40 (2), pp. 159–83.

Finkelpearl, P. J. 1980. 'The Comedian's Liberty: Censorship of the Jacobean Stage Reconsidered', in Kinney A. F. and Collins, D. S. *Renaissance Historicism. Selections from English Literary Renaissance* (Amherst: University of Massachusetts Press), pp. 191–206.

Foxe, John 1563. *Actes and Monuments of these Latter and Perillous Days, Touching Matters of the Church*. Numerous later editions. Online at https://www.johnfoxe.org (accessed 11.4.2018).

Frost, Ginger 1997. 'Bigamy and Cohabitation in Victorian England'. *Journal of Family History* 22, pp. 286–306.

Girling F. 1935. 'Chimneys of the Sixteenth Century', *The Queen* (August 14, 1935) p. 37, Monks Hall Archive.

Girling, F. A. 1934. 'Suffolk Chimneys of the 16th Century'. *Proceedings of the Suffolk Institute* 22, part 1, p. 104–7.

Gray, A. F. 1998. 'Mortality Crises in the Upper Waveney Valley 1539–1603: A preliminary study'. Unpublished paper courtesy of Mary Lewis, Syleham Parochial Church Council.

Gray, A. F. 2004. 'Syleham: A village history. Part 1: Glaciation to AD 1605'. Unpublished paper.

Gray, A. F. 1995. 'Monks Hall Syleham. A Vernacular Survey'. Unpublished paper Monks Hall Archive.

BIBLIOGRAPHY

Greenway, Diana E. (ed) 1971. 'Norwich: Bishops (originally of Elmham and Thetford)', in *Fasti Ecclesiae Anglicanae 1066–1300*: Vol. 2, *Monastic Cathedrals (Northern and Southern Provinces)* (London: Institute of Historical Research). Available at British History Online http://www.british-history.ac.uk/fasti-ecclesiae/1066-1300/vol2/pp55-58 (accessed 3.7.2017).

Hasler, P. W. (ed.) 1981. *The History of Parliament: The House of Commons 1558–1603* (Woodbridge: Boydell and Brewer).

Haward, W. I. 1926. 'Economic Aspects of the Wars of the Roses in East Anglia'. *English Historical Review* Vol XLI/CL:XII, pp. 170–89.

Head, D. M. 1995. *The Ebbs and Flows of Fortune: The Life of Thomas Howard, Third Duke of Norfolk*. (Athens, Ga: University of Georgia Press).

Hearn, Karen n.d. 'Netherlandish Painters Active in Britain in the 16th and 17th Centuries', article 17. Online at http://ezine.codart.nl/17/issue/46/artikel/netherlandish-painters-active-in-britain-in-the-16th-and-17th-centuries/?id=191#!/page/5, (accessed 11.9.2017).

Henson, Donald 1998. *A Guide to Late Anglo-Saxon England: From Ælfred to Eadgar II* (Ely: Anglo-Saxon Books)

Hilton, R. and Alton, T. H. 1987. *The English Rising of 1381* (Cambridge: Cambridge University Press).

Holmes, Clive (ed) 1970. 'The Suffolk Committee for Scandalous Ministers 1644-46'. *Suffolk Record Society* Vol XIII.

Holmes, Clive 1974. *The Eastern Association in the English Civil War* (Cambridge: Cambridge University Press).

Holt, H. M. E., and Kain, R. J. P. 1982. 'Land Use and Farming in Suffolk about 1840', *Proceedings of the Suffolk Institute for Archaeology & History* 35, part 2. Online at http://www.suffolkinstitute.org.uk/online-proceedings-contents (accessed 12.4.2018).

Holt, Richard 1988. *The Mills of Medieval England* (Oxford: Blackwell), pp 58, 61–3.

Hoppitt, Rosemary 1992. 'Suffolk's Deer Parks 11th–17th century' (unpublished PhD thesis, UEA).

Huscroft R. 2016. *Tales from the Long Twelfth Century: The Fall of the Angevin Empire* (New Haven: Yale).

Hyde, M. S. and Plummer, J. 1997. 'English Ancestry of New England Settlers, Joshua and Anthony Fisher'. *New England Historical and Genealogy Register* 151

Jardine, Lisa 2008. *Going Dutch: How England Plundered Holland's Glory*

(London: Harper Press).

Johnson, Matthew 1993. *Housing Culture: Traditional Architecture in an English Landscape* (London: UCL Press).

Jones, Dan 2010. *Summer of Blood: The Peasants' Revolt of 1381.* (London: Harper Press).

Karakacili, Eona 2004. *The Journal of Economic History* 64, pp. 24–60.

Keats-Rohan, K. 1998. 'Belvoir : the heirs of Robert and Beranger de Tosny', *Prosopon Newsletter*, 9.

Langdon, John 2004. *Mills in the Medieval Economy: England, 1300–1540* (Oxford: Oxford University Press), pp. 431, 441.

Latimer, Paul 2016. 'How to suppress a Rebellion', in Dalton and Luscombe. *Rulership and Rebellion*.

Lee, John S. 'Tracing Regional and Local Changes in Population and Wealth during the later Middle Ages using Taxation Records, Cambridgeshire 1334-1563' online at http://www.localpopulationstudies.org.uk/PDF/LPS69/LPS69_2002_32-50.pdf (accessed 9.4.2018).

Lewis, E. 1988. 'Medieval Hall Houses of the Winchester Area'. Winchester City Museum.

Lewis, Samuel 1840. *A Topographical Dictionary of England: Comprising the Several Counties* (4th edn, London).

Lucas, Adam 2014. *Ecclesiastical Lordship, Seigneurial Power and the Commercialization of Milling in Medieval England* (London and New York: Routledge).

Lyle, Margaret 2007. 'Regional agricultural wage variations in early nineteenth century England'. *Agricultural History Review AgHR* 55, I, pp. 95–106, online at www.bahs.org.uk/AGHR/ARTICLES/55_105Lyle.pdf (accessed 11.4.2018).

MacCulloch, Diarmaid 1975. 'Radulph Agas, Virtue Unrewarded'. *Suffolk Archaeology and History*, Vol XXXIII part 3 p. 283.

Mansfield, Nicholas 1988, 'Land and Labour', in Gliddon, G. (ed.), *Norfolk and Suffolk in the Great War* (Norwich: Gliddon Books), pp. 74–83.

Martin, E. and Satchell, M. 2008. '"Wheare most Inclosures be" East Anglian Fields: History, Morphology and Management', East Anglian Archaeology 124.

Martin, Thomas 1779. *History of Thetford* (London: J. Nichols)

BIBLIOGRAPHY

McIntosh, Marjorie K. 2013. *Poor Relief and Community in Hadleigh, Suffolk 1547–1600* (Hatfield: University of Hertfordshire Press).

Murphy, E. 2015. *The Moated Grange: A history of south Norfolk through the story of one home 1300–2000* (Hove: Book Guild).

Murphy, E. 2017. 'A Walk along the Medieval King's Highway from Scole to Thorpe Abbotts and Brockdish.' *Mardler, Brockdish and Thorpe Abbotts Village Magazine* 210, pp. 15–17.

Nickells, J. (ed.) 1743. Original Letters and Papers of State: Addressed to Oliver Cromwell found in collection of John Milton.

Ordericus Vitalis (1075–c.1143) *The ecclesiastical history of England and Normandy*, translated 1853 by Forester, Thomas (London: HG Bohn). Available at https://archive.org/details/ecclesiasticalhi03orde (accessed 4.7.2017).

Overton, Mark 1985. 'The Diffusion of Agricultural Innovations in Early Modern England: Turnips and Clover in Norfolk and Suffolk, 1580-1740'. *Transactions of the Institute of British Geographers* 10, pp. 205–21.

Page, Augustine 1841. *A Supplement to the Suffolk Traveller or Topographical and Genealogical Collections concerning that County. Hundred of Hoxne, Syleham or Seilam* (Ipswich: Joshua Page).

Page, William (ed), 1906. *A History of the County of Norfolk*, Vol. 2 (London: Victoria County History), pp. 363–9.

Paston Family Letters, online at http://www.medievalhistories.com/the-paston-letters-online/ (accessed 21.7.2017).

Pearce, Christopher 2016. 'Who were the Cluniacs? Monastic Wales Project'. School of Archaeology, History and Anthropology, University of Wales Trinity St David, Lampeter, available at http://www.monasticwales.org/article/7 (accessed 10.7.2017).

Pepys, S. *The Diary of Samuel Pepys* October 4th 1661.

Perren, R. 1995. *Agriculture in Depression 1870–1940* (Cambridge: Cambridge University Press).

Poos, L. R. 1991. *A Rural Society after the Black Death* (Cambridge: Cambridge University Press).

Porter, Roy 1982. *English Society in the 18th Century* (1st edn Allen Lane; rev. edn 1990, London: Penguin).

Prescott, Andrew 2004. (The Hand of God: the Suppression of the Peasants' Revolt in 1381). In Morgan, Nigel. *Prophecy, Apocalypse and the Day of Doom* (Donington, UK: Shaun Tyas).

Protestation Returns 1642. Parliamentary Archive. Online at http://archivesmapsearch.labs.parliament.uk (accessed 10.4.2018).

Roffe, D. 2000. *Domesday: the Inquest and the Book* (Oxford: Oxford University Press).

Rubin, Miri 2005. *The Hollow Crown: A History of Britain in the Late Middle Ages* (London: Penguin).

Sandon, E. 1977. *Suffolk Houses. A Study in Domestic Architecture* (Woodbridge: Baron Publishing).

Sharpe, Richard 2004. *1088 – William II and the Rebels*. Anglo-Norman Studies XXVI (Woodbridge: Boydell and Brewer).

Shirley, Kevin L. 2004. *The Secular Jurisdiction of Monasteries in Anglo-Norman and Angevin England* (Woodbridge: Boydell and Brewer).

Sisson, C. J. (ed) 1933. *Thomas Lodge and Other Elizabethans* (Cambridge, Mass.: Harvard University Press).

Skeat, Walter W. 1843 (later edn online 1913). *The place-names of Suffolk* (Cambridge Antiquarian Society, Cambridge). Available at https://archive.org/details/placenamesofsuff00skearich (accessed 9.4.2018).

Skinner, Patricia *Challenging the Boundaries of Medieval History: The Legacy of Timothy Reuter* (Turnhout, Belgium: Brepols).

Smith, A. H. 1956. *English Place Name Elements*, Vol. 2 (Cambridge University Press, Cambridge).

Starr, A. J. 1941. '18th Century Agriculture in Suffolk'. *Geography* 26, pp. 116–25.

Stephen, Leslie 'William Wollaston (1660-1724)', Dictionary of National Biography 1885-1900. Vol. 62.

Stevenson, J. and Fr. Michel (eds) 1886. *Chronicle of the reigns of Stephen*. (London: Longman)

Streitberger, W. R. 1978. 'On Edmund Tilney's Biography'. *The Review of English Studies* 29 (113) p. 18.

Suckling, A. I. 1846–48. *The History and Antiquities of the County of Suffolk*, Vol. 1.

Tate, W. E. 1952. 'A Handlist of Suffolk Enclosure Acts and Awards.' *Proceedings of the Suffolk Institute of Archaeology and Natural History* Vol. XXV, Part 33.

Theobald, J. (2001). "Distant Lands": The Management of Absentee Estates

BIBLIOGRAPHY

in Woodland High Suffolk, 1660–1800'. *Rural History*, 12 (1), pp. 1-18.

Tweyman, Stanley 1976. 'Truth, Happiness and Obligation: The Moral Philosophy of William Wollaston'. *Philosophy* Vol. 51, pp. 35–46.

Tylney, Emery Dogmata eiusdem Georgij. (translation, The dogmas of the same George), in Foxe, *Actes and Monuments*.

Venn, J. (ed). 1924. *Alumni Cantabrigienses: A Biographical List of All Known Students, Graduates and Holders of Office at the University of Cambridge from the earliest times to 1900*. Vol. 1. (Cambridge: Cambridge University Press); Vol. 2, ed. Venn, J. A. and Venn, J. 1952–4.

Whetham, Edith 1978. *The Agrarian History of England and Wales. Vol Vlll: 1914–39* (Cambridge: Cambridge University Press).

White, W. 1844. *White's Directory* (Sheffield: R. Leader).

Whitelock, E. H. D. 1930. *Anglo-Saxon Wills* (Cambridge: Cambridge University Press)

Williamson, M. 2013. 'Destruction in the Wars of the Roses'. Online at http://weaponsandwarfare.com (accessed 17.11.13)

Wollaston, Francis 1793. *The Secret History of a Private Man*. Facsimile edition published by Ecco Prints.

Yarde, L. 2011. '15 minutes of Fame: The Rebellion of 1088', http://unusualhistoricals.blogspot.it/2011/05/15-minutes-of-fame-rebellion-of-1088.html (accessed 3.7.2017).

Young, Arthur 1804. *General View of the Agriculture of the County of Suffolk* (London: Board of Agriculture).

Index

Aldous
    John, 120
Aldwell,
    S. W. H. (Vicar of Wingfield and Syleham), 129-130, 133, 141, 242
Algar
    Thomas, 85
Allen, alias Fuller
    Agnes/Ann/Anna, 105, 109, 127
Andrews
    Lancelot, 113
Anglo-Saxons, 11
Arthur (Prince of Wales), 74
Austen
    Jane, 155
Babington Conspiracy, 73
Backhouse
    Amy, 188
    Ethel, 188
    Harriet (née Merrells), 187-188, 190-191, 194
    James, ix, 180, 187-192
    Mabel, 188
    Sarah, 188
Backler
    Ezekiel, 146, 148
Bailey
    Mark (historian), 39, 51, 242
Balding, 144
Baldwin (Abbot of St Edmunds), 19
Banerynghale
    John, 37, 51
Barry
    Anthony (Sr. & Jr., Captain), 114, 119, 122, 127-128, 148
    Christopher, 112, 120, 123, 127
    Lambe, 153-155
    Miss, 146
Basse
    Katherine, 64
Battle of Hastings, 20
Baxter
    Esther, 168

Beaton
    David (Cardinal Archbishop of St Andrew's Scotland), 81
Becket
    Thomas (Archbishop of Canterbury), 27, 29
Benedictine, 33-34, 36, 50, 242
Berkeley
    George, 133
Bigod
    Hugh, 26, 28-32, 34
    Roger, 19-22, 51
    William, 28
Black Death, 39-41, 51, 247
Bland
    Arthur Taylor, 201
Bloomfield
    Joseph, 165
    Sarah, 168
Bole
    John, 37, 53, 58
    Robert, 58
    William, 58
Boleyn
    Ann, 68, 74
Bond
    John, 146
    Lewis, 181-182
Boston (Lincolnshire), 75
Brandon
    Charles (1st Duke of Suffolk), 62, 238
Bristol, 81, 140-141, 151
Browning
    Rose, 120
    Samuel, 148, 160
Buck
    George, 85, 89
Bullingham
    Agnes, 187
    Arthur, 181, 186
    Eliza, 177, 181-187, 198
    George (GB), ix, 180-181, 183-187, 195, 198,
    George (son of GB), 181

INDEX

John, 181
Maria (née Miller, wife of GB), 181-183
Robert, 181
Bullman
    Mary, 119, 129
Burlage
    Robert, 83, 88
Buttram
    Mary, 176
    William, 168, 179
Cambridge
    Caius College (later Gonville and Caius), 114, 118, 161
    Corpus Christi College, 50, 80
    Emmanuel College, 113-114, 153
    Jesus College, 63
    Pembroke College, 113
    Sidney Sussex College, 136, 138-139
Cardinall
    William, 82, 88
Carter
    James, 168
    Robert, 47
    Sarah, 168
Catholicism, 81
Caton
    Philippa, 150, 161
Cavendish
    John de, 42
    Hotel (Yarmouth), 204
Charles
    Elianora *also* Alianora, 39
    Thomas (of Essham), 24, 39
Charnel
    Caterina, 39
Charterhouse
    School, 139
    Square (London), 134, 136
Chislehurst (Kent), 137-138, 142
Christ Church (Oxford), 63
Clapton, 140
Cluniac Order, 21-25, 33, 35-36, 50, 71
Cluny Abbey (Cluny France), 21-22, 33-35

Cobbett
    William, 155, 162
Cobden
    Richard, 170
Cold Norton (Essex), 139
Coleman
    Philip, 85
Collett
    John, 67
Colman, Mr, (neighbour of GB), 186
Cooper
    Augustus, 168-169, 179
Corbould
    Catherine (née Lorimer, later Catherine Walne), 151-158
    Edward Henry, 150, 161
    Elizabeth (later Theobald), 151-152
    Martha, 150
    Pelham, 151-152, 161-162
    Richard, 150
    Sarah, 152
    Susannah, 151
    William, 151-152
Corn Laws, 169-170
Cornwallis
    Charles (2nd Marquess of,) 146, 154, 238
Cossey
    Alice (AC), 64
    Beatrice, 62
    John, 59-61
    John (JC) (older son of RC), 64-67, 71
    Robert (RC), 62-63
    Robert (son of JC and AC), 65
    Rose, 59, 61
    Thomas, 65
Cotton
    Mary, 119
Court of Chancery, 83, 88, 129, 149
Craig
    John, 82, 88, 243
Cranfield
    George, 195
    Reginald *also* Cranford, 198

Cromwell
    Oliver, 128, 247
    Thomas, 63, 68
Cult of St Edmund, 19
Cutting
    Eliza, 174
D'Ewes
    Symonds (High Sheriff of Suffolk), 115
Dade
    Alice, 175-176
Daines
    Thomas, 107
dairying, 6, 8, 56, 102, 112, 191
Davis
    Winifred, 83
Davy
    Sir Humphrey, 139
De la Pole
    Edmund 63
    John, 61
Deakin
    Roger, vii, 2, 4
Defoe
    Daniel, 103, 126, 243
Dengie (Essex), 137
Denny
    Richard, 168
Despenser *also* le Despencer
    Henry (Bishop of Norwich), 43
Disraeli
    Benjamin, 174, 241
Diss and Colchester Railway, 168, 179
Dollond
    Peter, (FRS, optical instrument maker), 138
Domesday book and survey, 6-7, 13, 20, 23, 248
Douvrend (Normandy), 20
Dowsing
    William (Provost Marshall), 117, 128, 243
Dye
    George, 169

Dyer,
    Christopher, 41, 52, 243
Dymond
    David, 11, 51, 57-58, 61, 71, 127, 244
Dyson
    John, 240
    Thomas, 169
East Anglia, 9-11, 13, 17-18, 20, 23, 29, 36-37, 39-41, 59-61, 63, 65, 67, 82, 104, 124, 127, 143, 156, 219, 239, 244-245
Eastern Association, 116-117, 127, 245
Eastgate
    Agnes, 57
    Roger, 57
    Walter de, 46-47, 49-50
Edric (a Saxon nobleman), 10
Eleanor of Aquitaine, 26
Elmham
    Johanne de, 39
Elsey
    Jethro, 196
Elvin
    Rose, 44
    Stephen, 44
enclosure, 62, 144, 160, 171, 179, 248
English Civil War, 127-128, 245
Esham, Manor of *also* Essham *or* Essam, 13, 16-17, 23, 25, 39
Estrithson
    Sweyn, 20
Evans
    Thomas, 168
Fauquier
    Elizabeth, 135
    Francis, 134
    John, 134
    Mary, 136
    William, 136
Fenner
    John, 83, 88
Fisher
    Anthony, 89, 121, 245
    Edmund, 129
    Gregory, 121, 129

INDEX

Robert, 89
William, 84, 89
Fitzroy
    Henry, 69
flax, 64, 103-104, 195
Fordham
    John de (Prior of Thetford), 45
Fountains Abbey, 68
Foxe
    John, 81-82
Framlingham
    Francis, 79
Fuller
    Ann (née Farrow), 121-122, 129
    Anna. *See* Puckell
    Benjamin (Sr.) (BF), 113, 115, 118, 127
    Benjamin (Jr.), 118
    Buckminster, 105
    Clare *also* Cleere, 107
    Edward (of Redenhall, Mayflower Compact signatory), 104
    Frances, 129
    Judith, 107, 110
    Lydia, 107, 110
    Margaret, 129
    Mary (of Bardwell) (MF), 119-120
    Robert, 110, 120, 122-123, 129, 141
    Samuel (of Redenhall, Mayflower Compact signatory), 104
    Samuel (son of WF and MF), 119, 129
    Sarah (SF), 113-115, 119, 129
    Sarah (daughter of WF and MF), 119-120
    Sybill (née Spalding), 108
    Thomas (of Redenhall), 110
    William, 121
    William (*alias* Alen *also* Allen), 77, 109-110, 127
    William (of Bardwell) (WF), 118-119. 127
    William (of Bradwell), 108, 110
    William (of Monks Hall), 107-109, 112, 126
    William (of Syleham), 83, 86, 104-106, 118, 129
    William (son of BF and SF), 118
Gainsborough
    Thomas, 134-135, 153-154
Galton
    Mary Ann, 174
Gamen
    Katherine, 42
Geoffrey (son of Henry II), 27
Geste
    Laurence, 58
Glebe terriers, 122, 129, 145-147
Glover
    Elizabeth, 120
Godbold
    Charles, 169
Gooch
    Sir Thomas, 198
Gosnold
    Bartholomew (Captain), 86-87
    Elizabeth (née Tilney), 86-87
Gould
    William, 153
Gowing
    John, 122
Gray
    Andrew Francis, ii, viii
Great Famine, 38
Groom
    William (of Rattlesden), 147, 160
    William, 191
Guild of St Margaret, 59
Habergham
    Samuel, 115, 128
Hall
    John, 57
Hammond
    Nat, 168
Hanseatic League, 97
Harte
    Elizabeth, 86, 89
Harvard
    John, 114

Hatton
    John, 166
Hearth Tax Records, 119, 129
Heberden
    Thomas, 134
    William, 141
hemp, 65, 103-104, 112, 123, 143
Henniker
    Lord, 168
Henry the Younger, 27
Herfast, 13, 18
Herryng
    Thomas, 85, 89
Herschel
    William, 138
Hill Top House (Wheathampstead Hertfordshire), 202
Hogarth
    William, 132, 134
Holt
    Sir John, 134, 148, 151
Holy Sepulchre, 34
Hopkins
    Matthew, 116, 127, 244
Howard
    Catherine, 68
    John (1st Duke of Norfolk), 59
    John, 120
    Sir Thomas (Earl of Surrey, later 2nd Duke of Norfolk), vii, 66, 69, 74
    Thomas (3rd Duke of Norfolk), 68-69, 72, 245
    Thomas, 28
Huggins
    Walter, 185
Hume
    David, 133
Hundred Years War, 41
Hurren
    Edward, 192
Hyde
    Althea, 136
Hynke
    William, 43, 46-47
Inner Temple, 75, 83

James of Bedingfield, 42
Jeffreys
    Julian, 173
Joan of Arc, 53
Johnson
    Matthew, 94, 101, 246
Josling
    Ellen, 177
Juby
    Robert, 171
Kerrison
    Sir Edward, 146, 159
King
    Charles I, 111, 128
    Charles II, 118
    Edmund the Elder, 7
    Edred, 7
    Edward I, 17
    Edward III, 23, 35
    Edward VI, 73, 81-82
    George III, 156
    Henry I, 21, 24-25, 28, 51
    Henry II, 26, 28-29, 31-32
    Henry III, 93
    Henry VII, 60
    Henry VIII, 18, 61-63, 68, 71-74, 87, 242
    Richard II, 41
    William II, 17, 20, 24, 248
Kingswaye, 31
Kiss
    John, 65
Lakenheath
    John de, 42
Lamb family, 106
Land Tax Redemption Records, 145
Large
    Richard, 58
Laud
    William (Archbishop of Canterbury), 111
Layton
    Richard, 68
le Cotelar
    John, 43

INDEX

Leader
  John Temple Bouverie, 209-210, 213
Leicester, 28-29, 51, 132, 142
Leigh (*also* Legh)
  Thomas, 68
Lewes (Sussex), 22, 34
Limmer, 201
Lewis
  E., 101, 246
  Mary, v, 11, 87, 160, 244
  Samuel, 127
Locke
  John, 133
London
  John, 68
Losinga
  Herbert de, 17-19, 22-24
  Robert de, 18
Lucas
  Adam, 52, 246
  Lord (President of the Board of Agriculture), 194
Malgod (1st Prior of Thetford), 22
Mann
  William, 146, 154-155, 162, 165, 169, 240
Marshall
  Thomas, 69
Matilda, 24, 28
Maynard
  Thomas, 157
Meriton
  George (Rector of Hadleigh), 85
Midhurst (Sussex), 83, 88
Mildmay
  Sir Walter, 113
Montrose (Scotland) 81
Moore
  Garrard and Sons, Auctioneers, 177, 196, 200-201, 208
  Mary, 123
Morley
  Edgar, 188-189, 190
Mosell
  Thomas, 85

Mully *also* Molly
  family, 160
  Richard, 122, 146-147
  Sara, 147
Mutimer
  Henry, 191-194
  Hettie, 194
Myllsent
  John, 69
New England, 73, 89, 104, 111, 113, 121, 245
Norfolk
  Billingford, 110
  Brockdish, 3, 9, 43-44, 52, 64, 110, 115, 119, 122, 129, 146, 148-150, 152, 154-156, 160-162, 169, 185, 247
    Grove, 148-149, 152, 154,
  Dickleburgh, 110, 201
  East Dereham, 137
  Harleston, 24, 105, 109-110, 127, 152, 156-157, 185, 197-198, 203
    Swan Inn, 157
    Railway Tavern, 185
  Hedenham, 192
  Kenninghall Place, 70
  Kings Lynn, 116
  Lakenheath, 42
  Loddon Parish Church, 192
  Lynford Manor, 34, 69
  Lynton Santon Manor, 34
  Monks Wyk, 34
  Needham, 64, 110, 148, 160, 186
  North Elmham, 19
  Norwich, 12, 18-19, 22-24, 28, 36, 40, 42-43, 59-60, 64, 67, 87, 103, 111, 122, 142, 147, 149, 153, 155, 160-162, 168, 173, 178-179, 198-199, 203, 229, 239, 242, 245-246
    Castle, 19, 21, 28-31, 35, 42, 59, 72, 74, 98, 155, 191, 225, 238-239
    Cathedral, 18-19, 22-25, 64, 137, 243
  Rushall, 110
  Scole, 1, 44, 52, 156, 185, 247
  South Lopham, 21

Starston, 152, 154, 159, 162
Thetford, 2, 4, 9-10, 13, 15-17, 19-25, 31, 33-37, 42, 44-45, 48-51, 54, 56-57, 59, 61-62, 64-65, 68-71, 83, 198, 239, 243-246
    Castle, 19, 21, 28-31, 35, 42, 59, 72, 74, 98, 155, 191, 225, 238-239
    Priory, 2, 4, 9, 13, 15, 17, 19, 21-25, 33-38, 42, 44, 46, 50-51, 57-65, 67-71, 83, 239, 243-244
Thorpe Abbotts, 44, 52, 149, 247
Thorpe Parva, 44
Weston Longville, 153
Yarmouth, Great, 1, 108, 157, 199, 204
Norman Conquest, 5, 9, 13
O'Toole
    Peter, 26
Oman
    Charles, 41, 52
Osgood (a Saxon), 7-8, 11
Page
    John, 43, 54
Paris
    Matthew (Benedictine chronicler), 34
Paston family, 60-61, 63, 247
Peasants' Revolt, 40
Peel
    Sir Robert, 170
Pelham
    Sir John, 151
Pepys
    Samuel, 103, 126, 247
Peter the Venerable (Abbot of Cluny), 33
Pevsner
    Nikolaus, 2
Philip Augustus (King of France), 26-27
Philip of Flanders, 27
Pilgrimage of Grace, 69
Poray-Swinarski
    Matthew Woodrow, 90, 223, 235
Pretty
    George, 185
Primrose League, 174

Prince Albert, 167
Protestantism, 71, 80-82, 88, 243
Puckell
    Anna, 102, 107, 105-106, 113
Puritans, 102, 111, 118
Queen
    Catherine of Aragon, 68, 74
    Eadgiva, 7
    Elizabeth I, 73-74, 84
    Mary I, 67, 82
    Mary (of Scots), 82
    Victoria, 25, 50, 150, 163, 231, 247
Read
    Alfred (AR), 159, 163, 165-166, 168-171, 178-179
    Edgar, 168, 171, 173
    Elizabeth (daughter of AR), 163, 165, 172
    Elizabeth Manby (née Cracknell), 163, 172, 168, 171-172
    Ernest Capon, 177
    James (the elder) (JR), 4, 133, 141, 178
    James (the younger), 171-172, 174, 175-176, 178-179, 240
    John, 171-172
    Mary (*later* Mrs William Buttram), 168
    Mary Kate, 172
    Percy James, 174, 176
    Sarah (wife of JR), 163
    Sarah (daughter of AR), 163, 165, 168
    Sophia, 172
    Susan, 172, 174, 179
Redgrave
    Anna, 192-194
    Henry, 180, 191-194, 196, 242
    Henry John, 180, 192, 196
    James, 192-193
    Rosa, 192-193
Reformation, 61, 63, 80-81, 88, 126-127, 238, 243
Restoration, 118, 124, 197, 200-201, 204, 222-223, 240

INDEX

Revill
    Harry, 187
Rice
    John ap, 68
Richards
    John, 146
Riches
    Helen, 177
riots, 40, 157, 170, 216
Rix
    Henry (curate at Syleham), 122
Robert of Normandy, 20
Roberts
    John (churchwarden at Syleham), 122
Rous
    William (constable of Hoxne), 42
Royal Agricultural Society, 179
Royal Society, 133, 136, 138-139, 142
Royalist, 116
Rush
    William, 165
Saghar
    John, 7, 12
Sakanovic
    Mischa, 92, 101
Sayer
    Thomas (Vicar of Hoxne), 115
Scarlett
    William, 188-189
Schylle
    Edward, 58
Segges
    Agnes, 76-78
    Thomas, 78-79, 87
    William, 87, 109
Seymour, *also* St Maur
    family (of Wingfield), 17
Sharman
    Eliza. *See* Bullingham
Shaxton
    Nicholas, 82
Shepherd
    Thomas, 114
Skidbrooke (Lincolnshire), 85, 89

Skirbeck (Lincolnshire), 75, 80, 88
Smyth
    William, 174, 179
    Susan. *See under* Read, Susan
Smythe
    George, 156, 162
South Weald (Essex), 139
Spalding
    Agnes, 110
    John, 108, 110, 126-127
    Margaret, 110, 149
    Sybill. *See under* Fuller, Sybill
St Margaret of Scotland, 31
St Mary Aldermary, (church of, London), 86, 89
St Radegund's Priory, 63
Stannard
    Henry, 169
Stephen (2nd Prior of Thetford), 22-23
Stigand (Archbishop of Canterbury), 10, 13, 16
Stratford
    Richard, 65
Stratforde
    Agnes, 84
    Nicholas, 84-85
    Richard, 84-85
Stuntley
    John, 57
Sudbury
    Simon (Archbishop of Canterbury), 40, 42
Suffolk
    Agricultural Association, 167
    Aldham
        Manor of, 85-86
    Aldringham, 190
    Bardwell, 108, 118-120, 127-129
        Bardwell Hall, 118, 128
        St Peter and St Paul, 118
    Benacre Estate, 190
    Botesdale, 121, 129
    Bradwell, 108, 110, 127, 129
    Brent Eleigh, 63
    Brome, 64, 144, 146, 154, 238

Brome Hall, 146, 154, 238
Brundish, 192
   Button's Farm, 192
Bungay, 21, 28-31, 42, 115, 149, 155, 239
   Bungay Castle, 29, 31
Bury St Edmunds, 19, 29-30, 41, 52, 71, 239
Chediston, 163, 174, 176, 179, 191
   Grove Farm, 174, 179
cheese, 11, 48, 52, 77, 102-103, 144, 173
Chickering, 8, 17, 50, 57, 59, 120, 224, 235
Cookley, 163
Cotton, 8, 51, 122, 146, 150-151, 154, 162
   Harts Farm, 150
Cratfield, 116, 128, 242
Darsham, 34
Denham, 57, 193, 232
Dennington, 36, 163, 184
Dun (cattle), 144
East Suffolk Agricultural Protection Society, 170
Edwardstone, 75, 86, 88
Eye, 29, 36, 94, 103, 117, 138, 144, 149, 151, 155-157, 161-162, 168, 174, 186-187, 194, 196-198, 201-202, 218, 220, 239
   Depperhaugh Wood, 36
   Langton Green, 197
   White Lion, 155, 157, 162
Felixstowe
   Walton Castle, 21
Finborough, 134-135
   Finborough Hall, 135
Flixton
   Priory, 67
Framlingham
   Castle, 29, 74, 98
Frostenden, 192
Great Ashfield, 5
Hadleigh, 75, 79, 82, 87-88, 243, 247
Halesworth, 5, 192, 199, 203

Hartismere Hospital, 174
Hazlewood Estate, 188
Holton, 75, 88
Hoxne, 1, 5, 8, 13, 19, 25, 31, 36, 39-40, 42-43, 50, 57-58, 64, 71, 104, 110, 114-115, 117-120, 127-129, 146, 148-150, 152, 154, 156-157, 161-163, 165-166, 168, 173-174, 177-179, 182, 185, 187, 193, 196-197, 200-201, 208, 218, 232, 238-239, 247
   Hoxne Abbey, 148-150, 152, 161
   Laurels (The), 177
   Poor Law Union, 174
Huntingfield, 163
Instead, 2, 8, 28-29, 49, 120, 195, 230
Ipswich, 1, 11, 17, 20, 25, 32, 38, 51-52, 60, 63, 71, 86, 103, 118, 126-127, 129-130, 133-135, 141, 148, 155-158, 161-162, 165, 168, 178-179, 198, 242, 244, 247
   Ipswich Grammar School, 63
Kelsale, 192-193
Kersey, 121
Knodishall, 188, 198
   Bull's Hall, 188
Lavenham, 63
Laxfield, 117, 165, 185, 192-193
Layham, 75, 86, 88
Leiston, 41, 188, 190
   Conservative Club, 190
Linstead Magna, 163
Lowestoft, 116
Melford, 144
Mellis, 2, 123, 129, 168, 181
Mendham, 8, 71, 105, 109, 127, 144, 239
Metfield, 117
Mettingham, 42
   Mettingham Castle, 42
Oakley, 144, 146, 154, 197, 238
   Oakley Park, 146, 154, 238
Occold, 117, 161
Onehouse, 151
Orford, 29, 59
   Orford Castle, 29

INDEX

Polstead, 75, 86, 88
Red Poll (cattle), 144
Rendlesham, 170, 179
Reydon, 75, 88
Ringsfield, 41
Rishangles, 36, 117
   Rishangles Green, 36
Shadingfield, 190
Shelley, 74-75, 79-80, 82, 85-88
   Church, 75
   Hall, 75, 79, 82, 85-88
South Elmham
   St James, 36
   St Peter's Hall, 66
South Elmhams, 5
Stoke, 59, 75, 86, 88
Stowlangtoft, 115
Stradbroke, 23, 84, 135, 146, 148, 156, 163, 181-182, 198, 220, 239
Syleham, 1-11, 13-17, 19-21, 23-27, 29-31, 33-34, 37-40, 43-45, 50-51, 57-65, 71, 76-77, 79-80, 83-88, 94, 98, 101, 103-115, 117-123, 126-129, 132-134, 137, 141, 144-148, 151-156, 158-162, 164-166, 168-169, 171-177, 179, 181, 185-187, 190-191, 195-196, 198-199, 201, 208-209, 220-222, 228, 230, 235-239, 242, 244, 247
   Comitis, 11, 16-17, 20, 39, 43, 50, 57, 59, 63, 146, 169, 239
   Cross, 7, 9, 17, 19, 30, 40, 46, 55, 57, 59, 65, 91, 93-94, 97, 124, 152, 182-183
   Gate House Farm, 172, 176-177, 196
   glebe land, 34, 122, 146
   Green, 6-7, 11, 36, 103, 120, 144, 169, 179, 197, 230, 238
   Hall, 1-12, 14, 16-18, 20, 22, 24, 26, 28, 30-32, 34, 36-40, 42-46, 48, 50-80, 82-102, 104-110, 112-116, 118-126, 128-136, 138-182, 184-188, 190-192, 194-242, 244, 246, 248, 252
   Lamps, 165
   Mill, 9, 16, 31, 33, 43-46, 49, 52, 56-58, 122, 154, 186, 195, 206
   Park Farm, 36, 196
   St Margaret's Church, 59, 105-106, 115, 172, 220, 222, 230, 236
   tithe records, 112, 123
   White Horse Inn, 169
   Wygnotts Croft, 84
Thorndon, 36, 161, 181
Thornham Parva, 181, 183
Thorpe Abbotts, 44, 52, 149, 247
Thrandeston, 24, 144, 177
Ufford, 91-92, 203, 225
   Ufford Place, 91-92, 225
West Stow, 9
Wetheringsett, 36
Weybread, 17, 23, 154, 191
Whepstead, 201
   Manston Hall, 201
Whittingham, 8
Wilby, 161, 163
Wingfield, 7, 9, 13, 17, 23, 50, 59, 61, 63, 71, 110, 113-114, 118-119, 126, 129, 153, 162, 171, 191, 225, 230, 238-240, 242
   Castle, 19, 21, 28-31, 35, 42, 59, 72, 74, 98, 155, 191, 225, 238-239
   Wingfield Castle Farm, 191
Withersdale, 119, 129
Wrentham, 190
   North Hall, 190, 199
Yaxley, 144, 181-183
Syggs
   Thomas. *See* Segges
Tasburgh
   family (of St Peter South Elmham), 67
Taylor
   Rowland, 82
Teder
   Thomas, 85
Thellusson
   Colonel, 188-190
Theobald
   (Bishop of London), 12

Jonathan, 146, 152
John of Starston, 152, 159, 162
Sarah. *See* Corbould
Thetford Way, 44
Thomas of Walsingham, 43
Threadkell
    family, 178
Thurston
    John *also* Thruston, 149-150, 161
    Thomas, 181-182
    Anna, 192
Thurtell
    Caroline, 169
Tilney *also* Tylney
    Agnes, 74
    Anne, 75
    Charles, 82-83
    Edmund, 73, 85
    Elizabeth (3rd wife of PT), 74
    Elizabeth (daughter of PT), 75
    Emery (ET), 4, 71, 73-77, 79-90, 239, 249
    Frederick *also* Frarye (FT), 75, 82, 87, 89
    Margaret, 75
    Margaret (wife of FT), 75, 85
    Philip (son of FT), 82, 85
    Sir Philip (PT), 73-75, 79, 88
    Thomas (eldest son of PT), 4, 71, 73, 75-76, 79, 87
    Thomas (eldest son of ET), 85-86, 89, 110
Tithe Commutation Act, 164
Tosti of St Omer, 30
Tosny
    Adelise *also* Adelicia de, 20-21
    Robert of, 11, 16
Tuthill
    Charles, 152
Tyler
    Wat, 40-41
Vaughan
    Edward, 153
Vyknell
    Peter (of Pockthorp), 67

Waldegrave
    Sir William, 82
Walne
    Catherine, 152, 158, 162
    James, v, 131, 137, 143, 146-147, 150, 152, 155-157, 159, 162, 209
Warenne
    William de, 22
Wars of the Roses, 53, 59-61, 245, 249
Waveney
    River, vii, 1, 10, 40, 77, 120, 175, 220
Welling (Kent), 140
Welton
    Sarah, 151
Westminster, 103
Whitacre
    Revd, 146
Whitaker
    Thomas, 153
White Ship disaster, 21, 24
Whiting
    Richard (Abbot of Glastonbury Abbey), 69
William (Bishop of Thetford), 16-17
William de Warenne, 22
William of Ixworth, 62
Winn
    Richard Horry, 197, 200-203, 205, 207-208, 217
Wisbech (Cambridgeshire), 124
Wishart
    George, 80-81, 88
Witherell
    Brian *also* Briant, 107, 115
Wollaston
    Catherine, 134
    Charles Buchanan (Rector of Feltham), 141, 172
    Charlton, 134, 136
    Frances, 139
    Francis, 134-136
    Francis (astronomer), 136-138, 142, 156, 165, 171, 242
    Francis John Hyde, 138, 142, 243
    George, 136

    Henry Septimus Hyde, 139, 142,
        171-172
    William, 124, 130, 131-135, 141,
        148, 242, 248, 249
    William Henry, 136
    William Hyde, 139
    William Monro, 140
Wolrych
    John (Sr.), 54
    John (Jr.), 54
    Thomas, 43
Wolsey
    Cardinal, 63, 67-68
Woodforde
    James, 157, 162
woollen cloth industry, 112
Wrawe
    John (parson of Ringsfield), 41
Wren
    Matthew (Bishop of Norwich), 111
Wrench
    Sir Benjamin, 149, 161
Wright
    Katherine, see also Basse, 65
Wright
    Ralph, 64
Wyberton (Lincolnshire), 75, 80, 88
Wythe
    Charles, 148-149, 160-161
Young
    Arthur, 6, 144, 160, 249

Further details of Poppyland Publishing titles can be found at **www.poppyland.co.uk** where clicking on the 'Support and Resources' button will lead to pages specially compiled to support this book.

Join us for more Norfolk and Suffolk history at **www.facebook.com/poppylandpublishing** and follow **@poppylandpub** on Twitter.